THE SOVEREIGNTY OF GOD

ARTHUR W. PINK

Baker Books

A Division of Baker Book House Co.
Grand Rapids, Michigan 49516

First published 1930 by I. C. Herendeen

Trade paperback edition first published 1984 by Baker Books
a division of Baker Book House Company
P.O. Box 6287, Grand Rapids, MI 49516-6287

ISBN: 0-8010-7088-0

Seventeenth printing, July 1999

Printed in the United States of America

For information about academic books, resources for Christian leaders, and all
new releases available from Baker Book House, visit our web site:
http://www.bakerbooks.com/

CONTENTS

FOREWORD TO THE FIRST EDITION

IN the following pages an attempt has been made to examine anew in the light of God's Word some of the profoundest questions which can engage the human mind. Others have grappled with these mighty problems in days gone by and from their labors we are the gainers. While making no claim for originality the writer, nevertheless, has endeavored to examine and deal with his subject from an entirely independent viewpoint. We have studied diligently the writings of such men as Augustine and Acquinas, Calvin and Melancthon, Jonathan Edwards and Ralph Erskine, Andrew Fuller and Robert Haldane.* And sad it is to think that these eminent and honored names are almost entirely unknown to the present generation. Though, of course, we do not endorse all their conclusions, yet we gladly acknowledge our deep indebtedness to their works. We have purposely refrained from quoting freely from these deeply taught theologians, because we desired that the faith of our readers should stand not in the wisdom of men but in the power of God. For this reason we *have* quoted freely from the Scriptures and have sought to furnish proof-texts for *every* statement we have advanced.

It would be foolish for us to expect that this work will meet with general approval. The trend of modern theology —if theology it can be called—is ever toward the deification of the creature rather than the glorification of the Creator, and the leaven of present-day Rationalism is rapidly permeating the whole of Christendom. The malevolent effects of Darwinianism are more far reaching than most are aware. Many of those among our religious leaders who are still regarded as orthodox would, we fear, be found to be very heterodox if they were weighed in the balances of the Sanctuary. Even those who are clear, intellectually, upon other truth, are rarely sound in *doctrine*. Few, very few, today, really believe in the *complete* ruin and *total* depravity of man. Those who speak of man's "free will," and insist upon his inherent power to either accept or reject the Saviour, do but voice their ignorance of the real condition of Adam's

---

*Among those who have dealt most helpfully with the subject of God's Sovereignty in recent years we mention Drs. Rice, J. B. Moody, and Bishop, from whose writings we have also received instruction.

fallen children. And if there are few who believe that, so far as *he* is concerned, the condition of the sinner is *entirely hopeless,* there are fewer still who really believe in the *absolute Sovereignty* of God.

In addition to the widespread effects of unscriptural teaching, we also have to reckon with the deplorable *superficiality* of the present generation. To announce that a certain book is a treatise on doctrine is quite sufficient to prejudice against it the great bulk of church-members and most of our preachers as well. The craving today is for something light and spicy, and few have patience, still less desire, to examine carefully that which would make a *demand* both upon their hearts and their mental powers. We remember, also, how that it is becoming increasingly difficult in these strenuous days for those who *are* desirous of studying the deeper things of God to find the time which such study requires. Yet, it is still true that "Where there's a will, there's a way," and in spite of the discouraging features referred to, we believe there is even now a godly remnant who will take pleasure in giving this little work a careful consideration, and such will, we trust, find in it "Meat in due season."

We do not forget the words of one long since passed away, namely, that "Denunciation is the last resort of a defeated opponent." To dismiss this book with the contemptuous epithet—"Hyper-Calvinism"! will not be worthy of notice. For controversy we have no taste, and we shall not accept any challenge to enter the lists against those who might desire to debate the truths discussed in these pages. So far as our personal reputation is concerned, that we leave our Lord to take care of, and unto Him we would now commit this volume and whatever fruit it may bear, praying Him to use it for the enlightening of His own dear people (insofar as it is in accord with His Holy Word) and to pardon the writer for and preserve the reader from the injurious effects of any false teaching that may have crept into it. If the joy and comfort which have come to the author while penning these pages are shared by those who may scan them, then we shall be devoutly thankful to the One whose grace alone enables us to discern spiritual things.

June 1918.   ARTHUR W. PINK.

FOREWORD TO THE SECOND EDITION

It is now two years since the first edition of this work was presented to the Christian public. Its reception has been far more favorable than the author had expected. Many have notified him of the help and blessing received from a perusal of his attempts to expound what is admittedly a difficult subject. For every word of appreciation we return hearty thanks to Him in Whose light we alone "see light." A few have condemned the book in unqualified terms, and these we commend to God and to the Word of His grace, remembering that it is written, "a man can receive nothing, except it be given him from heaven" (John 3:27). Others have sent us friendly criticisms and these have been weighed carefully, and we trust that, in consequence, this revised edition will be unto those who are members of the household of faith more profitable than the former one.

One word of explanation seems to be called for. A number of respected brethren in Christ feel that our treatment of the Sovereignty of God was too extreme and one-sided. It has been pointed out that a fundamental requirement in expounding the Word of God is the need of *preserving the balance of Truth*. With this we are in hearty accord. Two things are beyond dispute: God is sovereign, and man is a responsible creature. But in this book we are treating of the Sovereignty of God, and while the responsibility of man is readily owned, yet, we do not pause on every page to *insist* on it; instead, we have sought to stress that side of the Truth which in these days is almost universally neglected. Probably 95 per cent. of the religious literature of the day is devoted to a setting forth of the duties and obligations of men. The fact is that those who undertake to expound the Responsibility of man are the very ones who have *lost* 'the balance of Truth' by ignoring, very largely, the Sovereignty of God. It is perfectly right to insist on the responsibility of man, but what of God?—has *He* no claims, no rights! A hundred such works as this are needed, ten thousand sermons would have to be preached throughout the land on this subject, if the 'balance of Truth' is to be regained. The 'balance of Truth' has been lost, lost through a disproportionate emphasis being thrown on the human side, to the minimizing, if not the exclusion, of the Divine side. We grant that this book *is* one-sided, for it only pretends to deal with one side of the Truth, and that is, the neglected side, the Divine side. Furthermore, the question might be raised: Which is the more to be deplored—an over emphasizing of the human side and an insufficient emphasis on the Divine side, or, an over emphasizing of the Divine side and an insufficient emphasis on the human side? Surely, if we err at all it is on the right side. Surely, there is far more danger of making too much of man and too little of God, than there is of making too much of God and too little of man. Yea, the question might well be asked, *Can we* press *God's* claims too far? Can we be too extreme in insisting upon the absoluteness and universality of the Sovereignty of God?

It is with profound thankfulness to God that, after a further two years diligent study of Holy Writ, with the earnest desire to discover what almighty God has been pleased to reveal to His children on this subject, we are able to testify that we see no reason for making any retractions from what we wrote before, and while we have re-arranged the material of this work, the substance and doctrine of it remains unchanged. May the One Who condescended to bless the first edition of this work be pleased to own even more widely this revision.   ARTHUR W. PINK,
1921.   SWENGEL, PA.

FOREWORD TO THE THIRD EDITION

That a third edition of this work is now called for, is a cause of fervent praise to God. As the darkness deepens and the pretentions of men are taking on an ever-increasing blatancy, the need becomes greater for the claims of God to be emphasised. As the twentieth century Babel of religious tongues is bewildering so many, the duty of God's servants to point to the one sure anchorage for the heart, is the more apparent. Nothing is so tranquillising and so stabilising as the assurance that the Lord Himself is on the Throne of the universe, "working *all* things after the counsel of His own will".

The Holy Spirit has told us that there are in the Scriptures "some things hard to be understood", but mark it is "hard" *not* "impossible"! A patient waiting on the Lord, a diligent comparison of scripture with scripture, often issues in a fuller apprehension of that which before was obscure to us. During the last ten years it has pleased God to grant us further light on certain parts of His Word, and this we have sought to use in improving our expositions of different passages. But it is with unfeigned thanksgiving that we find it unnecessary to either change or modify any *doctrine* contained in the former editions. Yea, as time goes by, we realise (by Divine grace) with ever-increasing force, the truth, the importance, and the value of the Sovereignty of God as it pertains to every branch of our lives.

Our hearts have been made to rejoice again and again by unsolicited letters which have come to hand from every quarter of the earth, telling of help and blessing received from the former editions of this work. One Christian friend was so stirred by reading it and so impressed by its testimony, that a check was sent to be used in sending free copies to missionaries in fifty foreign countries, "that its glorious message may encircle the globe"; numbers of whom have written us to say how much they have been strengthened in their fight with the powers of darkness. To God alone belongs *all* the glory. May He deign to use this third edition to the honour of His own great

Name, and to the feeding of His scattered and starved
sheep. A. W. P.
Morton's Gap, 1929
Kentucky.

FOREWORD TO THE FOURTH EDITION

It is with profound praise to God "most high" that another
edition of this valuable and helpful book is now called for.
Though its teaching runs directly counter to much that is
being promulgated on every hand today, yet we are happy
to be able to say that its circulation is increasing to the
strengthening of the faith, comfort and hope of an increasing
number of God's elect. We commit this new edition to Him
whom we "delight to honour," praying that He may be
pleased to bless its circulation to the enlightening of many
more of His own, to the "praise of the glory of His grace,"
and a clearer apprehension of the majesty of God and His
sovereign mercy.

1949 I. C. Herendeen

INTRODUCTION

WHO is regulating affairs on this earth today—God, or the Devil? That God reigns supreme in Heaven, is generally conceded; that He does so over this world, is almost universally denied—if not directly, then indirectly. More and more are men in their philosophisings and theorisings, relegating God to the background. Take the material realm. Not only is it denied that God *created* everything, by personal and direct action, but few believe that He has any immediate concern in *regulating* the works of His own hands. Everything is supposed to be ordered according to the (impersonal and abstract) "laws of Nature". Thus is the Creator banished from His own creation. Therefore we need not be surprised that men, in their degrading conceptions, exclude Him from the realm of human affairs. Throughout Christendom, with an almost negligible exception, the theory is held that man is "a free agent", and therefore, lord of his fortunes and the determiner of his destiny. That Satan is to be blamed for much of the evil which is in the world, is freely affirmed by those who, though having so much to say about "the responsibility of man", often *deny* their *own* responsibility, by attributing to the Devil what, in fact, proceeds from their *own* evil hearts (Mark 7:21-23).

But who *is* regulating affairs on this earth today—God, or the Devil? Attempt to take a serious and comprehensive view of the world. What a scene of confusion and chaos confronts us on every side! Sin is rampant; lawlessness abounds; evil men and seducers *are* waxing "worse and worse" (2 Tim. 3:13). Today, everything appears to be *out of joint*. Thrones are creaking and tottering, ancient dynasties are being overturned, democracies are revolting, civilization is a demonstrated failure; half of Christendom was but recently locked-together in a death grapple; and now that the titanic conflict is over, instead of the world having been made "safe for democracy", we have discovered that democracy is very *unsafe* for the world. Unrest, discontent, and lawlessness are rife every where, and none can say how soon another great war will be set in motion. Statesmen are perplexed and staggered. Men's hearts are

11

"failing them for fear, and for looking after those things which are coming on the earth" (Luke 21:26). Do *these* things look as though *God* had full control?

But let us confine our attention to the religious realm. After nineteen centuries of Gospel preaching, Christ is still "despised and rejected of men". Worse still, *He* (the Christ of Scripture) is proclaimed and magnified by very few. In the majority of modern pulpits He is dishonoured and disowned. Despite frantic efforts to attract the crowds, the majority of the churches are being emptied rather than filled. And what of the great masses of non-church goers? In the light of Scripture we are compelled to believe that the "many" are on the Broad Road that leadeth to destruction, and that only "few" are on the Narrow Way that leadeth unto life. Many are declaring that Christianity is a failure, and despair is settling on many faces. Not a few of the Lord's own people are bewildered, and their faith is being severely tried. *And what of God?* Does He see and hear? Is He impotent or indifferent? A number of those who are regarded as leaders of Christian-thought told us that, God could not help the coming of the late awful War, and that He was *unable* to bring about its termination. It was said, and said openly, that conditions were *beyond* God's control. Do these things look as though *God* were ruling the world?

Who *is* regulating affairs on this earth today—God, or the Devil? What impression is made upon the minds of those men of the world who, occasionally, attend a Gospel service? What are the conceptions formed by those who hear even those preachers who are counted as "orthodox"? Is it not that a *disappointed* God is the One whom Christians believe in? From what is heard from the average evangelist today, is not any serious hearer *obliged* to conclude that he professes to represent a God who is filled with benevolent intentions, yet unable to carry them out; that He is earnestly desirous of blessing men, but that they will not let Him? Then, *must not* the average hearer draw the inference that the Devil has gained the upper hand, and that God is to be pitied rather than blamed?

But does not everything seem to show that the Devil *has*

far more to do with the affairs of earth than God has?
Ah, it all depends upon whether we are walking by faith,
or walking by sight. Are your thoughts, my reader, concerning this world and God's relation to it, based upon what
you *see?* Face this question seriously and honestly. And
if you are a Christian, you will, most probably, have cause
to bow your head with shame and sorrow, and to acknowledge that it *is* so. Alas, in reality, we walk very little "by
faith". But what does "walking by faith" signify? It
means that our thoughts are formed, our actions regulated,
our lives moulded by the Holy Scriptures, for, "faith cometh by hearing, and hearing *by the Word of God"* (Rom.
10:17). It is from the Word of Truth, and that alone, that
we can learn what is *God's* relation to this world.

Who is regulating affairs on this earth today—God or the
Devil? *What saith the Scriptures?* Ere we consider the
direct reply to this query, let it be said that, the Scriptures
predicted just what we now see and hear. The prophecy
of Jude is in course of fulfillment. It would lead us too
far astray from our present inquiry to fully amplify this
assertion, but what we have particularly in mind is a sentence
in verse 8—"Likewise also these dreamers defile the flesh,
despise dominion and speak evil of dignities." Yes, they
"speak evil" of the Supreme Dignity, the "Only Potentate,
the King of kings, and Lord of lords." Ours is peculiarly
an age of irreverence, and as the consequence, the spirit of
lawlessness, which brooks no restraint and which is desirous
of casting off everything which interferes with the free
course of self-will, is rapidly engulfing the earth like some
giant tidal wave. The members of the rising generation are
the most flagrant offenders, and in the decay and disappearing of parental authority we have the certain precursor of
the abolition of civic authority. Therefore, in view of the
growing disrespect for human law and the refusal to "render honor to whom honor is due," we need not be surprised
that the recognition of the majesty, the authority, the sovereignty of the Almighty Law-giver should recede more and
more into the background, and that the masses have less and
less patience with those who insist upon them. And conditions will not improve; instead, the more sure Word of
Prophecy makes known to us that they will grow worse and

worse. Nor do we expect to be able to stem the tide — it
has already risen much too high for that. All we can now
hope to do is warn our fellow-saints against the spirit of the
age, and thus seek to counteract its baneful influence upon
them.

Who is regulating affairs on this earth today—God, or
the Devil? What saith the Scriptures? If we believe their
plain and positive declarations, no room is left for uncertainty. They affirm, again and again, that God is on the
throne of the universe; that the sceptre is in His hands;
that He is directing *all things* "after the counsel of His own
will". They affirm, not only that God created all things, but
also that God is ruling and reigning over all the works of
His hands. They affirm that God is the "Almighty", that
His will is irreversible, that He is absolute sovereign in every realm of all His vast dominions. And surely it *must* be
so. Only two alternatives are possible: God must either
rule, or be ruled; sway, or be swayed; accomplish His own
will, or be thwarted by His creatures. Accepting the fact
that He is the "Most High", the only Potentate and King
of kings, vested with perfect wisdom and illimitable power,
and the conclusion is irresistible that He must be God *in
fact*, as well as in name.

It is in view of what we have briefly referred to above,
that we say, Present-day conditions call loudly for a new
examination and new presentation of God's omnipotence,
God's sufficiency, God's sovereignty. From every pulpit in
the land it needs to be thundered forth that God still lives,
that God still observes, that God still reigns. Faith is now
in the crucible, it is being tested by fire, and there is no fixed
and sufficient resting-place for the heart and mind but in
the Throne of God. What is needed now, as never before,
is a full, positive, constructive setting forth of the Godhood
of God. Drastic diseases call for drastic remedies. People
are weary of platitudes and mere generalizations—the call
is for something definite and specific. Soothing-syrup may
serve for peevish children, but an iron tonic is better suited
for adults, and we know of nothing which is more calculated
to infuse spiritual vigor into our frames than a scriptural
apprehension of the full character of God. It is written,

"The people that do *know their God* shall be strong and do exploits" (Dan. 11:32).

Without a doubt a world-crisis is at hand, and everywhere men are alarmed. But God is not! *He* is never taken by surprise. It is no un-expected emergency which now confronts Him, for He is the One who "worketh all things after the counsel of His own will" (Eph. 1:11). Hence, though the world is panic-stricken, the word to the believer is, "Fear not"! "All things" are subject to His immediate control: "all things" are moving in accord with His eternal purpose, and therefore, "all things" are "working together *for good* to them that love God, to them who are the called according to His purpose." It *must* be so, for "of Him, and through Him, and to Him are *all things*" (Rom. 11:36). Yet how little is this realised today even by the people of God! Many suppose that He is little more than a far-distant Spectator, taking no immediate hand in the affairs of earth. It is true that man has a will, but so also has God. It is true that man is endowed with power, but God is all-powerful. It is true that, speaking generally, the material world is regulated by law, but behind that law is the law-Giver and law-Administrator. Man is but the creature. God is the Creator, and endless ages before man first saw the light "the mighty God" (Isa. 9:6) existed, and ere the world was founded, made His plans; and being infinite in power and man only finite, His purpose and plan cannot be withstood or thwarted by the creatures of His own hands.

We readily acknowledge that life is a profound problem, and that we are surrounded by mystery on every side; but we are not like the beasts of the field—ignorant of their origin, and unconscious of what is before them. No: *"We have* also a more sure Word of Prophecy", of which it is said ye do well that ye "take heed, as unto a light that shineth in a dark place, until the day dawn, and the day star arise in your hearts" (2 Pet. 1:19). And it is to this Word of Prophecy we indeed do well to "take heed," to that Word which had not its origin in the mind of man but in the Mind of God, for, "the prophecy came not at any time by the will of man: but holy men of God spake moved by the Holy Spirit." We say again, it is to *this "Word"* we do well to take heed. As we turn to this Word and are instructed thereout, we discover a fundamental principle which must be applied to every problem: Instead of beginning with man and his world and working back to God, we must begin with God and work down to man—"In the beginning *God*"! Apply this principle to the present situation. Begin with the world as it is today and try and work back to God, and everything will seem to show that God has no connection with the world at all. But begin with God and work down to the world and light, much light, is cast on the problem. Because God is *holy* His anger burns against sin; because God is *righteous* His judgments fall upon those who rebel against Him; because God is *faithful* the solemn threatenings of His Word are fulfilled; because God is *omnipotent* none can successfully resist Him, still less overthrow His counsel; and because God is *omniscient* no problem can master Him and no difficulty baffle His wisdom. It is just because God is who He is and what He is that we are now beholding on earth what we do—the beginning of His outpoured judgments: in view of His inflexible justice and immaculate holiness we could not expect anything other than what is now spread before our eyes.

But let it be said very emphatically that the heart can only rest upon and *enjoy* the blessed truth of the absolute sovereignty of God as *faith is in exercise*. Faith is ever occupied with *God*. That is the character of it; that is what differentiates it from intellectual theology. Faith *endures* "as seeing Him who is invisible" (Heb. 11:27): endures the disappointments, the hardships, and the heart-aches of life, by recognising that *all* comes from the hand of Him who is too wise to err and too loving to be unkind. But so long as we are occupied with any other object than God Himself, there will be neither rest for the heart nor peace for the mind. But when we receive all that enters our lives as from *His* hand, then, no matter what may be our circumstances or surroundings—whether in a hovel, a prison-dungeon, or a martyr's stake—we shall be enabled to say, "The lines are fallen unto me in *pleasant* places" (Psa. 16:6). But *that* is the language of *faith,* not of sight or of sense.

But if instead of bowing to the testimony of Holy Writ, if instead of walking by faith, we follow the evidence of our eyes, and *reason* therefrom, we shall fall into a quagmire of virtual atheism. Or, if we are regulated by the opinions and views of others, peace will be at an end. Granted that there *is* much in this world of sin and suffering which appals and saddens us; granted that there is much in the providential dealings of God which startle and stagger us; that is no reason why we should unite with the unbelieving worldling who says, "If I were God, I would not allow this or tolerate that" etc. Better far, in the presence of bewildering mystery, to say with one of old, "I was dumb, I opened not my mouth; because Thou didst it" (Psa. 39:9). Scripture tells us that God's judgments *are* "unsearchable", and His ways "past finding out" (Rom. 11:33). It must be so if faith is to be tested, confidence in His wisdom and righteousness strengthened, and submission to His holy will fostered.

Here is the fundamental difference between the man of faith and the man of unbelief. The unbeliever is "of the world," judges everything by worldly standards, views life from the standpoint of time and sense, and weighs everything in the balances of his own carnal making. But the man of faith *brings in God,* looks at everything from *His* standpoint, estimates values by spiritual standards, and views life in the light of eternity. Doing this, he receives whatever comes as from the hand of God. Doing this, his heart is calm in the midst of the storm. Doing this, he rejoices in hope of the glory of God.

In these opening paragraphs we have indicated the lines of thought followed out in this book. Our first postulate is that because God *is God,* He does as He pleases, only as He pleases, always as He pleases; that His great concern is the accomplishment of His own pleasure and the promotion of His own glory; that He is the Supreme Being, and therefore Sovereign of the universe. Starting with this postulate we have contemplated the *exercise* of God's Sovereignty, first in Creation, second in Governmental Administration over the works of His hands, third in the Salvation of His own elect, fourth in the Reprobation of the wicked, and fifth in Operation upon and within men. Next we have viewed the Sovereignty of God as it relates to the human Will in particular and human Responsibility in general, and have sought to show what is the only becoming attitude for the creature to take in view of the majesty of the Creator. A separate chapter has been set apart for a consideration of some of the difficulties which are involved, and to answering the questions which are likely to be raised in the minds of our readers; while one chapter has been devoted to a more careful yet brief examination of God's Sovereignty in relation to prayer. Finally, we have sought to show that the Sovereignty of God is a truth revealed to us in Scripture for the comfort of our hearts, the strengthening of our souls, and the blessing of our lives. A due apprehension of God's Sovereignty promotes the spirit of worship, provides an incentive to practical godliness, and inspires zeal in service. It is deeply humbling to the human heart, but in proportion to the degree that it brings man into the dust before his Maker, to that extent is God glorified.

We are well aware that what we have written is in open opposition to much of the teaching that is current both in religious literature and in the representative pulpits of the land. We freely grant that the postulate of God's Sovereignty with all its corollaries is at direct variance with the opinions and thoughts of the natural man, but the truth is, *we* are quite *unable* to think upon these matters: we are *incompetent* for forming a proper estimate of God's character and ways, and it is because of this that God has given us a revelation of *His* mind, and in that revelation He plainly declares, "My thoughts are not your thoughts, neither are your ways My ways, saith the Lord. For as the heavens are higher than the earth, so are My ways higher than your ways, and My thoughts than your thoughts" (Is. 55:8, 9). In view of this scripture, it is only to be expected that much of the contents of the Bible *conflicts* with the sentiments of the carnal mind, which is *enmity* against God. Our appeal then is not to the popular beliefs of the day, nor to the creeds of the churches, but to the Law and Testimony of Jehovah. All that we ask for is an impartial and attentive examination of what we have written, and that, made prayerfully in the light of the Lamp of Truth. May the reader heed the Divine admonition to "prove all things; hold fast that which is good" (1 Thess. 5:21).

I

GOD'S SOVEREIGNTY DEFINED

"Thine, O Lord, is the greatness, and the power, and the glory, and the victory, and the majesty: for all that is in the heaven and in the earth is Thine; Thine is the kingdom, O Lord, and Thou art exalted as Head above all" (I Chron. 29:11).

THE Sovereignty of God is an expression that once was generally understood. It was a phrase commonly used in religious literature. It was a theme frequently expounded in the pulpit. It was a truth which brought comfort to many hearts, and gave virility and stability to Christian character. But, today, to make mention of God's sovereignty is, in many quarters, to speak in an unknown tongue. Were we to announce from the average pulpit that the subject of our discourse would be the sovereignty of God, it would sound very much as though we had borrowed a phrase from one of the dead languages. Alas! that it should be so. Alas! that the doctrine which is the key to history, the interpreter of Providence, the warp and woof of Scripture, and the foundation of Christian theology, should be so sadly neglected and so little understood.

The sovereignty of God. What do we mean by this expression? We mean the supremacy of God, the kingship of God, the godhood of God. To say that God is sovereign is to declare that God *is* God. To say that God is sovereign is to declare that He is the Most High, doing according to His will in the army of heaven, and among the inhabitants of the earth, so that none can stay His hand or say unto Him what doest Thou? (Dan. 4:35). To say that God is sovereign is to declare that He is the Almighty, the Possessor of all power in heaven and earth, so that none can defeat His counsels, thwart His purpose, or resist His will (Ps. 115:3). To say that God is sovereign is to declare that He is "The Governor among the nations" (Ps. 22:28), setting up kingdoms, overthrowing empires, and determining the course of dynasties as pleaseth Him best. To say that God is sovereign is to declare that He is the "Only Potentate, the King of kings, and Lord of lords" (1 Tim. 6:15). Such is the God of the Bible.

How different is the God of the Bible from the God of

modern Christendom! The conception of Deity which prevails most widely today, even among those who profess to
give heed to the Scriptures, is a miserable caricature, a blasphemous travesty of the Truth. The God of the twentieth
century is a helpless, effeminate being who commands the
respect of no really thoughtful man. The God of the popular mind is the creation of a maudlin sentimentality. The
God of many a present-day pulpit is an object of pity rather
than of awe-inspiring reverence.* To say that God the Father has purposed the salvation of all mankind, that God
the Son died with the express intention of saving the whole
human race, and that God the Holy Spirit is now seeking
to win the world to Christ; when, as a matter of common
observation, it is apparent that the great majority of our
fellow-men are dying in sin, and passing into a hopeless
eternity: is to say that God the Father is *disappointed,* that
God the Son is *dis-satisfied,* and that God the Holy Spirit is
defeated. We have stated the issue baldly, but there is no
escaping the conclusion. To argue that God is "trying His
best" to save all mankind, but that the majority of men will
not let Him save them, is to insist that the will of the Creator is impotent, and that the will of the creature is omnipotent. To throw the blame, as many do, upon the Devil, does
not remove the difficulty, for if Satan is defeating the purpose of God, then, Satan is Almighty and God is no longer
the Supreme Being.

To declare that the Creator's original plan has been frustrated by sin, is to *dethrone* God. To suggest that God was
taken by surprise in Eden and that He is now attempting
to remedy an unforeseen calamity, is to *degrade* the Most
High to the level of a finite, erring mortal. To argue that
man is a free moral agent and the determiner of his own
destiny, and that therefore he has the power to checkmate
his Maker, is to *strip* God of the attribute of Omnipotence.
To say that the creature has burst the bounds assigned by his
Creator, and that God is now practically a helpless Spectator before the sin and suffering entailed by Adam's fall, is to

---

*Some years ago an evangelical (?) preacher of nation-wide repu-
tation visited the town in which we then were, and during the course
of his address kept repeating, "Poor God! Poor God!" Surely it is
this "preacher" who needs to be pitied.

repudiate the express declaration of Holy Writ, namely, "Surely the wrath of man shall praise Thee: the remainder of wrath *shalt Thou restrain"* (Ps. 76:10). In a word, to deny the sovereignty of God is to enter upon a path which, if followed to its logical terminus, is to arrive at blank atheism.

The sovereignty of the God of Scripture is absolute, irresistible, infinite. When we say that God is sovereign we affirm His right to govern the universe, which He has made for His own glory, just as He pleases. We affirm that *His right* is the right of the Potter over the clay, i.e., that He may mould that clay into whatsoever form He chooses, fashioning out of *the same lump* one vessel unto honor and another unto dishonor. We affirm that He is under no rule or law outside of His own will and nature, *that God is a law unto Himself,* and that He is under no obligation to give an account of His matters to any.

Sovereignty characterises the whole Being of God. He is sovereign in all His attributes. *He is sovereign in the exercise of His power.* His power is exercised *as* He wills, *when* He wills, *where* He wills. This fact is evidenced on every page of Scripture. For a long season that power appears to be dormant, and then it is put forth in irresistible might. Pharaoh dared to hinder Israel from going forth to worship Jehovah in the wilderness—what happened? God exercised His power, His people were delivered and their cruel task-masters slain. But a little later, the Amalekites dared to attack these same Israelites in the wilderness, and what happened? Did God put forth His power on this occasion and display His hand as He did at the Red Sea? Were these enemies of His people promptly overthrown and destroyed? No, on the contrary, the Lord swore that He would "have war with Amalek *from generation to generation"* (Ex. 17:16). Again, when Israel entered the land of Canaan, God's power was signally displayed. The city of Jericho barred their progress—what happened? Israel did not draw a bow nor strike a blow: the Lord stretched forth His hand and the walls fell down flat. But the miracle was never repeated! *No other city fell after this manner.* Every other city had to be captured by the sword!

Many other instances might be adduced illustrating the

sovereign exercise of God's power. Take one other example. God put forth His power and David was delivered from Goliath, the giant; the mouths of the lions were closed and Daniel escaped unhurt; the three Hebrew children were cast into the burning fiery furnace and came forth unharmed and unscorched. *But God's power did not always interpose for the deliverance of His people,* for we read: *"And others* had trial of cruel mockings and scourgings, yea, moreover of bonds and imprisonment: they were stoned, they were sawn asunder, were tempted, were slain with the sword; they wandered about in sheepskins and goatskins; being destitute, afflicted, tormented" (Heb. 11:36, 37). But why? Why were not these men of faith delivered like the others? Or, why were not the others suffered to be killed like these? Why should God's power interpose and rescue some and not the others? Why allow Stephen to be stoned to death, and then deliver Peter from prison?

God is sovereign in the *delegation of His power to others.* Why did God endow Methuselah with a vitality which enabled him to outlive all his contemporaries? Why did God impart to Samson a physical strength which no other human has ever possessed? Again; it is written, "But thou shalt remember the Lord thy God: for it is He that *giveth thee power* to get wealth" (Deut. 8:18), but God does not bestow this power on all alike. Why not? Why has He given such power to men like Morgan, Carnegie, Rockefeller? The answer to all of these questions, is, Because God is Sovereign, and being Sovereign He does as He pleases.

God is sovereign in the exercise of His mercy. Necessarily so, for mercy is directed by the *will* of Him that showeth mercy. Mercy is not a *right* to which man is entitled. Mercy is that adorable attribute of God by which He pities and relieves the wretched. But under the righteous government of God no one is wretched who does not *deserve* to be so. The objects of mercy, then, are those who are miserable, and all misery is the result of *sin,* hence the miserable are deserving of punishment not mercy. To speak of *deserving mercy* is a contradiction of terms.

God bestows His mercies on whom He pleases and withholds them as seemeth good unto Himself. A remarkable illustration of this fact is seen in the manner that God responded to the prayers of two men offered under very similar circumstances. Sentence of death was passed upon Moses for one act of disobedience, and he besought the Lord for a reprieve. But was his desire gratified? No; he told Israel, 'The Lord is wroth with me for your sakes, *and would not hear me:* and the Lord said unto me, Let it suffice thee" (Deut. 3:26). Now mark the second case:—"In those days was Hezekiah sick unto death. And the prophet Isaiah the son of Amoz came to him, and said unto him, Thus saith the Lord, Set thine house in order; for thou shalt die, and not live. Then he turned his face to the wall, and prayed unto the Lord, saying, I beseech Thee, O Lord, remember now how I have walked before Thee in truth and with a perfect heart, and have done that which is good in Thy sight. And Hezekiah wept sore. And it came to pass, afore Isaiah was gone out into the middle court, that the word of the Lord came to him, saying, Turn again, and tell Hezekiah the captain of my people, Thus saith the Lord, the God of David thy father, *I have heard thy prayer,* I have seen thy tears: behold, I will heal thee: on the third day thou shalt go up unto the house of the Lord. And I will add unto thy days fifteen years" (2 Kings 20:1-6). Both of these men had the sentence of death in themselves, and both prayed earnestly unto the Lord for a reprieve: the one wrote: "The Lord would not hear me," and died; but to the other it was said, "I have heard thy prayer", and his life was spared. What an illustration and exemplification of the truth expressed in Rom. 9:15!—"For He saith to Moses, I will have mercy *on whom I will have mercy,* and I will have compassion *on whom I will have compassion.*"

The sovereign exercise of God's mercy—pity shown to the wretched—was displayed when Jehovah became flesh and tabernacled among men. Take one illustration. During one of the Feasts of the Jews, the Lord Jesus went up to Jerusalem. He came to the Pool of Bethesda, where lay *"a great multitude* of impotent folk, of blind, halt, withered, waiting for the moving of the water." Among this "great multitude" there was "a certain man which had an infirmity thirty and eight years." What happened? "When Jesus saw *him* lie, and knew that he had been now a long time in that case, he saith *unto him,* Wilt thou be made whole? The impotent man answered Him, Sir, I have no man, when the water is troubled, to put me into the pool: but while I am coming, another steppeth down before me. Jesus saith unto him, Rise, take up thy bed, and walk. And immediately the man was made whole, and took up his bed, and walked" (John 5:3-9). Why was this one man singled out from all the others? We are not told that he cried "Lord, have mercy *on me.*" There is not a word in the narrative which intimates that this man possessed any qualifications which entitled him to receive special favor. Here then was a case of the sovereign exercise of Divine mercy, for it was just as easy for Christ to heal the whole of that "great multitude" as this one "certain man." But He did not. He put forth His power and relieved the wretchedness of this one particular sufferer, and for some reason known only to Himself, He declined to do the same for the others. Again, we say, what an illustration and exemplification of Rom. 9:15!—"I will have mercy on whom I will have mercy, and I will have compassion on whom I will have compassion."

God is sovereign in the exercise of His love. Ah! that is a hard saying, who then can receive it? It is written, "A man can receive nothing, except it be given him from heaven" (John 3:27). When we say that God is sovereign in the exercise of His love, we mean that He loves whom He chooses. God does not love everybody*; if He did, He would love the Devil. Why does not God love the Devil? Because there is nothing in him *to love;* because there is nothing in him to *attract* the heart of God. Nor is there anything to *attract* God's love in any of the fallen sons of Adam, for *all* of them are, by nature, "children of *wrath*" (Eph. 2:3). If then there is nothing in any member of the human race to attract God's love, and if, notwithstanding, He *does* love *some,* then it necessarily follows that the *cause* of His love must be found in Himself, which is only another way of saying that the exercise of God's love to-

---

*John 3:16 will be examined on pages 202-205 and App. III, pages 253-255.

wards the fallen sons of men is according to His own good pleasure.†

In the final analysis, the exercise of God's love *must* be traced back to His sovereignty, or, otherwise, He would *love by rule;* and if He loved by rule, then is He under *a law of love,* and if He is under a *law* of love then is He not supreme, but is Himself *ruled* by law. "But," it may be asked, "Surely you do not *deny* that God loves the entire human family?" We reply, it is written, "Jacob have I loved, but Esau have I hated" (Rom. 9:13). If then God loved Jacob and hated Esau, and that before they were born or had done either good or evil, then the *reason* for His love was not in them, but in Himself.

That the exercise of God's love *is* according to His own sovereign pleasure is also clear from the language of Eph. 1:3-5, where we read, "Blessed be the God and Father of our Lord Jesus Christ, who hath blessed us with all spiritual blessings in heavenly places in Christ: According as He hath chosen us in Him before the foundation of the world, that we should be holy and without blame before Him. *In love having predestinated us* unto the adoption of children by Jesus Christ to Himself *according to the good pleasure of His will."* It was *"in love"* that God the Father predestined His chosen ones unto the adoption of children by Jesus Christ to Himself, "according"—according to what? According to *some excellency* He discovered in them? No. What then? According to what He *foresaw* they would become? No; mark carefully the inspired answer—"According to the good pleasure *of His will."*

God is sovereign in the exercise of His grace. This of necessity, for grace is favor shown to the *un-deserving,* yea, to the Hell-deserving. Grace is the antithesis of justice. Justice demands the impartial enforcement of law. Justice requires that each shall receive his legitimate due, neither

†We are not unmindful of the fact that men have invented the distinction between God's love of *complacency* and His love of *compassion,* but this *is* an invention pure and simple. *Scripture* terms the latter God's "pity" (see Matt. 18:33), and "He is *kind* unto the unthankful and the evil" (Luke 6:35)!

more nor less. Justice bestows no favors and is no respecter of persons. Justice, as such, shows no pity and knows no mercy. But after justice has been fully satisfied, grace flows forth. Divine grace is not exercised at the expense of justice, but "grace reigns through righteousness" (Rom. 5:21), and if grace *"reigns"*, then is grace sovereign.

Grace has been defined as the unmerited favor of God;* and if unmerited, then none can claim it as their inalienable *right*. If grace is unearned and undeserved, then none are *entitled* to it. If grace is a gift, then none can *demand* it. Therefore, as salvation is by grace, the free gift of God, then He bestows it on whom He pleases. Because salvation is by grace, the very chief of sinners is not beyond the reach of Divine mercy. Because salvation is by grace, boasting is excluded and God gets all the glory.

The sovereign exercise of grace is illustrated on nearly every page of Scripture. The Gentiles are left to walk in their own ways, while Israel becomes the covenant people of Jehovah. Ishmael the firstborn is cast out comparatively unblest, while Isaac the son of his parents' old age is made the child of promise. Esau the generous-hearted and forgiving-spirited is denied the blessing, though he sought it carefully with tears, while the worm Jacob receives the inheritance and is fashioned into a vessel of honor. So in the New Testament. Divine truth is hidden from the wise and prudent, but is revealed to babes. The Pharisees and Sadducees are left to go their own way, while publicans and harlots are drawn by the cords of love.

In a remarkable manner Divine grace was exercised at the time of the Saviour's birth. The incarnation of God's Son was one of the greatest events in the history of the universe, and yet its actual occurrence was not made known to all mankind; instead, it was specially revealed to the Bethlehem shepherds and wise men of the East. And this was pro-

---

*An esteemed friend who kindly read through this book in its manuscript form, and to whom we are indebted for a number of excellent suggestions, has pointed out that, grace is something more than "unmerited favor." To feed a tramp who calls on me is "unmerited favor," but it is scarcely *grace*. But suppose that after *robbing* me I should feed this starving tramp—*that* would be "grace." Grace, then, is favor shown where there is positive *de*-merit in the one receiving it.

phetic and indicative of the entire course of this dispensation, for even today Christ is not made known to all. It would have been an easy matter for God to have sent a company of angels to *every nation* and announced the birth of His Son. But He did not. God could have readily attracted the attention of all mankind to the "star;" but He did not. Why? Because God is sovereign and dispenses His favors as He pleases. Note particularly the two classes to whom the birth of the Saviour *was* made known, namely, the most *unlikely* classes—illiterate shepherds and heathen from a far country. No angel stood before the Sanhedrin and announced the advent of Israel's Messiah! No "star" appeared unto the scribes and lawyers as they, in their pride and self-righteousness, searched the Scriptures! They searched diligently to find out where He should be born, and yet it was not made known *to them* when He was actually come. What a display of Divine sovereignty—the illiterate shepherds singled out for peculiar honor, and the learned and eminent passed by! And why was the birth of the Saviour revealed to these foreigners, and not to those in whose midst He was born? See in this a wonderful foreshadowing of God's dealings with our race throughout the entire Christian dispensation—sovereign in the exercise of His grace, bestowing His favors on whom He pleases, often on the most unlikely and unworthy.*

*It has been pointed out to us that God's sovereignty was signally displayed in His choice of *the place* where His Son was born. Not to Greece or Italy did the Lord of Glory come, but to the insignificant land of Palestine! Not in Jerusalem—the royal city—was Immanuel born, but in Bethlehem, which was *"little* among the thousands (of towns and villages) in Judah" (Micah 5:2)! And it was in despised *Nazareth* that He grew up!! Truly, God's ways are not ours.

II

THE SOVEREIGNTY OF GOD IN CREATION

"Thou art worthy, O Lord, to receive glory, and honor, and power: for Thou hast created all things, and for Thy pleasure they are and were created" (Rev. 4:11).

HAVING shown that sovereignty characterises the whole Being of God, let us now observe how it marks all His ways and dealings.

In the great expanse of eternity, which stretches behind Genesis 1:1, the universe was unborn and creation existed only in the mind of the great Creator. In His sovereign majesty God dwelt all alone. We refer to that far distant period before the heavens and the earth were created. There were then no angels to hymn God's praises, no creatures to occupy His notice, no rebels to be brought into subjection. The great God was all alone amid the awful silence of His own vast universe. But even at that time, if time it could be called, God was sovereign. He might create or not create *according to His own good pleasure.* He might create this way or that way; He might create one world or one million worlds, and who was there to resist His will? He might call into existence a million different creatures and place them on *absolute equality,* endowing them with the same faculties and placing them in the same environment; or, He might create a million creatures each *differing* from the others, and possessing nothing in common save their creaturehood, and who was there to challenge His right? If He so pleased, He might call into existence a world so immense that its dimensions were utterly beyond finite computation; and were He so disposed, He might create an organism so small that nothing but the most powerful microscope could reveal its existence to human eyes. It was His sovereign right to create, on the one hand, the exalted seraphim to burn around His throne, and on the other hand, the tiny insect which dies the same hour that it is born. If the mighty God chose to have *one vast gradation* in His universe, from loftiest seraph to creeping reptile, from revolving worlds to floating atoms, from macrocosm to microcosm, *instead of making everything uniform,* who was there to question His sovereign pleasure?

28

Behold then the exercise of Divine sovereignty long before man ever saw the light. With whom took God counsel in the creation and disposition of His creatures. See the birds as they fly through the air, the beasts as they roam the earth, the fishes as they swim in the sea, and then ask, Who was it that made them to differ? Was it not their Creator who *sovereignly* assigned their various locations and adaptations to them!

Turn your eye to the heavens and observe the mysteries of Divine sovereignty which there confront the thoughtful beholder: "There is one glory of the sun, and another glory of the moon, and another glory of the stars: for one star *differeth from* another star in glory" (1 Cor. 15:41). But why should they? Why should the sun be more glorious than all the other planets? Why should there be stars of the first magnitude and others of the tenth? Why such amazing *inequalities?* Why should some of the heavenly bodies be *more favorably placed* than others in their relation to the sun? And why should there be 'shooting stars,' falling stars, "wandering stars" (Jude 13), in a word, *ruined* stars? And the only possible answer is, "For Thy pleasure they are and were created" (Rev. 4:11).

Come now to our own planet. Why should two thirds of its surface be covered with water, and why should so much of its remaining third be unfit for human cultivation or habitation? Why should there be vast stretches of marshes, deserts and ice-fields? Why should one country be so inferior, topographically, from another? Why should one be fertile, and another almost barren? Why should one be rich in minerals and another own none? Why should the climate of one be congenial and healthy, and another uncongenial and unhealthy? Why should one abound in rivers and lakes, and another be almost devoid of them? Why should one be constantly troubled with earthquakes, and another be almost entirely free from them? Why? Because thus it pleased the Creator and Upholder of all things.

Look at the animal kingdom and note the wondrous variety. What comparison is possible between the lion and the lamb, the bear and the kid, the elephant and the mouse? Some, like the horse and the dog, are gifted with great intelligence; while others, like sheep and swine, are almost devoid of it. Why? Some are designed to be beasts of burden, while others enjoy a life of freedom. But why should the mule and the donkey be shackled to a life of drudgery, while the lion and tiger are allowed to roam the jungle at their pleasure? Some are fit for food, others unfit; some are beautiful, others ugly; some are endowed with great strength, others are quite helpless; some are fleet of foot, others can scarcely crawl—contrast the hare and the tortoise; some are of use to man, others appear to be quite valueless; some live for centuries, others a few months at most; some are tame, others fierce. But why all these variations and differences?

What is true of the animals is equally true of the birds and fishes. But consider now *the vegetable kingdom*. Why should roses have thorns, and lilies grow without them? Why should one flower emit a fragrant aroma and another have none? Why should one tree bear fruit which is wholesome and another that which is poisonous? Why should one vegetable be capable of enduring frost and another wither under it? Why should one apple tree be loaded with fruit, and another tree of the same age and in the same orchard be almost barren? Why should one plant flower a dozen times in a year and another bear blossoms but once a century? Truly, *"whatsoever the Lord pleased,* that did He in heaven, and in the earth, in the seas, and all deep places" (Ps. 135: 6).

Consider the angelic hosts. Surely we shall find uniformity here. But no; there, as elsewhere, the same sovereign pleasure of the Creator is displayed. Some are higher in rank than others; some are more powerful than others; some are nearer to God than others. Scripture reveals a definite and well-defined gradation in the angelic orders. From arch-angel, past seraphim and cherubim, we come to "principalities and powers" (Eph. 3:10), and from principalities and powers to "rulers" (Eph. 6:12), and then to the angels themselves, and even among them we read of "the *elect* angels" (1 Tim. 5:21). Again we ask, Why this *inequality,* this difference in rank and order? And all we can say is "Our God is in the heavens, He hath done whatsoever He hath pleased" (Ps. 115:3).

If then we see the sovereignty of God displayed throughout all creation why should it be thought a strange thing if we behold it operating in the midst of *the human family?* Why should it be thought strange if to one God is pleased to give five talents and to another only one? Why should it be thought strange if one is born with a robust constitution and another of the same parents is frail and sickly? Why should it be thought strange if Abel is cut off in his prime, while Cain is suffered to live on for many years? Why should it be thought strange that some should be born black and others white; some be born idiots and others with high intellectual endowments; some be born constitutionally lethargic and others full of energy; some be born with a temperament that is selfish, fiery, egotistical, others who are naturally self-sacrificing, submissive and meek? Why should it be thought strange if some are qualified by nature to lead and rule, while others are only fitted to follow and serve? Heredity and environment cannot account for all these variations and inequalities. No; it is *God* who maketh one to differ from another. Why should He? "Even so, Father, for so it seemed good in Thy sight" must be our reply.

Learn then this basic truth, that the Creator is absolute Sovereign, executing His own will, performing His own pleasure, and considering nought but His own glory. *"The Lord hath made all things FOR HIMSELF"* (Prov. 16:4). And had He not a perfect *right* to? Since God *is* God, who dare challenge His prerogative? To murmur against Him is rank rebellion. To question His ways is to impugn His wisdom. To criticise Him is sin of the deepest dye. Have we forgotten *who* He is? Behold, "All nations before Him are as nothing; and they are counted to Him less than nothing, and vanity. To whom then will ye liken God?" (Isaiah 40:17, 18).

III

THE SOVEREIGNTY OF GOD IN ADMINISTRATION

"The Lord hath prepared His Throne in the heavens;
and His Kingdom ruleth over all" (Psalm 103:19).

FIRST, a word concerning the *need* for God to govern *the material world.* Suppose the opposite for a moment. For the sake of argument, let us say that God created the world, designed and fixed certain laws (which men term "the laws of Nature"), and that He then *withdrew,* leaving the world to its fortune and the out-working of these laws. In such a case, we should have a world over which there was no intelligent, presiding Governor, a world controlled by nothing more than *impersonal* laws—a concept worthy of gross Materialism and blank Atheism. But, I say, suppose it for a moment; and in the light of such a supposition, weigh well the following question:—What guaranty have we that some day ere long the world will not be destroyed? A very superficial observation of 'the laws of Nature' reveals the fact that they are *not uniform* in their working. The proof of this is seen in the fact that no two seasons are alike. If then Nature's laws are irregular in their operations, what guaranty have we against some dreadful catastrophe striking our earth? "The wind bloweth *where it listeth"* (pleaseth), which means that man can neither harness nor hinder it. Sometimes the wind blows with great fury, and it might be that it should suddenly gather in volume and velocity, until it became a hurricane earth-wide in its range. If there is nothing more than the laws of Nature regulating the wind, then, perhaps tomorrow, there may come a terrific tornado and sweep everything from the surface of the earth! What assurance have we against such a calamity? Again; of late years we have heard and read much about clouds bursting and flooding whole districts, working fearful havoc in the destruction of both property and life. Man is helpless before them, for science can devise no means to *prevent* clouds bursting. Then how do we know that these bursting-clouds will not be multiplied indefinitely and the whole earth be deluged by their downpour? This would be nothing new: why should not the Flood of Noah's day be repeated? And what of earthquakes?

33

Every few years, some island or some great city is swept
out of existence by one of them—and what can man do?
Where is the guaranty that ere long a mammoth earthquake
will not destroy the whole world? Science tells us of great
subterranean fires burning beneath the comparatively thin
crust of our earth, how do we know but what these fires will
not suddenly burst forth and consume our entire globe?
Surely every reader now sees the point we are seeking to
make: Deny that God is *governing* matter, deny that *He* is
"upholding all things by the word of His power" (Heb. 1:
3), *and all sense of security is gone!*

Let us pursue a similar course of reasoning in connection
with *the human race*. Is God governing this world of ours?
Is He shaping the destinies of nations, controlling the course
of empires, determining the limits of dynasties? Has He
prescribed the limits of evil-doers, saying, Thus far shalt
thou go and no further? Let us suppose the opposite for a
moment. Let us assume that God has delivered over the
helm into the hand of His creatures, and see where such a
supposition leads us. For the sake of argument we will say
that every man enters this world endowed with a will that is
absolutely free, and that it is *impossible* to compel or even
coerce him without *destroying* his freedom. Let us say that
every man possesses a knowledge of right and wrong, that he
has the power to choose between them, and that he is left entirely free to make his own choice and go his own way. Then
what? Then it follows that man is *sovereign,* for he does as
he pleases and is the architect of his own fortune. But in
such a case we can have no assurance that ere long every
man will reject the good and choose the evil. In such a case
we have no guaranty against the entire human race committing moral suicide. Let all Divine restraints be removed
and man be left absolutely free, and all ethical distinctions
would immediately disappear, the spirit of barbarism would
prevail universally, and pandemonium would reign supreme.
Why not? If one nation deposes its rulers and repudiates
its constitution, what is there to prevent all nations from doing the same? If little more than a century ago the streets
of Paris ran with the blood of rioters, what assurance have
we that before the present century closes every city throughout the world will not witness a similar sight? What is

there to hinder earthwide lawlessness and universal anarchy? Thus we have sought to show the *need,* the imperative need, for God to occupy the Throne, take the government upon *His* shoulder, and control the activities and destinies of His creatures.

But has the man of faith any difficulty in perceiving the government of God over this world? Does not the anointed eye discern, even amid much seeming confusion and chaos, the hand of the Most High controlling and shaping the affairs of men, even in the common concerns of every day life? Take for example farmers and their crops. Suppose God left them to themselves: what would then prevent them, one and all, from grassing their arable lands and devoting themselves exclusively to the rearing of cattle and dairying? In such a case there would be a world-famine of wheat and corn! Take the work of the post-office. Suppose that everybody decided to write letters on Mondays only, could the authorities cope with the mail on Tuesdays? and how would they occupy their time the balance of the week? So again with storekeepers. What would happen if *every* housewife did her shopping on Wednesday, and stayed at home the rest of the week? But instead of such things happening, farmers in different countries both raise sufficient cattle and grow enough grain of various kinds to supply the almost incalculable needs of the human race; the mails are almost evenly distributed over the six days of the week; and some women shop on Monday, some on Tuesday, and so on. Do not these things clearly evidence the overruling and controlling hand of God!

Having shown, in brief, the imperative need for God to reign over our world, let us now observe still further the *fact* that God *does* rule, actually rule, and that His government extends to and is exercised over all things and all creatures. And,

1. GOD GOVERNS INANIMATE MATTER.

That God governs inanimate matter, that inanimate matter performs His bidding and fulfils His decrees, is clearly shown on the very frontispiece of Divine revelation. God said, Let there be light, and we read, *"There was light."* God said, "Let the waters under the heaven be gathered to-

gether unto one place, and let the dry land appear," and
"it was so." And again, "God said, Let the earth bring
forth grass, the herb yielding seed, and the fruit tree yielding
fruit after his kind, whose seed is in itself, upon the earth:
and it was so." As the Psalmist declares, "He spake, and it
was done; He commanded, and it stood fast."

What is stated in Genesis one is afterwards illustrated all
through the Bible. After the creation of Adam, sixteen centuries went by before ever a shower of rain fell upon the
earth, for before Noah "there went up a mist from the earth,
and watered the whole face of the ground" (Gen. 2:6).
But, when the iniquities of the antediluvians had come to
the full, then God said, "And, behold, *I, even I, do bring a
flood of waters upon the earth,* to destroy all flesh, wherein
is the breath of life, from under heaven; and everything
that is in the earth shall die;" and in fulfillment of this we
read, "In the six hundredth year of Noah's life, in the second month, the seventeenth day of the month, the same day
were all the fountains of the great deep broken up, and the
windows of heaven were opened. And the rain was upon
the earth forty days and forty nights" (Gen. 6:17 and 7:
11, 12).

Witness God's absolute (and *sovereign)* control of inanimate matter in connection with the plagues upon Egypt. At
His bidding the light was turned into darkness and rivers
into blood; hail fell, and death came down upon the godless
land of the Nile, until even its haughty monarch was compelled to cry out for deliverance. Note particularly how
the inspired record here emphasises God's absolute control
over the elements—"And Moses stretched forth his rod
toward heaven: *and the Lord sent* thunder and hail, and the
fire ran along upon the ground; *and the Lord* rained hail
upon the land of Egypt. So there was hail, and fire mingled
with the hail, very grievous, such as there was none like it
in all the land of Egypt since it became a nation. And the
hail smote throughout all the land of Egypt all that was in
the field, both man and beast; and the hail smote every herb
of the field, and brake every tree of the field. *Only in the
land of Goshen, where the children of Israel were, was there
no hail"* (Ex. 9:23-26). The same distinction was observed
in connection with the ninth plague: "And the Lord said

unto Moses, Stretch out thine hand toward heaven, that there may be darkness over the land of Egypt, even darkness which may be felt. And Moses stretched forth his hand toward heaven; and there was a thick darkness in all the land of Egypt three days: They saw not one another, neither rose any from his place for three days: *but all the children of Israel had light in their dwellings"* (Ex. 10:21-23).

The above examples are by no means *isolated* cases. At God's decree fire and brimstone descended from heaven and the cities of the Plain were destroyed, and a fertile valley was converted into a loathsome sea of death. At His bidding the waters of the Red Sea parted asunder so that the Israelites passed over dry shod, and at His word they rolled back again and destroyed the Egyptians who were pursuing them. A word from Him, and the earth opened her mouth and Korah and his rebellious company were swallowed up. The furnace of Nebuchadnezzar was heated seven times beyond its normal temperature, and into it three of God's children were cast, but the fire did not so much as scorch their clothes, though it slew the men who cast them into it.

What a demonstration of the Creator's governmental control over the elements was furnished when He became flesh and tabernacled among men! Behold Him asleep in the boat. A storm arises. The winds roar and the waves are lashed into fury. The disciples who are with Him, fearful lest their little craft should founder, awake their Master, saying, "Carest Thou not that we perish?" And then we read, "And He arose, and rebuked the wind, and said unto the sea, Peace, be still. *And the wind ceased, and there was a great calm"* (Mark 4:39). Mark again, the sea, at the will of its Creator, bore Him up upon its waves. At a word from Him the fig-tree withered; at His touch disease fled instantly.

The heavenly bodies are also ruled by their Maker and perform His sovereign pleasure. Take two illustrations. At God's bidding the sun went back ten degrees on the dial of Ahaz to help the weak faith of Hezekiah. In New Testament times, God caused a star to herald the incarnation of His Son—the star which appeared unto the wise men of the East. This star, we are told, *"went before them* till it came and stood over where the young Child was" (Matt. 2:9).

What a declaration is this—"He sendeth forth His commandment upon earth: His word runneth very swiftly. *He giveth* snow like wool: *He scattereth* the hoar frost like ashes. *He casteth forth* His ice like morsels: who can stand before *His cold? He sendeth* out His word, and melteth them: *He causeth His wind to blow,* and the waters flow" (Ps. 147:15-18). The mutations of the elements are beneath God's sovereign control. It is *God* who withholds the rain, and it is *God* who gives the rain when He wills, where He wills, as He wills, and on whom He wills. Weather Bureaus may attempt to give forecasts of the weather, but how frequently God mocks their calculations! Sun 'spots,' the varying activities of the planets, the appearing and disappearing of comets (to which abnormal weather is sometimes attributed), atmospheric disturbances, are merely secondary causes, for behind them all is God Himself. Let His Word speak once more: "And also *I have withholden the rain* from you, when there were yet three months to the harvest: *and I caused it* to rain upon one city, and caused it not to rain upon another city: one piece was rained upon, and the piece whereon it rained not withered. So two or three cities wandered unto one city, to drink water; but they were not satisfied: yet have ye not returned unto Me, saith the Lord. *I have smitten you with blasting and mildew:* when your gardens and your vineyards and your fig trees and your olive trees increased, the palmerworm devoured them: yet have ye not returned unto Me, saith the Lord. *I have sent among you the pestilence* after the manner of Egypt: your young men have I slain with the sword, and have taken away your horses; and I have made the stink of your camps to come up into your nostrils: yet have ye not returned unto Me, saith the Lord" (Amos 4:7-10).

Truly, then, God governs inanimate matter. Earth and air, fire and water, hail and snow, stormy winds and angry seas, all perform the word of His power and fulfil His sovereign pleasure. Therefore, when we complain about the weather, we are, in reality, murmuring against God.

2. GOD GOVERNS IRRATIONAL CREATURES.

What a striking illustration of God's government over the animal kingdom is found in Gen. 2:19! "And out of the ground the Lord God formed every beast of the field, and every fowl of the air; *and brought them unto Adam* to see what he would call them: and whatsoever Adam called every living creature, that was the name thereof." Should it be said that this occurred in Eden, and took place before the fall of Adam and the consequent curse which was inflicted on every creature, then our next reference fully meets the objection: God's control of the beasts was again openly displayed at the Flood. Mark how God caused to "come unto" Noah every specie of living creature "of every living thing of all flesh, two of every sort shalt thou bring into the ark, to keep them alive with thee; they shall be male and female. Of fowls after their kind, of every creeping thing after his kind: two of every sort *shall come unto thee*" (Gen. 6:19, 20)—all were beneath God's sovereign control. The lion of the jungle, the elephant of the forest, the bear of the polar regions; the ferocious panther, the untameable wolf, the fierce tiger; the high-soaring eagle and the creeping crocodile—see them all in their native fierceness, and yet, quietly submitting to the will of their Creator, and coming two by two into the ark!

We referred to the plagues sent upon Egypt as illustrating God's control of inanimate matter, let us now turn to them again to see how they demonstrate His perfect rulership over irrational creatures. At His word the river brought forth frogs abundantly, and these frogs entered the palace of Pharaoh and the houses of his servants and, contrary to their natural instincts, they entered the beds, the ovens and the kneadingtroughs (Ex. 8:13). Swarms of flies invaded the land of Egypt, but there were no flies in the land of Goshen! (Ex. 8:22). Next, the cattle were stricken. and we read, "Behold, *the hand of the Lord* is upon thy cattle which is in the field, upon the horses, upon the asses, upon the camels, upon the oxen, and upon the sheep: there shall be a very grievous murrain. And the Lord shall sever between the cattle of Israel and the cattle of Egypt: and there shall nothing die of all that is the children's of Israel. And the Lord appointed a set time, saying, Tomorrow the Lord shall do this thing in the land. And the Lord did that thing on the morrow, and all the cattle of Egypt died: but of the cattle of the children of Israel *died not one*"

(Ex. 9:3-6). In like manner God sent clouds of locusts to plague Pharaoh and his land, appointing the time of their visitation, determining the course and assigning the limits of their depredations.

Angels are not the only ones who do God's bidding. The brute beasts equally perform His pleasure. The sacred ark, the ark of the covenant, is in the country of the Philistines. How is it to be brought back to its home land? Mark the servants of God's choice, and how completely they were beneath His control: "And the Philistines called for the priests and the diviners saying, What shall we do to the ark of the Lord? tell us wherewith we shall send it to his place. And they said. . . . Now therefore make a new cart, and take two milch kine, on which there hath come no yoke, and tie the kine to the cart, and bring their calves home from them: And take the ark of the Lord, and lay it upon the cart; and put the jewels of gold, which ye return Him for a trespass offering, in a coffer by the side thereof, and send it away that it may go. And see, if it goeth up by the way of his own coast to Bethshemesh, then He hath done us this great evil: but if not, then we shall know that it is not His hand that smote us; it was a chance that happened to us." And what happened? How striking the sequel! "And the kine *took the straight way to the way of Bethshemesh,* and went along the highway, lowing as they went, *and turned not aside to the right hand or to the left*" (1 Sam. 6:12). Equally striking is the case of Elijah: "And the word of the Lord came unto him, saying, Get thee hence, and hide thyself by the brook Cherith, that is before Jordan. And it shall be, that thou shalt drink of the brook; *and I have commanded the ravens to feed thee there.*" (1 Kings 17:2-4). The natural instinct of these birds of prey was held in subjection, and instead of consuming the food themselves, they carried it to Jehovah's servant in his solitary retreat.

Is further proof required? then it is ready to hand. God makes a dumb ass to rebuke the prophet's madness. He sends forth two she-bears from the woods to devour forty and two of Elijah's tormentors. In fulfillment of His word, He causes the dogs to lick up the blood of the wicked Jezebel. He seals the mouths of Babylon's lions when Daniel is cast into the den, though, later, He causes them to devour the prophet's accusers. He prepares a great fish to swallow the disobedient Jonah and then, when His ordained hour struck, compelled it to vomit him forth *on dry land*. At His bidding a fish carries a coin to Peter for tribute money, and in order to fulfil His word He makes the cock to crow twice after Peter's denial. Thus we see that God reigns over irrational creatures: beasts of the field, birds of the air, fishes of the sea, all perform His sovereign *bidding*.

3. GOD GOVERNS THE CHILDREN OF MEN.

We fully appreciate the fact that this is the most difficult part of our subject, and, accordingly, it will be dealt with at greater length in the pages that follow; but at present we consider the *fact* of God's government over men in general, before we attempt to deal with the problem in detail.

Two alternatives confront us, and between them we are obliged to choose: either God governs, or He is governed; either God rules, or He is ruled; either God has His way, or men have theirs. And is our choice between these alternatives hard to make? Shall we say that in man we behold a creature so unruly that he is *beyond* God's control? Shall we say that sin has *alienated* the sinner so far from the thrice Holy One that he is *outside* the pale of His jurisdiction? Or, shall we say that man has been endowed with moral responsibility, and therefore God must leave him entirely free, at least during the period of his probation? Does it necessarily follow because the natural man is an outlaw against heaven, a rebel against the Divine government, that God is unable to fulfil His purpose through him? We mean, not merely that He may *overrule* the effects of the actions of evil-doers, nor that He will yet bring the wicked to stand before His judgment-bar so that sentence of punishment may be passed upon them—multitudes of non-Christians believe these things—but, we mean, that every action of the most lawless of His subjects is entirely beneath His control, yea that the actor is, though unknown to himself, carrying out the secret decrees of the Most High. Was it not thus with Judas? and is it possible to select a more extreme case? If then the arch-rebel was performing the counsel of God is it any greater tax upon our faith to believe the same of all rebels?

Our present object is not philosophic inquiry nor metaphysical causistry, but to ascertain the teaching of Scripture upon this profound theme. To the Law and the Testimony, for there only can we learn of the Divine government —its character, its design, its modus operandi, its scope. What then has it pleased God to reveal to us in His blessed Word concerning His rule over the works of His hands, and particularly, over the one who originally was made in His own image and likeness?

"In Him we live, *and move,* and have our being" (Acts 17:28). What a sweeping assertion is this! These words, be it noted, were addressed, not to one of the churches of God, not to a company of saints who had reached an exalted plane of spirituality, but to a heathen audience, to those who worshipped "the unknown God" and who "mocked" when they heard of the resurrection of the dead. And yet, to the Athenian philosophers, to the Epicureans and Stoics, the apostle Paul did not hesitate to affirm that they lived and moved and had their being in God, which signified not only that they owed their existence and preservation to the One who made the world and all things therein, but also that their very actions were encompassed and therefore controlled by the Lord of heaven and earth. Compare Dan. 5:23, last clause!

"The *disposings* (margin) of the heart, and the answer of the tongue is from the Lord" (Prov. 16:1). Mark that the above declaration is of general application—it is of "man," not simply of believers, that this is predicated. "A man's heart deviseth his way: *but the Lord directeth his steps*" (Prov. 16:9). If the Lord *directs* the steps of a man, is it not proof that he is being controlled or governed by God? Again; "There are many devices in a man's heart; *nevertheless the counsel of the Lord, that shall stand*" (Prov. 19:21). Can this mean anything less than, that no matter what man may desire and plan, it is the will of his Maker which is executed? As an illustration take the "Rich Fool" The "devices" of his heart are made known to us—"And he thought within himself, saying, What shall I do, because

I have no room where to bestow my fruits? And he said, This will I do: *I will* pull down my barns, and build greater; and there *I will* bestow all my fruits and my goods. And *I will* say to my soul, Soul, thou hast much goods laid up for many years; take thine ease, eat, drink, and be merry." Such were the "devices" of *his* heart, nevertheless it was "the counsel of the Lord" that stood. The "I will's" of the rich man came to nought, for *"God said unto him,* Thou fool, this night shall thy soul be required of thee" (Luke 12:17-20).

"The king's heart is in the hand of the Lord, as the rivers of water: *He turneth it whithersoever He will"* (Prov. 21:1). What could be more explicit? Out of the heart are "the issues of life" (Prov. 4:23), for as a man "thinketh *in his* heart, so is he" (Prov. 23:7). If then the heart is in the hand of the Lord, and if "He turneth it whithersoever He will," then is it not clear that men, yea, governors and rulers, and so *all men,* are completely beneath the governmental control of the Almighty!

No limitations must be placed upon the above declarations. To insist that *some* men, at least, *do* thwart God's will and overturn His counsels, is to repudiate other scriptures equally explicit. Weigh well the following: "But He is in one mind, and who can turn Him? and what His soul desireth, *even that He doeth"* (Job 23:13). "The counsel of the Lord *standeth for ever,* the thoughts of His heart to all generations" (Psa. 33:11). "There is no wisdom nor understanding nor counsel against the Lord" (Prov. 21:30). "For the Lord of hosts hath purposed, *and who shall disannul it?* And His hand is stretched out, and who shall turn it back?" (Isa. 14:27). "Remember the former things of old: for I am God, and there is none else! I am God, and there is none like Me, declaring the end from the beginning, and from ancient times the things that are not yet done, saying, *My counsel shall stand, and I will do all My pleasure"* (Isa. 46:9,10). There is no ambiguity in these passages. They affirm in the most unequivocal and unqualified terms that it is impossible to bring to naught the purpose of Jehovah.

We read the Scriptures in vain if we fail to discover that the actions of men, evil men as well as good, are governed by the Lord God. Nimrod and his fellows determined to erect the tower of Babel, but ere their task was accomplished God frustrated their plans. God called Abraham "alone" (Isa. 51:2), but his kinsfolk accompanied him as he left Ur of the Chaldees. Was then the will of the Lord defeated? Nay, verily. Mark the sequel. Terah *died* before Canaan was reached (Gen. 11:31), and though Lot accompanied his uncle into the land of promise, he soon separated from him and settled down in Sodom. Jacob was the child to whom the inheritance was promised, and though Isaac sought to reverse Jehovah's decree and bestow the blessing upon Esau, his efforts came to naught. Esau again swore vengeance upon Jacob, but when next they met they wept for joy instead of fighting in hate. The brethren of Joseph determined his destruction, but their evil counsels were overthrown. Pharaoh refused to let Israel carry out the instructions of Jehovah and perished in the Red Sea for his pains. Balak hired Balaam to curse the Israelites, but God *compelled* him to bless them. Haman erected a gallows for Mordecai but was hanged upon it himself. Jonah resisted the revealed will of God, but what became of his efforts?

Ah, the heathen may "rage" and the people imagine a "vain thing"; the kings of the earth may "set themselves", and the rulers take counsel together *against* the Lord and against His Christ, saying, "Let us break Their bands asunder, and cast away Their cords from us" (Psa. 2:1-3). But is the great God perturbed or disturbed by the rebellion of His puny creatures? No, indeed: "He that sitteth in the heavens shall *laugh:* the Lord shall have them *in derision*" (v. 4). He is infinitely exalted above all, and the greatest confederacies of earth's pawns, and their most extensive and vigorous preparations to defeat His purpose are, in *His* sight, altogether purile. He looks upon their puny efforts, not only without any alarm, but He "laughs" at their folly; He treats their impotency with "derision." He knows that He can crush them like moths when He pleases, or consume them in a moment with the breath of His mouth. Ah, it is but "a *vain* thing" for the potsherds of the earth to strive with the glorious Majesty of Heaven. Such is our God; worship ye Him.

Mark, too, the *sovereignty* which God displayed in His dealings with men! Moses who was slow of speech, and not Aaron his elder brother who was not slow of speech, was the one chosen to be His ambassador in demanding from Egypt's monarch the release of His oppressed people. Moses again, though greatly beloved utters one hasty word and was excluded from Canaan; whereas Elijah, passionately murmurs and suffers but a mild rebuke, and was afterwards taken to heaven without seeing death! Uzzah merely touched the ark and was instantly slain, whereas the Philistines carried it off in insulting triumph and suffered no immediate harm. Displays of grace which would have brought a doomed Sodom to repentance, failed to move an highly privileged Capernaum. Mighty works which would have subdued Tyre and Sidon, left the upbraided cities of Galilee under the curse of a rejected Gospel. If they would have prevailed over the former, why were they not wrought there? If they proved ineffectual to deliver the latter then why perform them? What exhibitions are these of the sovereign will of the Most High!

4. GOD GOVERNS ANGELS: BOTH GOOD AND EVIL ANGELS.

The angels are God's servants, His messengers, His chariots. They ever hearken to the word of His mouth and do His commands. "And God *sent* an angel unto Jerusalem to destroy it: and as he was destroying, the Lord beheld, and He repented Him of the evil, and said to the angel that destroyed, It is enough, Stay now thine hand. . . . And the Lord commanded the angel; *and he put his sword* again into the sheath thereof" (1 Chron. 21:15, 27). Many other scriptures might be cited to show that the angels are in subjection to the will of their Creator and perform His bidding—"And when Peter was come to himself, he said, Now I know of a surety, that the Lord *hath sent His angel*, and hath delivered me out of the hand of Herod" (Acts 12:11). "And the Lord God of the holy prophets *sent His angel* to shew unto His servants the things which must shortly be done" (Rev. 22:6). So it will be when our Lord returns: "The Son of Man shall *send forth His angels* and they shall gather out of His kingdom all things that offend, and them which do iniquity" (Matt. 13:41). Again, we read,

"He shall *send His angels* with a great sound of a trumpet, and they shall gather together His elect from the four winds, from one end of heaven to the other" (Matt. 24:31).

The same is true of *evil* spirits: they, too, fulfil God's sovereign decrees. An evil spirit is sent by God to stir up rebellion in the camp of Abimelech: "Then *God sent an evil spirit* between Abimelech and the men of Shechem, . . . which aided him in the killing of his brethren" (Judges 9:23). Another evil spirit He sent to be a lying spirit in the mouth of Ahab's prophets—"Now therefore, behold, *the Lord hath put* a lying spirit in the mouth of all these thy prophets, and the Lord hath spoken evil concerning thee" (1 Kings 22:23). And yet another was sent by the Lord to trouble Saul—"But the Spirit of the Lord departed from Saul, and *an evil spirit from the Lord* troubled him" (1 Sam. 16:14). So, too, in the New Testament: a whole legion of the demons go not out of their victim until the Lord gave them *permission* to enter the herd of swine.

It is clear from Scripture, then, that the angels, good and evil, are under God's control, and willingly or unwillingly carry out God's purpose. Yea, *SATAN himself* is absolutely subject to God's control. When arraigned in Eden, he listened to the awful sentence, but answered not a word. He was *unable* to touch Job until God granted him leave. So, too, he had to gain our Lord's consent before he could "sift" Peter. When Christ commanded him to depart— "Get thee hence, Satan"—we read, *"Then* the Devil leaveth Him"* (Matt. 4:11). And, in the end, he will be cast into the Lake of Fire, which has been prepared for him and his angels.

The Lord God omnipotent reigneth. His government is exercised over inanimate matter, over the brute beasts, over the children of men, over angels good and evil, and over Satan himself. No revolving world, no shining of star, no storm, no creature moves, no actions of men, no errands of angels, no deeds of Devil—*nothing in all the vast universe can come to pass otherwise than God has eternally purposed*. Here is a foundation for faith. Here is a resting place for the intellect. Here is an anchor for the soul, both sure and steadfast. It is not blind fate, unbridled evil, man or Devil, but the Lord Almighty who is ruling the world, ruling it according to His own good pleasure and for His own eternal glory.

> "Ten thousand ages ere the skies
> Were into motion brought;
> All the long years and worlds to come,
> Stood present to His thought:
> There's not a sparrow nor a worm,
> But's found in His decrees,
> He raises monarchs to their thrones
> And sinks as He may please."

IV

THE SOVEREIGNTY OF GOD IN SALVATION

"O the depths of the riches both of the wisdom and knowledge of God! how unsearchable are His judgments, and His ways past finding out" (Rom. 11:33).

"SALVATION is of the Lord" (Jonah 2:9); but the Lord does not save all. Why not? He *does* save some; then if He saves some, why not others? Is it because they are too sinful and depraved? No; for the apostle wrote, "This is a faithful saying, and worthy of all acceptation, that Christ Jesus came into the world to save sinners; *of whom I am chief*" (1 Tim. 1:15). Therefore, if God saved the "chief" of sinners, none are excluded because of their depravity. Why then does not God save all? Is it because some are too stony-hearted to be won? No; because of the most stony-hearted people of all it is written, that God will yet "take the stony heart out of their flesh, and will give them a heart of flesh" (Ezek. 11:19). Then is it because some are so stubborn, so intractable, so defiant that God is *unable* to woo them to Himself? Before we answer this question let us ask another; let us appeal to the experience of the Christian reader.

Friend; was there not a time when *you* walked in the counsel of the ungodly, stood in the way of sinners, sat in the seat of the scorners, and with them said, *"We will not have this Man to reign over us"* (Luke 19:14)? Was there not a time when *you* "would not come to Christ that you might have life" (John 5:40)? Yea, was there not a time when you mingled *your* voice with those who said unto God, "Depart from us; for we desire not the knowledge of Thy ways. What is the Almighty, that we should serve Him? and what profit should we have, if we pray unto Him?" (Job 21:14, 15)? With shamed face you have to acknowledge *there was.* But how is it that all is now changed? What was it that brought you from haughty self-sufficiency to a humble suppliant, from one that was at enmity with God to one that is at peace with Him, from lawlessness to subjection, from hate to love? And, as one 'born of the Spirit,' you will readily reply, *"By the grace of God I am what I*

am" (1 Cor. 15:10). Then do you not see that it is due to
no lack of power in God, nor to His refusal to coerce man,
that *other rebels* are not saved too? If God was able to
subdue *your* will and win *your* heart, and that *without* interfering with your moral responsibility, then is He not
able to do the same for others? Assuredly He is. Then
how inconsistent, how illogical, how foolish of you, in seeking *to account for* the present course of the wicked and their
ultimate fate, to argue that God is *unable* to save them,
that they will not let Him. Do you say, "But the time
came when *I was willing*, willing to receive Christ as my
Saviour"? True, but it was *the Lord* who *made* you willing
(Ps. 110:3; Phil. 2:13); why then does He not make *all*
sinners willing? Why, but for the fact that He is sovereign
and does as He pleases! But to return to our opening inquiry.

Why is it that all are not saved, particularly all who
hear the Gospel? Do you still answer, Because the majority
refuse to believe? Well, that is true, but it is only a part
of the truth. It is the truth *from the human side*. But there
is a Divine side too, and this side of the truth needs to be
stressed or God will be robbed of His glory. The unsaved
are lost because they refuse to believe; the others are saved
because they believe. But *why* do these others believe?
What is it that causes them to put their trust in Christ? Is
it because they are more intelligent than their fellows, and
quicker to discern their *need* of salvation? Perish the
thought—*"Who maketh thee to differ from another?* And
what hast thou that thou didst not receive? Now if thou
didst receive it, why dost thou glory, as if thou hadst not
received it?" (1 Cor. 4:7). It is God Himself who maketh
the difference between the elect and the non-elect, for of
His own it is written, "And we know that the Son of God
is come, *and hath given us an understanding*, that we may
know Him that is true" (1 John 5:20).

Faith is God's *gift*, and "all men have not faith" (2 Thess.
3:2); therefore, we see that God does not bestow this gift
upon all. Upon whom then does He bestow this saving
favor? And we answer, upon His own elect—"As many
as were ordained to eternal life believed" (Acts 13:48).
Hence it is that we read of "the faith of God's elect" (Ti-

tus 1:1). But is God partial in the distribution of His favors? *Has He not the right to be?* Are there still some who 'murmur against the Good-Man of the house'? Then His own words are sufficient reply—"Is it not lawful for Me *to do what I will with Mine own?"* (Matt. 20:15). God is sovereign in the bestowment of His gifts, both in the natural and in the spiritual realms. So much then for a general statement, and now to particularize.

1. THE SOVEREIGNTY OF GOD THE FATHER IN SALVATION.

Perhaps the one scripture which most emphatically of all asserts the absolute sovereignty of God in connection with His determining the destiny of His creatures, is the ninth of Romans. We shall not attempt to review here the entire chapter, but will confine ourselves to vv. 21-23—"Hath not the potter power over the clay of the same lump, to make one vessel unto honor, and another unto dishonor? What if God, willing to show His wrath, and to make His power known, endured with much long-suffering the vessels of wrath fitted to destruction: And that He might make known the riches of His glory on the vessels of mercy, which He had afore prepared unto glory?" These verses represent fallen mankind as inert and as impotent as a lump of lifeless clay. This scripture evidences that there is "no difference," in themselves, between the elect and the non-elect: they are clay of "the same lump," which agrees with Eph. 2:3, where we are told, that all are *by nature* "children of wrath." It teaches us that the ultimate destiny of every individual is decided by the will of God, and blessed it is that such be the case; if it were left to *our* wills, the ultimate destination of us all would be the Lake of Fire. It declares that God Himself *does* make a difference in the respective destinations to which He assigns His creatures, for one vessel is made *"unto* honor and another *unto* dishonor;" some are "vessels of wrath fitted to destruction," others are "vessels of mercy, which He had afore prepared unto glory."

We readily acknowledge that it is very humbling to the proud heart of the creature to behold all mankind in the hand of God as the clay is in the potter's hand, yet this is precisely how the Scriptures of Truth represent the case. In this day of human boasting, intellectual pride, and deification of man, it needs to be insisted upon that the potter forms his vessels for himself. Let man strive with his Maker as he will, the fact remains that he is nothing more than clay in the Heavenly Potter's hands, and while we know that God will deal justly with His creatures, that the Judge of all the earth *will do right,* nevertheless, He shapes His vessels for His own purpose and according to His own pleasure. God claims the indisputable right to do as He wills with His own.

Not only has God the right to do as He wills with the creatures of His own hands, but *He exercises this right,* and nowhere is that seen more plainly than in His predestinating grace. Before the foundation of the world God made a choice, a selection, an election. Before His omniscient eye stood the whole of Adam's race, and from it He singled out a people and predestinated them "unto the adoption of children," predestinated them "to be conformed to the image of His Son," "ordained" them unto eternal life. Many are the scriptures which set forth this blessed truth, seven of which will now engage our attention.

"As many as were ordained to eternal life, believed" (Acts 13:48). Every artifice of human ingenuity has been employed to blunt the sharp edge of this scripture and to explain away the obvious meaning of these words, but it has been employed in vain, though nothing will ever be able to reconcile this and similar passages to the mind of the natural man. "As many as were ordained to eternal life, believed." Here we learn four things: First, that believing is the consequence *and not the cause* of God's decree. Second, that a limited number only are "ordained to eternal life," for if all men without exception were thus ordained by God, then the words "as many as" are a meaningless qualification. Third, that this "ordination" of God is not to mere external privileges but to "eternal life," not to service but to salvation itself. Fourth, that all—"as many as," not one less—who are thus ordained by God to eternal life will most certainly believe.

The comments of the beloved Spurgeon on the above passage are well worthy of our notice. Said he, "Attempts have been made to prove that these words do not teach predestination, but these attempts so clearly do violence to language that I shall not waste time in answering them. I read: 'As many as were ordained to eternal life believed', and I shall not twist the text but shall glorify the grace of God by ascribing to that grace the faith of every man. Is it not God who gives the disposition to believe? If men are disposed to have eternal life, does not He—in every case—dispose them? Is it wrong for God to give grace? If it be right for Him to give it, is it wrong for Him to *purpose* to give it? Would you have Him give it by accident? If it is right for Him to purpose to give grace today, it was right for Him to purpose it before today—and, since He changes not—from eternity."

"Even so then at this present time also there is a remnant *according to the election of grace*. And if by grace, then it is no more of works: otherwise grace is no more grace. But if it be of works, then is it no more grace: otherwise work is no more work" (Rom. 11:5, 6). The words "Even so" at the beginning of this quotation refer us to the previous verse where we are told, "I have reserved to Myself seven thousand men who have not bowed the knee to Baal." Note particularly the word "reserved." In the days of Elijah there were seven thousand—a small minority—who were Divinely preserved from idolatry and brought to the knowledge of the true God. This preservation and illumination was not from anything in themselves, but solely by God's special influence and agency. How highly favored such individuals were to be thus "reserved" by God! Now says the apostle, Just as there was a "remnant" in Elijah's days "reserved by God", even so there is in this present dispensation.

"A remnant according to the election of grace." Here the *cause* of election is traced back to its source. The basis upon which God elected this "remnant" was not faith foreseen in them, because a choice founded upon the foresight of good works is just as truly made on the ground of *works* as any choice can be, and in such a case, it would not be *"of grace;"* for, says the apostle, "if by grace, then it is no more of works: otherwise grace is no more grace;" which means that grace and works are opposites, they have nothing in common, and will no more mingle than will oil and water. Thus the idea of inherent good foreseen in those chosen, or of anything meritorious performed by them, is rigidly excluded. "A remnant according to the election *of grace"*, signifies an unconditional choice resulting from the sovereign favor of God; in a word, it is absolutely a *gratuitous* election.

"For ye see your calling, brethren, how that not many wise men after the flesh, not many mighty, not many noble, are called: But God hath chosen the foolish things of the world to confound the wise; and God hath chosen the weak things of the world to confound the things which are mighty: and base things of the world, and things which are despised, hath God chosen, yea, and things which are not, to bring to nought things that are: That no flesh should glory in His presence" (1 Cor. 1:26-29). Three times over in this passage reference is made to *God's choice,* and choice necessarily supposes a selection, the taking of some and the leaving of others. The Chooser here is God Himself, as said the Lord Jesus to the apostles, "Ye have not chosen Me, but I have chosen you" (John 15:16). The number chosen is strictly defined—"*not many* wise men after the flesh, *not many* noble," etc., which agrees with Matt. 20:16, "So the last shall be first, and the first last; for many be called, *but few chosen."* So much then for *the fact* of God's choice; now mark the *objects* of His choice.

The ones spoken of above as chosen of God are "the weak things of the world, base things of the world, and things which are despised." But why? To demonstrate and magnify His grace. God's *ways* as well as His thoughts are utterly at variance with man's. The carnal mind would have supposed that a selection had been made from the ranks of the opulent and influential, the amiable and cultured, so that Christianity might have won the approval and applause of the world by its pageantry and fleshly glory. Ah! but "that which is highly esteemed among men is abomination in the sight of God" (Luke 16:15). God chooses the *"base* things." He did so in Old Testament times. The nation which He singled out to be the depository of His holy oracles and the channel through which the promised Seed should come, was not the ancient Egyptians, the imposing Babylonians, nor the highly civilized and cultured Greeks. No; that people upon whom Jehovah set

His love and regarded as 'the apple of His eye', were the despised, nomadic Hebrews. So it was when our Lord tabernacled among men. The ones whom He took into favored intimacy with Himself and commissioned to go forth as His ambassadors, were, for the most part, unlettered fishermen. And so it has been ever since. So it is today: at the present rates of increase, it will not be long before it is manifested that the Lord has more in despised China who are really His, than He has in the highly favored U. S. A ; more among the uncivilized blacks of Africa, than He has in cultured (?) Germany! And the purpose of God's choice, the *raison d'etre* of the selection He has made is, "that no flesh should glory in His presence"—there being nothing whatever in the objects of His choice which should entitle them to His special favors, then, all the praise will be freely ascribed to the exceeding riches of His manifold grace.

"Blessed be the God and Father of our Lord Jesus Christ, who hath blessed us with all spiritual blessings in the heavenlies in Christ: *According as He hath chosen us in Him before the foundation of the world,* that we should be holy and without blame before Him; In love having predestinated us unto the adoption of children by Jesus Christ to Himself, according to the good pleasure of His will. . . . In whom also we have obtained an inheritance, being predestinated according to the purpose of Him who worketh all things after the counsel of His own will" (Eph. 1:3-5, 11). Here again we are told at what point in time—if time it could be called—when God made choice of those who were to be His children by Jesus Christ. It was not after Adam had fallen and plunged his race into sin and wretchedness, but long ere Adam saw the light, even before the world itself was founded, that God chose us in Christ. Here also we learn the *purpose* which God had before Him in connection with His own elect: it was that they "should be holy and without blame before Him;" it was "unto the adoption of children;" it was that they should "obtain an inheritance." Here also we discover the *motive* which prompted Him. It was *"in love* that He predestinated us unto the adoption of children by Jesus Christ to Himself" —a statement which refutes the oft made and wicked charge that, for God to decide the eternal destiny of His creatures before they are born, is tyrannical and unjust. Finally, we are informed here, that in this matter He took counsel with none, but that we are "predestinated according to the good pleasure of His will."

"But we are bound to give thanks always to God for you, brethren beloved of the Lord, *because God hath from the beginning chosen you to salvation* through sanctification of the Spirit and belief of the truth" (2 Thess. 2:13). There are three things here which deserve special attention. First, the fact that we are expressly told that God's elect are "chosen to salvation." Language could not be more explicit. How summarily do these words dispose of the sophistries and equivocations of all who would make election refer to nothing but external privileges or rank in service! It is to "salvation" itself that God hath chosen us. Second, we are warned here that election unto salvation does not disregard the use of appropriate means: salvation is reached through "sanctification of the Spirit and belief of the truth." It is not true that because God has chosen a certain one to salvation that he will be saved willy-nilly, whether he believes or not: nowhere do the scriptures so represent it. The same God who predestined the end, also appointed the means; the same God who "chose unto salvation", decreed that His purpose should be realized through the work of the Spirit and belief of the truth. Third, that God has chosen us unto salvation is a profound cause for fervent praise. Note how strongly the apostle expresses this—"*we are bound* to give thanks *always* to God for you, brethren beloved of the Lord, *because* God hath from the beginning chosen you to salvation," etc. Instead of shrinking back in horror from the doctrine of predestination, the believer, when he sees this blessed truth as it is unfolded in the Word, discovers a ground for gratitude and thanksgiving such as nothing else affords, save the unspeakable gift of the Redeemer Himself.

"Who hath saved us, and called us with an holy calling, not according to our works, but according to His own purpose and grace, which was given us in Christ Jesus before the world began" (2 Tim. 1:9). How plain and pointed is the language of Holy Writ! It is man who, by his words, darkeneth counsel. It is impossible to state the case more clearly, or strongly, than it is stated here. Our salvation is not "according to *our* works;" that is to say, it is not due to anything in us, nor the rewarding of anything from us; instead, it is the result of God's own "purpose and grace;" and this grace was given us in Christ Jesus before the world began. It is by *grace* we are saved, and in the purpose of God this grace was bestowed upon us not only before we saw the light, not only before Adam's fall, but even before that far distant "beginning" of Genesis 1:1. And herein lies the unassailable comfort of God's people. If His choice has been from eternity it will last to eternity! "Nothing can survive to eternity but what came from eternity, and what *has* so come, will" (G. S. Bishop).

"Elect according to the foreknowledge of God the Father, through sanctification of the Spirit, unto obedience and sprinkling of the blood of Jesus Christ" (1 Peter 1:2). Here again election by the Father precedes the work of the Holy Spirit in, and the obedience of faith by, those who are saved; thus taking it entirely off creature ground, and resting it in the sovereign pleasure of the Almighty. The "foreknowledge of God the Father" does not here refer to His prescience of all things, but signifies that the saints were all eternally present in Christ before the mind of God. God did not "foreknow" that certain ones who heard the Gospel would believe it *apart from the fact that He had "ordained" these certain ones to eternal life.* What God's prescience saw in all men was, love of sin and hatred of Himself. The "foreknowledge" of God *is based upon His own decrees* as is clear from Acts 2:23—"Him, being delivered by the determinate counsel and foreknowledge of God, ye have taken, and by wicked hands have crucified and slain"—note the order here: first God's "determinate counsel" (His decree), and second His "foreknowledge." So it is again in Rom. 8: 28, 29, "For whom He did foreknow, He also did predestinate to be conformed to the image of His Son," but the first word here, *"for,"* looks back to the preceding verse and the last clause of it reads, "to them who are the called according to His purpose"—these are the ones whom He did "foreknow and predestinate." Finally, it needs to be pointed out that when we read in Scripture of God "knowing" cer-

tain people, the word is used in the sense of knowing with
approbation and love: "But if any man love God, the same
is *known* of Him" (1 Cor. 8:3). To the hypocrites Christ
will yet say "I never knew you"—He never loved them.
"Elect according to the foreknowledge of God the Father"
signifies, then, chosen by Him as the special objects of His
approbation and love.

Summarizing the teaching of these seven passages we
learn that, God has "ordained to eternal life" certain ones,
and that in consequence of His ordination they, in due time,
"believe;" that God's ordination to salvation of His own
elect, is not due to any good thing in them nor to anything
meritorious from them, but solely of His "grace;" that God
has designedly selected the most *unlikely* objects to be the
recipients of His special favors, in order that "no flesh
should glory in His presence;" that God chose His people
in Christ before the foundation of the world, not because
they were so, but in order that they *"should be,* holy and
without blame before him"; that having selected certain
ones to salvation, He also decreed the means by which His
eternal counsel should be made good; that the very "grace"
by which we are saved was, in God's purpose, "given us in
Christ Jesus before the world began;" that long before they
were actually created, God's elect stood present before His
mind, were "foreknown" by Him, i.e., were the definite objects of His eternal love.

Before turning to the next division of this chapter, a
further word concerning the *subjects* of God's predestinating grace. We go over this ground again because it is at
this point that the doctrine of God's sovereignty in pre-
destining certain ones to salvation is most frequently as-
saulted. Perverters of this truth invariably seek to find
some cause *outside* God's own will, which *moves* Him to
bestow salvation on sinners; something or other is attributed
to the creature which entitles him to receive mercy at the
hands of the Creator. We return then to the question, *Why*
did God choose the ones He did?

What was there in the elect themselves which attracted
God's heart to them? Was it because of certain virtues
they possessed? because they were generous-hearted, sweet-
tempered, truth-speaking? in a word, because they were

"good," that God chose them? No; for our Lord said, "There is none good but one, that is God" (Matt. 19:17). Was it because of any good works they had *perfomed?* No; for it is written, "There is none that doeth good, no, not one" (Rom. 3:12). Was it because they evidenced an earnestness and zeal in inquiring after God? No; for it is written again, "There is none that seeketh after God" (Rom. 3:11). Was it because God foresaw they would believe? No; for how can those who are *"dead* in trespasses and sins" believe in Christ? How could God foreknow some men as believers when belief was impossible to them? Scripture declares that we "believe *through grace"* (Acts 18:27). Faith is God's gift, and apart from this gift none would believe. The *cause* of His choice then lies within Himself and not iń the objects of His choice. He chose the ones He did simply because He chose to choose them.

> "Sons we are by God's election
> Who on Jesus Christ believe,
> By eternal destination,
>
> Sovereign grace we now receive,
> Lord Thy mercy,
> Doth both grace and glory give!"

2. THE SOVEREIGNTY OF GOD THE SON IN SALVATION.

For whom did Christ die? It surely does not need arguing that the Father had an express purpose in giving Him to die, or that God the Son had a definite design before Him in laying down His life—"Known unto God are all His works from the beginning of the world" (Acts 15:18). What then was the purpose of the Father and the design of the Son? We answer, Christ died for "God's elect."

We are not unmindful of the fact that the *limited design* in the death of Christ has been the subject of much controversy—what great truth revealed in Scripture has not? Nor do we forget that anything which has to do with the person and work of our blessed Lord requires to be handled with the utmost reverence, and that a "Thus saith the Lord" must be given in support of every assertion we make. Our appeal shall be to the Law and to the Testimony.

For whom did Christ die? Who were the ones He intended to redeem by His blood-shedding? Surely the Lord Jesus had some *absolute determination* before Him when He went to the Cross. If He had, then it necessarily follows that the *extent* of that purpose was *limited,* because an *absolute* determination or purpose *must be effected.* If the absolute determination of Christ included all mankind, then all mankind would most certainly be saved. To escape this inevitable conclusion many have affirmed that there was no such absolute determination before Christ, that in His death a merely *conditional provision* of salvation has been made for all mankind. The refutation of this assertion is found in the *promises* made by the Father to His Son *before* He went to the Cross, yea, before He became incarnate. The Old Testament Scriptures represent the Father as promising the Son a certain *reward* for His sufferings on behalf of sinners. At this stage we shall confine ourselves to one or two statements recorded in the well known fifty-third of Isaiah. There we find God saying, "When Thou shalt make His soul an offering for sin, He shall see His seed," that "He shall see of the travail of His soul, and shall be satisfied," and that God's righteous Servant "should justify many" (vv. 10 and 11). But here we would pause and ask, How could it be *certain* that Christ *should* "see His seed," and "see of the travail of His soul and be *satisfied,*" unless the salvation of certain members of the human race had been *Divinely decreed,* and therefore was sure? How could it be *certain* that Christ *should* "justify many," if no *effectual* provision was made that *any* should receive Him as their Saviour? On the other hand, to insist that the Lord Jesus *did* expressly purpose the salvation of *all mankind,* is to charge Him with that which no intelligent being should be guilty of, namely, to *design* that which by virtue of His omniscience He *knew would never come to pass.* Hence, the only alternative left us is that, so far as the pre-determined purpose of His death is concerned, Christ died for the elect only. Summing up in a sentence, which we trust will be intelligible to every reader, we would say, Christ died not merely to *make possible* the salvation of all mankind, but to *make certain* the salvation of all that the Father had given to Him. Christ died not simply to render sins pardonable, but "to *put away sin* by the sacrifice of Himself" (Heb. 9:26). As to *who's* "sin" (i.e., *guilt,* as in 1 John 1:7, etc.) *has been* "put away," Scripture leaves us in no doubt—it was that of the elect, the "world" (John 1:29) of God's people!

(1.) The *limited design* in the Atonement follows, necessarily, from the eternal choice of the Father of certain ones unto salvation. The Scriptures inform us that, before the Lord became incarnate He said, "Lo, I come, to do *Thy will O God*" (Heb. 10:7), and after He had become incarnate He declared, "For I came down from heaven, not to do Mine own will, but the will of Him that sent Me" (John 6: 38). If then God had from the beginning chosen certain ones to salvation, then, because the will of Christ was in perfect accord with the will of the Father, He would not seek to *enlarge* upon His election. What we have just said is not merely a plausible deduction of our own, but is in strict harmony with the express teaching of the Word. Again and again our Lord referred to those whom the Father had "given" Him, and concerning whom He was particularly exercised. Said He, "All that the Father giveth Me shall come to Me; and him that cometh to Me I will in no wise cast out. . . . And this is the Father's will which hath sent Me, that of all which He hath given Me I should lose nothing, but should raise it up again at the last day" (John 6:37, 39). And again, "These words spake Jesus, and lifted up His eyes to heaven, and said, Father, the hour is come; glorify Thy Son, that Thy Son also may glorify Thee; As Thou hast given Him power over all flesh, that He should give eternal life *to as many as Thou hast given Him.* . . . I have manifested Thy name *unto the men which Thou gavest Me out of the world:* Thine they were, and Thou gavest them Me; and they have kept Thy Word. . . . I pray for them: I pray not for the world, *but for them which Thou hast given Me;* for they are Thine. . . . Father, I will that they also, *whom Thou hast given Me,* be with Me where I am; that they may behold My glory, which Thou hast given Me: for Thou lovest Me before the foundation of the world" (John 17:1, 2, 6, 9, 24). Before the foundation of the world the Father predestinated a people to be conformed to the image of His Son, and the death and resurrection of the Lord Jesus was in order to the carrying out of the Divine purpose.

(2.) The very *nature* of the Atonement evidences that, in its application to sinners, it was *limited* in the *purpose* of God. The Atonement of Christ may be considered from two chief viewpoints—Godward and manward. Godwards, the Cross-work of Christ was a *propitiation,* an appeasing of Divine wrath, a satisfaction rendered to Divine justice and holiness; manwards, it was a *substitution,* the Innocent taking the place of the guilty, the Just dying for the unjust. But a strict substitution of a Person for persons, and the infliction upon Him of voluntary sufferings, involve the *definite recognition* on the part of the Substitute and of the One He is to propitiate *of the persons for whom He acts,* whose sins He bears, whose legal obligations He discharges. Furthermore, if the Law-giver accepts the satisfaction which is made by the Substitute then those for whom the Substitute acts, whose place He takes, must necessarily be acquitted. If I am in debt and unable to discharge it and another comes forward and pays my creditor in full and receives a receipt in acknowledgment, then, in the sight of the law, my creditor no longer has any claim upon me. On the Cross the Lord Jesus gave Himself a ransom, and that it was accepted by God was attested by the open grave three days later; the question we would here raise is, *For whom* was this ransom offered? If it was offered for all mankind then the debt incurred by every man has been cancelled. If Christ bore in His own body on the tree the sins of all men without exception, then none will perish. If Christ was "made a curse" for all of Adam's race then none are now "under condemnation." "Payment God cannot *twice* demand, first at my bleeding Surety's hand and then again at mine." But Christ *did not* discharge the debt of all men without exception, for some there are who will be "cast into prison" (cf. I Peter 3:19 where the same Greek word for "prison" occurs), and they shall "by no means come out thence, till they have *paid* the uttermost farthing" (Matt. 5:26), which, of course, will never be. Christ *did not* bear the sins of all mankind, for some there are who "die *in their sins*" (John 8:21), and whose "sin remaineth" (John 9:41). Christ *was not* "made a curse" for all of Adam's race, for some there are to whom He will yet say, "Depart from Me *ye cursed*" (Matt. 25:41). To say that Christ died for all alike, to say that He became the Substitute and Surety of the whole human race, to say that He suffered on behalf of and in the stead of all mankind, is to say that He "bore the curse for many who are now bearing the curse for themselves; that He suffered punishment for many who are now lifting up their own eyes in Hell, being in torments; that He paid the redemption price for many who shall yet pay in their own eternal anguish 'the wages of sin, which is death'" (G. S. Bishop). But, on the other hand, to say as Scripture says, that Christ was stricken for the transgressions *of God's people,* to say that He gave His life *for the sheep,* to say that He gave His life a ransom *for many,* is to say that He made an atonement which fully atones; it is to say He paid a price which actually ransoms; it is to say He was set forth a propitiation which really propitiates; it is to say He is a Saviour who truly saves.

(3.) Closely connected with, and confirmatory of what we have said above, is the teaching of Scripture concerning our Lord's *priesthood.* It is as the great High Priest that Christ now makes intercession. But *for whom* does He intercede? for the whole human race, or only for His own people? The answer furnished by the New Testament to this question is clear as a sunbeam. Our Saviour has entered into heaven itself "now to appear in the presence of God *for us*" (Heb. 9:24), that is, for those who are "partakers of the heavenly calling" (Heb. 3:1). And again it is written, "Wherefore He is able also to save them to the uttermost that come unto God by Him, seeing He ever liveth to make intercession *for them*" (Heb. 7:25). This is in strict accord with the Old Testament type. After slaying the sacrificial animal, Aaron went into the holy of holies as the representative and on behalf of the people of God: it was the names of *Israel's* tribes which were engraven on his breastplate, and it was in *their* interests he appeared before God. Agreeable to this are our Lord's words in John 17:9—"I pray for them: I pray *not for the world,* but for them which Thou hast given Me; for they are Thine." Another scripture which deserves careful attention in this connection is found in Romans 8. In verse 33 the question is asked, "Who shall lay anything to the charge *of God's elect?*" and then follows the inspired answer— "It is God that justifieth. Who is he that condemneth? It is Christ that died, yea, rather that is risen again, who is even at the right hand of God, who also maketh intercession *for us.*" Note particularly that the death and intercession of Christ have one and the same objects! As it was in the type so it is with the antitype—expiation and supplication are *co-extensive.* If then Christ intercedes for the elect only, and "not for the world," then He died for them only. And observe further, that the death, resurrection, exaltation and intercession of the Lord Jesus, are here assigned as the reason why none can lay any "charge" against God's *elect.* Let those who would still take issue with what we are advancing weigh carefully the following question—If the death of Christ extends equally to all, how does it become *security* against a "charge," seeing that all who believe not are "under condemnation"? (John 3:18).

(4.) The number of those who share the benefits of Christ's death is determined not only by the *nature* of the Atonement and the *priesthood* of Christ but also by His *power.* Grant that the One who died upon the cross was God manifest in the flesh, and it follows inevitably that what Christ has purposed that will He perform; that what He has purchased that will He possess; that what He has set His heart upon that will He secure. If the Lord Jesus possesses all power in heaven and earth, then none can successfully resist His will. But it may be said, This is true in the abstract, nevertheless, Christ refuses to exercise this power, inasmuch as He will never *force* anyone to receive Him as their Saviour. In one sense that is true, but in another sense it is positively untrue. The salvation of any sinner *is* a matter of Divine power. By nature the sinner is at enmity with God, and naught but Divine power operating within him, can *overcome* this enmity; hence it is written, "No man can come unto Me, *except* the Father which hath sent Me *draw* him" (John 6:44). It is the Divine power overcoming the sinner's innate enmity which makes him *willing to come* to Christ that he might have life. But this "enmity" is not overcome in all—why? Is it because the enmity is *too strong* to be overcome? Are there some hearts so steeled against Him that Christ is *unable* to gain entrance? To answer in the affirmative is to *deny His omnipotence.* In the final analysis it is not a question of the sinner's willingness or unwillingness, for by nature *all* are *unwilling.* Willingness to come to Christ is the finished product of Divine power operating in the human heart and will in overcoming man's inherent and chronic "enmity," as it is written, "Thy people shall be willing in the day *of Thy power"* (Ps. 110:3). To say that Christ is *unable* to win to Himself those who are unwilling is to deny that all power in heaven and earth is His. To say that Christ cannot put forth His power without destroying man's responsibility is a begging of the question here raised, for *He has* put forth His power and made willing those who *have* come to Him, and if He did this without destroying *their* responsibility, why "cannot" He do so with others? If He is able to win the heart of one sinner to Himself, why not that of another? To say, as is usually said, the others *will not let Him* is to impeach His sufficiency. It is a question of *His* will. If the Lord Jesus has decreed, desired, purposed the salvation of all mankind, then the entire human race *will be saved,* or, otherwise, He lacks the power to make good His intentions; and in such a case it could never be said, "He *shall* see of the travail of His soul and be *satisfied."* The issue raised involves *the deity* of the Saviour, for a *defeated* Saviour cannot be God.

Having reviewed some of the general principles which require us to believe that the death of Christ was *limited* in its design, we turn now to consider some of the explicit statements of Scripture which expressly affirm it. In that wondrous and matchless fifty-third of Isaiah God tells us concerning His Son, "He was taken from prison and from judgment: and who shall declare His generation? for He was cut off out of the land of the living: *for the transgression of My people was He stricken"* (v. 8). In perfect harmony with this was the word of the angel to Joseph, "Thou shalt call His name Jesus, for He shall save *His people* from their sins" (Matt. 1:21) i. e not merely Israel, but all whom the Father had "given" Him. Our Lord Himself declared, "The Son of Man came not to be ministered unto, but to minister, and to give His life a ransom *for many"* (Matt. 20:28), but why have said "for many" if *all without exception* were included? It was "His people" whom He "redeemed" (Luke 1:68). It was for "the sheep," and not the "goats", that the Good Shepherd gave His life (John 10:11). It was the "Church of God" which He purchased with His own blood" (Acts 20:28).

If there is one scripture more than any other upon which we should be willing to rest our case it is John 11:49-52. Here we are told, "And one of them, named Caiaphas, being the high priest that same year, said unto them, Ye know nothing at all, nor consider that it is expedient for us, that one man should die for the people, and that the whole nation perish not. And this spake he not of himself: but being high priest that year, he prophesied that Jesus should die for that nation; And not for that nation only, but that also He should gather together in one the children of God that were scattered abroad." Here we are told that Caiaphas "prophesied *not of himself*," that is, like those employed by God in Old Testament times (see 2 Pet. 1:21), his prophecy originated not with himself, but he spake as he was moved by the Holy Spirit; thus is the value of his utterance carefully guarded, and the Divine source of this revelation expressly vouched for. Here, too, we are definitely informed that Christ died *for* "that nation," i.e., Israel, and also for the One Body, His Church, for it is into the Church that the children of God—"scattered" among the nations—are now being "gathered together in one." And is it not remarkable that the members of the Church are here called "children of God" even before Christ died, and therefore before He commenced to build His Church! The vast majority of them had not then been born, yet were they regarded as "children of God;" children of God because they had been chosen in Christ before the foundation of the world, and therefore "predestinated *unto the adoption of children* by Jesus Christ to Himself" (Eph. 1:4, 5). In like manner, Christ said, "Other sheep *I have* (not "shall have") which are not of this fold" (John 10:16).

If ever the real design of the Cross was uppermost in the heart and speech of our blessed Saviour it was during the last week of His earthly ministry. What then do the Scriptures which treat of *this* portion of His ministry record in

connection with our present inquiry? They say, "When
Jesus knew that His hour was come that He should depart
out of this world unto the Father, *having loved His own*
which were in the world, *He loved them* unto the end"
(John 13:1). They tell us how He said, "Greater love
hath no man than this, that a man lay down His life *for His
friends"* (John 15:13). They record His word, *"For their
sakes* I sanctify Myself, that they also might be sanctified
through the truth" (John 17:19); which means, that for
the sake of His own, those "given" to Him by the Father,
He separated Himself unto the death of the Cross. One
may well ask, Why such discrimination of terms if Christ
died for all men indiscriminately?

Ere closing this section of the chapter we shall consider
briefly a few of those passages which *seem* to teach most
strongly an *unlimited* design in the death of Christ. In
2 Cor. 5:14 we read, "One died *for all."* But that is not all
this scripture affirms. If the entire verse and passage from
which these words are quoted be carefully examined, it will
be found that instead of teaching an unlimited atonement,
it emphatically argues a limited design in the death of
Christ. The whole verse reads, "For the love of Christ con-
straineth us; because we thus judge, that if One died for all,
then were all dead." It should be pointed out that in the
Greek there is the definite article before the last "all," and
that the verb here is in the aorist tense, and therefore should
read, "We thus judge: that if One died for all, then they
all died." The apostle is here drawing a conclusion as is
clear from the words "we thus judge, that if . . . then
were." His meaning is, that those for whom the One died
are regarded, *judicially,* as having died too. The next verse
goes on to say, "And He died for all, *that* they which live
should not henceforth live unto themselves, but unto Him
which died *for them,* and rose again." The One not only
died but "rose again," and so, too, did the "all" for whom
He died, for it is here said they "live." Those for whom
a substitute acts are legally regarded as having acted themselves. In the sight of the law the substitute and those
whom he represents are one. So it is in the sight of God.
Christ was identified *with His people* and His people were
identified with Him, hence when He died they died (judi-

cially) and when He rose they rose also. But further we are
told in this passage (v. 17), that if any man be in Christ
he is a new creation; he has received a new life in fact as
well as in the sight of the law, hence the "all" for whom
Christ died are here bidden to live henceforth no more unto
themselves, "but unto Him which died for them, and rose
again." In other words, those who belonged to this "all"
for whom Christ died, are here exhorted to manifest practically in their daily lives what is true of them judicially:
they are to "live unto Christ who died *for them.*" Thus
the "One died *for all*" is defined for us. The "all" for which
Christ died are the they which "live," and which are here
bidden to live "unto Him." This passage then teaches three
important truths, and the better to show its scope we mention them in their inverse order: certain ones are here bidden to live no more unto themselves but unto Christ; the
ones thus admonished are "they which live," that is live spiritually, hence, the children of God, for they alone of mankind possess spiritual life, all others being *dead* in trespasses and sins; those who *do* thus live are the ones, the "all,"
the "them," for whom Christ died and rose again. This
passage therefore teaches that Christ died for *all His people,*
the elect, those given to Him by the Father; that as the result of His death (and rising again *"for them"*) they "live"
—and the elect are the *only* ones who *do* thus "live;" and
this life which is theirs through Christ must be lived "unto
Him," Christ's *love* must now "constrain" them.

"For there is one God, and one Mediator, between God
and men (not "man", for this would have been a generic
term and signified mankind. O the accuracy of Holy
Writ!), the Man Christ Jesus; who gave Himself *a ransom
for all,* to be testified in due time" (1 Tim. 2:5, 6). It is
upon the words "who gave Himself a ransom for all" we
would now comment. In Scripture the word "all" (as
applied to humankind) is used in two senses—absolutely
and relatively. In some passages it means *all without exception;* in others it signifies *all without distinction.* As to
which of these meanings it bears in any particular passage,
must be determined by the context and decided by a comparison of parallel scriptures. That the word "all" *is* used

in a *relative and restricted* sense, and in such case means all
without distinction and *not* all without exception, is clear
from a number of scriptures, from which we select two or
three as samples. "And there went out unto him all the
land of Judea, and they of Jerusalem, and were *all* baptized
of him in the river Jordan, confessing their sins" (Mark
1 :5). Does this mean that *every man, woman and child*
from "*all* the land of Judea and they of Jerusalem" were
baptized of John in Jordan? Surely not. Luke 7 :30 distinctly says, "But the Pharisees and lawyers rejected the
counsel of God against themselves, *being not baptized of
him.*" Then what does "*all* baptized of him" mean? . We
answer it *does not mean* all without exception, *but* all without distinction, that is, all classes and conditions of men.
The same explanation applies to Luke 3 :21. Again we read,
"And early in the morning He came again into the Temple,
and *all the people* came unto Him ; and He sat down, and
taught them" (John 8 :2) ; are we to understand this expression absolutely or relatively? Does "all the people"
mean all without exception or all without distinction, that
is, all classes and conditions of people? Manifestly the
latter; for the Temple was not able to accommodate *everybody* that was in Jerusalem at this time, namely, the Feast
of Tabernacles. Again, we read in Acts 22 :15, "For thou
(Paul) shalt be His witness *unto all men* of what thou hast
seen and heard." Surely "all men" here does not mean every
member of the human race. Now we submit that the words
"who gave Himself a ransom *for all*" in 1 Tim. 2 :6 mean
all without distinction, and *not* all without exception. He
gave Himself a ransom for men of all nationalities, of all
generations, of all classes; in a word, for all the elect, as
we read in Rev. 5 :9, "For Thou wast slain, and hast redeemed us to God by Thy blood *out of every* kindred, and
tongue, and people, and nation." That this is not an *arbitrary* definition of the "all" in our passage is clear from
Matt. 20 :28 where we read, "The Son of Man came not to be
ministered unto, but to minister, and to give His life *a ransom for many*", which limitation would be quite meaningless
if He gave Himself a ransom for all without exception.
Furthermore, the qualifying words here, "to be testified in
due time", must be taken into consideration. If Christ gave

Himself a ransom for the whole human race, in what sense will this be *"testified* in due time"? seeing that multitudes of men will certainly be eternally lost. But if our text means that Christ gave Himself a ransom for God's elect, for all without distinction, without distinction of nationality, social prestige, moral character, age or sex, then the meaning of these qualifying words is quite intelligible, for in "due time" this *will be* "testified" in the actual and accomplished salvation of *every one of them*.

"But we see Jesus, who was made a little lower than the angels for the suffering of death, crowned with glory and honor; that He by the grace of God should *taste death for every man*" (Heb. 2:9). This passage need not detain us long. A false doctrine has been erected here on a false translation. There is no word whatever in the Greek corresponding to "man" in our English version. In the Greek it is left in the abstract—"He tasted death for every." The Revised Version has correctly *omitted* "man" from the text, but has wrongly inserted it in italics. Others suppose the word "thing" should be supplied—"He tasted death for every thing" —but this, too, we deem a mistake. It seems to us that the words which immediately follow explain our text: *"For* it became Him, for whom are all things, and by whom are all things, in bringing many sons unto glory, to make the captain of their salvation perfect through sufferings." It is of *"sons"* the apostle is here writing, and we suggest an *ellipsis* of "son"—thus: "He tasted death for every"—and supply *son* in italics. Thus instead of teaching the unlimited design of Christ's death, Heb. 2:9, 10 is in perfect accord with the other scriptures we have quoted which set forth the *restricted* purpose in the Atonement: it was for the "sons" and not the human race our Lord "tasted death."*

In closing this section of the chapter let us say that the only limitation in the Atonement we have contended for arises from pure *sovereignty;* it is a limitation not of value and virtue, but of *design* and *application*. We turn now to consider—

---

*I John 2:2 will be examined in detail in Appendix 4.

3. THE SOVEREIGNTY OF GOD THE HOLY SPIRIT IN SAL-VATION.

Since the Holy Spirit is one of the three Persons in the blessed Trinity, it necessarily follows that He is in full sympathy with the will and design of the other Persons of the Godhead. The eternal *purpose* of the Father in election, the *limited design* in the death of the Son, and the *restricted scope* of the Holy Spirit's operations are in perfect accord. If the Father chose certain ones before the foundation of the world and gave them to His Son, and if it was for them that Christ gave Himself a ransom, then the Holy Spirit is not now working to "bring the world to Christ." The mission of the Holy Spirit *in* the world today is to *apply* the benefits of Christ's redemptive sacrifice. The question which is now to engage us is not the *extent* of the Holy Spirit's *power*—on that point there can be no doubt, it is infinite—but what we shall seek to show is that, His power and operations are *directed* by Divine wisdom and sovereignty.

We have just said that the power and operations of the Holy Spirit are directed by Divine wisdom and indisputable sovereignty. In proof of this assertion we appeal first to our Lord's words to Nicodemus in John 3:8:—"The wind bloweth where it listeth, and thou hearest the sound thereof, but canst not tell whence it cometh, and whither it goeth; so is every one that is born of the Spirit." A comparison is here drawn between the wind and the Spirit. The comparison is a *double* one: first, both are *sovereign in their actions,* and second, both are *mysterious in their operations.* The comparison is pointed out in the word "so." The first point of analogy is seen in the words "where it listeth" or "pleaseth"; the second is found in the words "canst not tell." With the second point of analogy we are not now concerned, but upon the first we would comment further.

"The wind bloweth *where it pleaseth . . . so* is every one that is born *of the Spirit.*" The wind is an element which man can neither harness nor hinder. The wind neither consults man's pleasure nor can it be regulated by his devices. So it is with the Spirit. The wind blows when it pleases, where it pleases, as it pleases. So it is with the

Spirit. The wind is regulated by Divine wisdom, yet, so far
as man is concerned, it is absolutely *sovereign* in its operations. So it is with the Spirit. Sometimes the wind blows
so softly it scarcely rustles a leaf; at other times it blows so
loudly that its roar can be heard for miles. So it is in the
matter of the new birth; with some the Holy Spirit deals so
gently, that His work is imperceptible to human onlookers;
with others His action is so powerful, radical, revolutionary,
that His operations are patent to many. Sometimes the wind
is purely local in its reach, at other times wide-spread in its
scope. So it is with the Spirit: today He acts on one or two
souls, tomorrow He may, as at Pentecost, "prick in the
heart" a whole multitude. But whether He works on few or
many, He consults not man. He acts *as He pleases.* The
new birth is due to *the sovereign will* of the Spirit.

Each of the three Persons in the blessed Trinity is concerned with our salvation: with the Father it is predestination; with the Son propitiation; with the Spirit regenera-
tion. The Father chose us; the Son died for us; the Spirit
quickens us. The Father was concerned *about* us; the Son
shed His blood *for* us, the Spirit performs His work *within*
us. What the One did was *eternal,* what the Other did was
external, what the Spirit does is *internal.* It is with the
work of the Spirit we are now concerned, with His work in
the new birth, and particularly His *sovereign operations* in
the new birth. The Father purposed our new birth; the
Son has made possible (by His "travail") the new birth; but
it is the Spirit who *effects* the new birth—"Born *of the
Spirit*" (John 3:6).

The new birth is solely the work of God the Spirit and
man has no part or lot in it. This from the very nature of
the case. Birth altogether excludes the idea of any effort
or work on the part of the one who is born. Personally we
have no more to do with our spiritual birth than we had
with our natural birth. The new birth is a spiritual resurrection, a "passing from death unto life" (John 5:24) and,
clearly, resurrection is altogether *outside* of man's province.
No corpse can re-animate itself. Hence it is written, "It
is the Spirit that quickeneth; the flesh profiteth *nothing*"
(John 6:63). But the Spirit does not "quicken" everybody
—why? The usual answer returned to this question is,

Because everybody does not trust in Christ. It is supposed that the Holy Spirit quickens only those who believe. But this is to put the cart before the horse. Faith is not the cause of the new birth, but the consequence of it. This ought not to need arguing. Faith (in God) is an exotic, something that is not native to the human heart. If faith *were* a natural product of the human heart, the exercise of a principle common to human nature, it would never have been written, "All men have not faith" (2 Thess. 3 :2). Faith is a spiritual grace, the fruit of the spiritual nature, and because the unregenerate are spiritually dead—"dead in trespasses and sins"—then it follows that faith from them is impossible, for a dead man cannot believe anything. "So then they that are in the flesh cannot please God" (Rom. 8 :8)—but they *could* if it were possible for the flesh to believe. Compare with this last-quoted scripture Heb. 11 : 6—"But without faith it is impossible to please Him." Can God be "pleased" or satisfied with any thing which does not have its origin in Himself?

That the work of the Holy Spirit *precedes* our believing is unequivocally established by 2 Thess. 2 :13—"God hath from the beginning chosen you to salvation through sanctification of the Spirit and belief of the truth." Note that "sanctification of the Spirit" comes before and makes possible "belief of the truth." What then is the "sanctification of the Spirit"? We answer, *the new birth.* In Scripture "sanctification" *always* means "separation," separation from something and unto something or someone. Let us now amplify our assertion that the "sanctification of the Spirit" corresponds to the new birth and points to the positional effect of it.

Here is a servant of God who preaches the Gospel to a congregation in which are an hundred unsaved people. He brings before them the teaching of Scripture concerning their ruined and lost condition; he speaks of God, His character and righteous demands; he tells of Christ meeting God's demands, and dying the Just for the unjust, and declares that through "this Man" is now preached the forgiveness of sins; he closes by urging the lost to believe what God has said in His Word and receive His Son as their own personal Saviour. The meeting is over; the congrega-

tion disperses; ninety-nine of the unsaved have refused to
come to Christ that they might have life, and go out into the
night having no hope, and without God in the world. But the
hundredth heard the Word of life; the Seed sown fell into
ground which had been prepared by God; he believed the
Good News, and goes home rejoicing that his name is written in heaven. He has been "born again," and just as a
newly-born babe in the natural world begins life by clinging
instinctively, in its helplessness, to its mother, so this new-
born soul has clung to Christ. Just as we read, "The Lord
opened" the heart of Lydia *"that* she attended unto the
things which were spoken of Paul" (Acts 16:14), so in the
case supposed above, the Holy Spirit quickened that one
before he believed the Gospel message. Here then is the
"sanctification of the Spirit:" this one soul who has been
born again has, by virtue of his new birth, been *separated*
from the other ninety-nine. Those born again are, by the
Spirit, *set apart* from those who are *dead* in trespasses and
sins.

A beautiful type of the operations of the Holy Spirit *an-
tecedent* to the sinner's "belief of the truth", is found in the
first chapter of Genesis. We read in verse 2, "And the
earth was without form, and void; and darkness was upon
the face of the deep." The original Hebrew here might be
literally rendered thus: "And the earth *had become* a desolate ruin, and darkness was upon the face of the deep."
In "the *beginning*" the earth was not created in the condition described in verse 2. Between the first two verses of
Genesis 1 some awful catastrophe had occurred—possibly
the fall of Satan—and, as the consequence, the earth had
been blasted and blighted, and had become a "desolate ruin",
lying beneath a pall of "darkness." Such also is the history
of man. Today, man is not in the condition in which he
left the hands of his Creator: an awful catastrophe has
happened, and now man is a "desolate ruin" and in total
"darkness" concerning spiritual things. Next we read in
Genesis 1 how God refashioned the ruined earth and created new beings to inhabit it. First we read, *"And the
Spirit of God moved upon* the face of the waters." Next
we are told, *"And God said,* Let there be light; and there
was light." The order is the same in the new creation: there

is first the action of the Spirit, and then the Word of God giving light. *Before* the Word found entrance into the scene of desolation and darkness, bringing with it the light, the Spirit of God "moved." So it is in the new creation. "The entrance of Thy words giveth light" (Ps. 119:130), but *before* it can enter the darkened human heart the Spirit of God must operate upon it.*

To return to 2 Thess. 2:13: "But we are bound to give thanks always to God for you, brethren beloved of the Lord, because God hath from the beginning chosen you to salvation through sanctification of the Spirit and belief of the truth." The *order* of thought here is most important and instructive. First, God's eternal choice; second, the sanctification of the Spirit; third, belief of the truth. Precisely the same order is found in 1 Pet. 1:2—"Elect according to the foreknowledge of God the Father, through sanctification of the Spirit, unto obedience and sprinkling of the blood of Jesus Christ." We take it that the "obedience" here is the "obedience of faith" (Rom. 1:5), which appropriates the virtues of the sprinkled blood of the Lord Jesus. So then *before* the "obedience" (of faith, cf. Heb. 5:9), there is the work of the Spirit setting us apart, and behind that is the election of God the Father. The ones "sanctified of the Spirit" then, are they whom "God hath from the beginning chosen to salvation" (2 Thess. 2:13), those who are "elect according to the foreknowledge of God the Father" (1 Pet. 1:2).

But, it may be said, is not the present mission of the Holy Spirit to "convict *the world* of sin"? And we answer, It is not. The *mission* of the Spirit is threefold; to glorify Christ, to vivify the elect, to edify the saints. John 16:8-11

---

*The *priority* contended for above is rather in order of nature than of time, just as the effect *must* ever be preceded by the cause. A blind man must have his eyes opened before he can see, and yet there is *no interval* of time between the one and the other. As soon as his eyes are opened, he sees. So a man must be born again *before* he can "see the kingdom of God" (John 3:3). *Seeing* the Son is necessary to believing in Him. Unbelief is attributed to spiritual *blindness*—those who believed not the "report" of the Gospel "saw no beauty" in Christ that they should desire Him. The work of the Spirit in "quickening" the one dead in sins, *precedes* faith in Christ, just as cause ever precedes effect. But no sooner *is* the heart turned toward Christ by the Spirit, than the Saviour is embraced by the sinner.

does not describe the "mission" of the Spirit, but sets forth the *significance* of His *presence* here in the world. It treats not of His subjective work in sinners, showing them their need of Christ, by searching their consciences and striking terror to their hearts; what we have there is entirely objective. To illustrate. Suppose I saw a man hanging on the gallows, *of what* would that "convince" me? Why, that he was a murderer. *How* would I thus be convinced? By reading the record of his trial? by hearing a confession from his own lips? No; but by the fact that he *was* hanging there. So the fact that the Holy Spirit is *here* furnishes proof of the world's guilt, of God's righteousness, and of the Devil's judgment.

The Holy Spirit ought not to be here at all. That is a startling statement, but we make it deliberately. *Christ* is the One who *ought* to be here. He was sent here by the Father, but the world did not want Him, would not have Him, hated Him, and cast Him out. And the presence of the Spirit here instead *evidences its guilt*. The coming of the Spirit was a proof to demonstration of the resurrection, ascension, and glory of the Lord Jesus. His presence on earth reverses the world's verdict, showing that God has set aside the blasphemous judgment in the palace of Israel's high priest and in the hall of the Roman governor. The "reproof" of the Spirit abides, and abides altogether irrespective of the world's reception or rejection of His testimony.

Had our Lord been referring here to the gracious work which the Spirit would perform *in* those who should be brought to feel their need of Him, He had said that the Spirit would convict men of their *un*-righteousness, their lack of righteousness. But this is not the thought here at all. The descent of the Spirit from heaven establishes *God's* righteousness, Christ's righteousness. The proof of that is, Christ has gone *to the Father*. Had Christ been an Imposter, as the religious world insisted when they cast Him out, the Father had not received Him. The fact that the Father *did* exalt Him to His own right hand, demonstrates that He was innocent of the charges laid against Him; and the proof that the Father *has* received Him, is the presence now of the Holy Spirit on earth, for Christ has *sent* Him from the Father (John 16:7)! The world was unrighteous in casting Him out, the Father righteous in glorifying Him; and this is what the Spirit's presence here establishes.

"Of judgment, because the Prince of this world is judged" (v. 11). This is the logical and inevitable climax. The world is brought in guilty for their rejection of, for their refusal to receive, Christ. Its condemnation is exhibited by the Father's exaltation of the spurned One. Therefore nothing awaits the world, and its Prince, but judgment. The "judgment" of Satan is already established by The Spirit's presence here, for Christ, through death, set at nought him who had the power of death, that is, the Devil (Heb. 2:14). When God's time comes for the Spirit to depart from the earth, then His sentence will be *executed,* both on the world and its Prince. In the light of this unspeakably solemn passage, we need not be surprised to find Christ saying, "The Spirit of truth, whom the world *cannot* receive, because it seeth Him not, neither knoweth Him". No, the world wants Him not; He condemns the world.

"And when He is come, He will reprove (or, better, "convict"—bring in guilty) the world of sin, and of righteousness, and of judgment: Of sin, because they believe not on Me; Of righteousness, because I go to My Father, and ye see Me no more; Of judgment, because the prince of this world is judged" (John 16:8-11). Three things, then, the presence of the Holy Spirit on earth demonstrates to the world: first, its sin, because the world refused to believe on Christ; second, God's righteousness in exalting to His own right hand the One cast out, and now no more seen by the world; third, judgment, because Satan the world's prince is already judged, though execution of his judgment is yet future. Thus the Holy Spirit's presence here *displays* things as they really are.

The Holy Spirit is sovereign in His operations and His mission is confined to God's elect: they are the ones He "comforts," "seals," guides into all truth, shews things to come, etc. The work of the Spirit is *necessary* in order to the complete accomplishment of the Father's eternal purpose. Speaking hypothetically, but reverently, be it said, that if God had done nothing more than given Christ to die

for sinners, not a single sinner would ever have been saved.
In order for any sinner to see his *need* of a Saviour and be
willing *to receive* the Saviour he needs, the work of the Holy
Spirit upon and within him were imperatively required.
Had God done nothing more than given Christ to die for
sinners and then sent forth His servants to proclaim salvation through Christ, leaving sinners entirely to themselves
to accept or reject as *they* pleased, then *every* sinner would
have *rejected,* because at heart every man hates God and is
at enmity with Him. Therefore the work of the Holy Spirit
was needed to bring the sinner to Christ, to overcome his
innate opposition, and compel him to accept the provision
God has made. We say "compel" the sinner, for this is precisely what the Holy Spirit does, has to do, and this leads
us to consider at some length, though as briefly as possible,
the parable of the "Marriage Supper."

In Luke 14:16 we read, "A certain man made a great supper, and bade many." By comparing carefully what follows
here with Matt. 22:2-10 several important distinctions will
be observed. We take it that these passages are two independent accounts of the same parable, differing in detail
according to the distinctive purpose and design of the Holy
Spirit in each Gospel. Matthew's account—in harmony
with the Spirit's presentation there of Christ as the Son of
David, the King of the Jews—says, "A certain *king* made
a marriage for his son." Luke's account—where the Spirit
presents Christ as the Son of Man—says, "A certain *man*
made a great supper and bade many." Matt. 22:3 says,
"And sent forth His *servants;*" Luke 14:17 says, "And sent
His *servant.*" Now what we wish particularly to call attention to is, that all through Matthew's account it is "servants," whereas in Luke it is always "servant." The class
of readers for whom we are writing are those that believe,
unreservedly, in the *verbal* inspiration of the Scriptures,
and such will readily acknowledge there must be some reason for this change from the plural number in Matthew to
the singular number in Luke. We believe the reason is a
weighty one and that attention to this variation reveals an
important truth. We believe that the "servants" in Matthew, speaking generally, are *all* who go forth preaching the
Gospel, but that the "Servant" in Luke 14 is the Holy Spirit

Himself. This is not incongruous, or derogatory to the Holy
Spirit, for God the Son, in the days of His earthly ministry,
was the Servant of Jehovah (Isa. 42:1). It will be observed that in Matt. 22 the "servants" are sent forth to do
three things: first, to *"call"* to the wedding (v. 3); second,
to *"tell"* those which are bidden . . . all things are ready:
come unto the marriage" (v. 4); third, to *"bid* to the marriage" (v. 9); and these three are the things which those
who minister the Gospel today are now doing. In Luke 14
the Servant is also sent forth to do three things: first, He
is "to *say* to them that were bidden, Come: for all things
are now ready" (v. 17); second, He is to *"bring in* the poor,
and the maimed, and the halt, and the blind" (v. 21); third,
He is to *"compel* them to come in" (v. 23), and the last two
of these the Holy Spirit *alone* can do!

In the above scripture we see that *"the* Servant," the
Holy Spirit, *compels* certain ones to come in to the "supper"
and herein is seen His sovereignty, His omnipotency, His
Divine sufficiency. The clear implication from this word
"compel" is, that those whom the Holy Spirit *does* "bring
in" *are not willing* of themselves *to come.* This is exactly
what we have sought to show in previous paragraphs. By
nature, God's elect are children of wrath *even as others*
(Eph. 2:3), and as such their hearts are at enmity with
God. But this "enmity" of theirs is overcome by the Spirit
and He "compels" *them* to come in. Is it not clear then
that the reason why *others* are left outside, is not only because they are *unwilling* to go in, but also because the Holy
Spirit does not "compel" *them* to come in? Is it not manifest that the Holy Spirit is *sovereign* in the exercise of His
power, that as the wind "bloweth *where it pleaseth"*, so the
Holy Spirit *operates where He pleases?*

And now to sum up. We have sought to show the per-
fect consistency of God's ways: that each Person in the
Godhead acts in sympathy and harmony with the Others.
God the Father elected certain ones to salvation, God the
Son died for the elect, and God the Spirit quickens the elect.
Well may we sing,

> Praise God from whom all blessings flow,
> Praise Him all creatures here below,
> Praise Him above ye heavenly host,
> *Praise Father, Son, and Holy Ghost.*

V

THE SOVEREIGNTY OF GOD IN REPROBATION

"Behold therefore the goodness *and the severity* of God" (Rom. 11:22).

IN the last chapter when treating of the Sovereignty of God the Father in Salvation, we examined seven passages which represent Him as making a choice from among the children of men, and predestinating certain ones to be conformed to the image of His Son. The thoughtful reader will naturally ask, And what of those who were *not* "ordained to eternal life?" The answer which is usually returned to this question, even by those who profess to believe what the Scriptures teach concerning God's sovereignty, is, that God *passes by* the non-elect, *leaves them alone* to go their own way, and in the end casts them into the Lake of Fire because they refused *His* way, and rejected the Saviour of His providing. But this is only a part of the truth; the other part—that which is most offensive to the carnal mind—is either ignored or denied.

In view of the awful solemnity of the subject here before us, in view of the fact that today almost all—even those who profess to be Calvinists—reject and repudiate this doctrine, and in view of the fact that this is one of the points in our book which is calculated to raise the most controversy, we feel that an extended enquiry into this aspect of God's Truth is demanded. That this branch of the subject of God's sovereignty is profoundly mysterious we freely allow, yet, that is no reason why we should reject it. The trouble is that, nowadays, there are so many who receive the testimony of God *only so far* as they can satisfactorily account for all the reasons and grounds of His conduct, which means they will accept nothing but that which can be measured in the petty scales of *their own* limited capacities.

Stating it in its baldest form the point now to be considered is, Has God fore-ordained certain ones to damnation? That many *will be* eternally damned is clear from Scripture, that each one will be judged according to his works and reap as he has sown, and that in consequence his "damnation is just" (Rom. 3:8), is equally sure, and that God *decreed* that the non-elect *should* choose the course *they* follow we now undertake to prove.

From what has been before us in the previous chapter concerning the *election of some* to salvation, it would unavoidably follow, even if Scripture had been silent upon it, that there must be a *rejection of others*. Every choice, evidently and necessarily implies a refusal, for where there is no leaving out there can be no choice. If there be some whom God has elected unto salvation (2 Thess. 2:13), there must be others who are *not* elected unto salvation. If there are some that the Father gave to Christ (John 6:37), there must be others whom He did not give unto Christ. If there are some whose names are written in the Lamb's book of Life (Rev. 21:27), there must be others whose names are *not* written there. That this *is* the case we shall fully prove below.

Now all will acknowledge that from the foundation of the world God certainly fore-knew and fore-saw who would and who would not receive Christ as their Saviour, therefore in giving being and birth to those He *knew* would *reject* Christ, He necessarily created them *unto* damnation. All that can be said in reply to this is, No, while God did *foreknow* these ones would reject Christ, yet He did not *decree* that they *should*. But this is a begging of the real question at issue. God had a definite reason *why* He created men, a specific purpose why He created this and that individual, and in view of the eternal destination of His creatures, He *purposed* either that this one should spend eternity in Heaven or that this one should spend eternity in the Lake of Fire. If then He foresaw that in creating a certain person that that person would despise and reject the Saviour, yet knowing this beforehand He, nevertheless, brought that person into existence, then it is clear He designed and ordained that that person should be eternally lost. Again; faith is God's gift, and the purpose to give it only to some, involves the purpose *not* to give it to others. Without faith there is no salvation—"He that believeth not shall be damned"— hence if there were some of Adam's descendants to whom He purposed not to give faith, it must be because He ordained that *they* should be damned.

Not only is there no escape from these conclusions,

but history *confirms* them. Before the Divine Incarnation, for almost two thousand years, the vast majority of mankind were left destitute of even the external means of grace, being favored with no preaching of God's Word and with no written revelation of His will. For many long centuries Israel was the *only* nation to whom the Deity vouchsafed any special discovery of Himself—"Who in times past suffered *all* nations to walk in their own ways" (Acts 14:16) —"You *only* (Israel) have I known of all the families of the earth" (Amos 3:2). Consequently, as all other nations were deprived of the preaching of God's Word, they were strangers to the faith that cometh thereby (Rom. 10:17). These nations were not only ignorant of God Himself, but of the way to please Him, of the true manner of acceptance with Him, and the means of arriving at the everlasting enjoyment of Himself.

Now if God had willed their salvation, would He not have vouchsafed them the means of salvation? Would He not have given them all things necessary to that end? But it is an undeniable matter of fact that He *did not.*   If, then, Deity can, consistently, with His justice, mercy, and benevolence, deny to some the means of grace, and shut them up in gross darkness and unbelief (because of the sins of their forefathers, generations before), why should it be deemed incompatible with His perfections to exclude some persons, many, from grace itself, and from that eternal life which is connected with it? seeing that He is Lord and sovereign Disposer both of the end to which the means lead, and the means which lead to that end?

Coming down to our own day, and to those in our own country—leaving out the almost unnumberable crowds of unevangelized heathen—is it not evident that there are many living in lands where the Gospel *is* preached, lands which are full of churches, who die strangers to God and His holiness? True, the means of grace were close to their hand, but many of them knew it not. Thousands are born into homes where they are taught from infancy to regard all Christians as hypocrites and preachers as arch-humbugs. Others, are instructed from the cradle in Roman Catholicism, and are trained to regard Evangelical Christianity as deadly heresy, and the Bible as a book highly dangerous for them to read. Others, reared in "Christian Science" families, know no more of the true Gospel of Christ than do the unevangelized heathen. The great majority of these die in utter ignorance of the Way of Peace. Now are we not *obliged* to conclude that it was not God's will to communicate grace to *them?* Had His will been otherwise, would He not have *actually* communicated His grace to them? If, then, it was the will of God, in time, to *refuse* to them His grace, it must have been His will from all eternity, since His will is, as Himself, the same yesterday, and today and forever. Let it not be forgotten that God's *providences* are but the *manifestations* of His *decrees:* what God *does* in time is only what He *purposed* in eternity—His own will being the alone cause of all His acts and works. Therefore from His actually leaving some men in final impenitency and unbelief we assuredly gather it was His everlasting determination so to do; and consequently that He reprobated some from before the foundation of the world.

In the Westminster Confession it is said, "God from all eternity did by the most wise and holy counsel of His own will, freely and unchangeably *fore-ordain whatsoever* comes to pass". The late Mr. F. W. Grant—a most careful and cautious student and writer—commenting on these words said: "It is perfectly, divinely true, that God hath ordained for His own glory whatsoever comes to pass." Now if these statements are true, is not the doctrine of Reprobation established by them? What, in human history, is the one thing which *does* come to pass every day? What, but that men and women die, pass out of this world into a hopeless eternity, an eternity of suffering and woe. If then God *has* foreordained *whatsoever* comes to pass then He must have decreed that vast numbers of human beings should pass out of this world unsaved to suffer eternally in the Lake of Fire. Admitting the general premise, is not the specific conclusion inevitable?

In reply to the preceding paragraphs the reader may say, All this is simply *reasoning*, logical no doubt, but yet mere inferences. Very well, we will now point out that in addition to the above conclusions there are many passages in Holy Writ, which are most clear and definite in their teaching on this solemn subject; passages which are too plain to be misunderstood and too strong to be evaded. The marvel is that so many good men have denied their undeniable affirmations.

"Joshua made war a long time with all those kings. There was not a city that made peace with the children of Israel, save the Hivites the inhabitants of Gibeon: all other they took in battle. For it was of the Lord to harden their hearts, that they should come against Israel in battle, that He might destroy them utterly, and that they might have no favour, but that He might destroy them, as the Lord commanded Moses" (Josh. 11:18-20). What could be plainer than this? Here was a large number of Canaanites whose hearts the Lord hardened, whom He had purposed to utterly destroy, to whom He showed *"no favour"*. Granted that they were wicked, immoral, idolatrous; were they *any* worse than the immoral, idolatrous cannibals of the South Sea Islands (and many other places), to whom God gave the Gospel through John G. Paton! Assuredly not. Then why did not Jehovah command Israel to teach the Canaanites His laws and instruct them concerning sacrifices to the true God? Plainly, because He had marked *them* out for destruction, and if so, that from all eternity.

"The Lord hath made all things for Himself: yea, even the wicked for the day of evil." (Prov. 16:4). That the Lord *made* all, perhaps every reader of this book will allow: that He made all *for Himself* is not so widely believed. That God made us, not for our own sakes, but for Himself; not for our own happiness, but for His glory; is, nevertheless, repeatedly affirmed in Scripture—Rev. 4:11. But Prov. 16:4 goes even farther: it expressly declares that the Lord made the wicked *for* the Day of Evil: *that* was His *design* in giving them being. But *why?* Does not Rom. 9: 17 tell us, "For the Scripture saith unto Pharaoh, Even for this purpose have I raised thee up, that I might shew My power in thee, and that My name might be declared throughout all the earth"! God has made the wicked that, at the end, He may *demonstrate* "His power"—demonstrate it by showing what an easy matter it is for Him to subdue the stoutest rebel and to overthrow His mightiest enemy.

"And then will I profess unto them, I never knew you: Depart from Me, ye that work iniquity" (Matt. 7:23). In the previous chapter it has been shown that, the words "know" and "foreknowledge" when applied to God in the Scriptures, have reference not simply to His prescience (i.e. His *bare knowledge* beforehand), but to His knowledge of *approbation.* When God said to Israel, "You only have I *known* of all the families of the earth" (Amos 3:2), it is evident that He meant, "You only had I any favorable regard to." When we read in Rom. 11:2 "God hath not cast away His people (Israel) whom He *foreknew,*" it is obvious that what was signified is, "God has not finally rejected that people whom He has chosen as the objects of His *love* —cf. Deut. 7:7, 8. In the same way (and it is the *only* possible way) are we to understand Matt. 7:23. In the Day of Judgment the Lord will say unto many, "I never knew you". Note, it is more than simply "I know you not". His solemn declaration will be, "I *never* knew you"—you were never the objects of My approbation. Contrast this with "I *know* (love) My sheep, and am known (loved) of Mine" (John 10:14). The "sheep", His elect, the "few", He *does* "know"; but the reprobate, the non-elect, the "many" He knows *not*—no, not even before the foundation of the world did He know them—He "NEVER" knew them!

In Romans 9 the doctrine of God's sovereignty in its application to both the elect and the reprobate is treated of at length. A detailed exposition of this important chapter would be beyond our present scope; all that we can essay is to dwell upon the part of it which most clearly bears upon the aspect of the subject which we are now considering.

V. 17. *"For the Scripture saith unto Pharaoh, Even for this same purpose have I raised thee up, that I might show My power in thee, and that My name might be declared throughout all the earth."* These words refer us back to vv. 13 and 14. In v. 13 God's love to Jacob and His hatred to Esau are declared. In v. 14 it is asked "Is there unrighteousness with God?" and here in v. 17 the apostle *continues* his reply to the objection. We cannot do better now than quote from Calvin's comments upon this verse. "There are here two things to be considered,—the predestination of Pharaoh to ruin, which is to be referred to the past and yet the hidden counsel of God,—and then, the design of this, which was to make known the name of God. As many interpreters, striving to modify this passage, pervert it, we must first observe, that for the word 'I have raised thee up', or stirred up, in the Hebrew is, 'I have appointed', by which it appears, that God, designing to show that the contumacy of Pharaoh would not prevent Him to deliver His people, not only affirms that his fury had been foreseen by Him, and that He had prepared means for restraining' it, but that He had also thus *designedly ordained it* and indeed for this end,—that He might exhibit a more illustrious evidence of His own power." It will be observed that Calvin gives as the force of the Hebrew word which Paul renders "For this purpose *have I raised thee up,*"—"I have *appointed*". As this is the word on which the doctrine and argument of the verse turns we would further point out that in making this quotation from Ex. 9:16 the apostle significantly departs from the Septuagint—the version then in common use, and from which he most frequently quotes—and substitutes a clause for the first that is given by the Septuagint: instead of "On this account thou hast been preserved", he gives "For this very end have I raised thee up"!

But we must now consider in more detail the case of Pharaoh which sums up in concrete example the great controversy between man and his Maker. "For now I will stretch out My hand, that I may smite thee and thy people with pestilence; and thou shalt be cut off from the earth. *And in very deed for this cause* have I raised thee up, for to show in thee My power; and that My name may be declared throughout all the earth" (Exodus 9:15, 16). Upon these words we offer the following comments:

First, we know from Exodus 14 and 15 that Pharaoh *was* "cut off", that he was cut off by God, that he was cut off in the very midst of his wickedness, that he was cut off not by sickness nor by the infirmities which are incident to old age, nor by what men term an accident, but cut off by *the immediate hand of God in judgment.*

Second, it is clear that God raised up Pharaoh *for* this very end—*to* "cut him off," which in the language of the New Testament means "destroyed." God never does anything without a previous design. In giving him being, in preserving him through infancy and childhood, in raising him to the throne of Egypt, God had one end in view. That such *was* God's purpose is clear from His words to Moses before he went down to Egypt, to demand of Pharaoh that Jehovah's people should be allowed to go a three days' journey into the wilderness to worship Him—"And the Lord said unto Moses, When thou goest to return into Egypt, see that thou do all these wonders before Pharaoh, which I have put in thine hand: *but I will harden his heart,* that he shall not let the people go" (Exodus 4:21). But not only so, God's design and purpose was declared long before this. Four hundred years previously God had said to Abraham, "Know of a surety that thy seed shall be a stranger in a land that is not theirs, and shall serve them; and they shall afflict them four hundred years; and also that nation, whom they shall serve, *will I judge*" (Gen. 15:13, 14). From these words it is evident (a nation and its king being looked at as one in the O. T.) that God's purpose was formed long before He gave Pharaoh being.

Third, an examination of God's dealings with Pharaoh makes it clear that Egypt's king was indeed a "vessel of wrath fitted to destruction." Placed on Egypt's throne, with the reins of government in his hands, he sat as head of the nation which occupied the first rank among the peoples of the world. There was no other monarch on earth able to control or dictate to Pharaoh. To such a dizzy height did God raise this reprobate, and such a course was a natural and necessary step to prepare him for his final fate, for it is a Divine axiom that "pride goeth before destruction and a haughty spirit before a fall." Further,—and this is deeply important to note and highly significant—God removed from Pharaoh the one outward restraint which was calculated to act as a check upon him. The bestowing upon Pharaoh of the unlimited powers of a king was setting him above all legal influence and control. But besides this, *God removed Moses* from his presence and kingdom. Had Moses, who not only was skilled in all the wisdom of the Egyptians but also had been reared in Pharaoh's household, been suffered to remain in close proximity to the throne, there can be no doubt but that his example and influence had been a powerful check upon the king's wickedness and tyranny. This, though not the only cause, was plainly one reason why God sent Moses into Midian, for it was during his *absence* that

Egypt's inhuman king framed his most cruel edicts. God designed, by removing this restraint, to give Pharaoh full opportunity to fill up the full measure of his sins, and ripen himself for his fully-deserved but predestined ruin.

Fourth, God "hardened" his heart as He declared He would (Ex. 4:21). This is in full accord with the declarations of Holy Scripture—"The preparations of the heart in man, and the answer of the tongue, *is from the Lord*" (Prov. 16:1); "The king's heart is in the hand of the Lord, as the rivers of water, He turneth it *whithersoever He will*" (Prov. 21:1). Like all other kings, Pharaoh's heart was in the hand of the Lord; and God had both the right and the power to turn it whithersoever He pleased. And it pleased Him to turn it *against* all good. God determined to hinder Pharaoh from granting his request through Moses to let Israel go, until He had fully prepared him for his final overthrow, and because nothing short of this would fully fit him, God *hardened* his heart.

Finally, it is worthy of careful consideration to note how the *vindication* of God in His dealings with Pharaoh has been fully attested. Most remarkable it is to discover that we have Pharaoh's *own testimony* in favor of God and against himself! In Exodus 9:15 and 16 we learn how God had told Pharaoh for what purpose He had raised him up, and in verse 27 of the same chapter we are told that Pharaoh said, "I have sinned this time: *the Lord is righteous,* and I and my people are wicked." Mark that this was said by Pharaoh *after* he knew that God had raised him up in order to "cut him off", *after* his severe judgments had been sent upon him, *after* he had hardened his own heart. By this time Pharaoh was fairly ripened for judgment, and fully prepared to decide whether God had injured him, or whether he had sought to injure God; and he fully acknowledges that he had "sinned" and that God was "righteous". Again; we have the witness of Moses who was fully acquainted with God's conduct toward Pharaoh. He had heard at the beginning what was God's design in connection with Pharaoh; he had witnessed God's dealings with him; he had observed his "long-sufferance" toward this vessel of wrath fitted to destruction; and at last he had beheld him cut off in Divine judgment at the Red Sea. How then was Moses impressed?

Does he raise the cry of injustice? Does he dare to charge God with unrighteousness? Far from it. Instead, he says, "Who is like unto Thee, O Lord, among the gods? Who is like Thee, glorious in holiness, *fearful* in praises, doing wonders!" (Exodus 15:11).

Was Moses moved by a *vindictive* spirit as he saw Israel's arch-enemy "cut off" by the waters of the Red Sea? Surely not. But to remove forever all doubt upon this score, it remains to be pointed out how that *saints in heaven,* after *they* have witnessed the sore judgments of God, join in singing "the song of *Moses* the servant of God, and the song of the Lamb saying, Great and marvelous are Thy works, Lord God Almighty; *just and true* are Thy ways, Thou King of Nations" (Rev. 15:3). Here then is the climax, and the full and final vindication of God's dealings with Pharaoh. Saints in heaven join in singing the Song of Moses, in which that servant of God celebrated Jehovah's praise in overthrowing Pharaoh and his hosts, declaring that in so acting God was *not* unrighteous but *just and true.* We must believe, therefore, that the Judge of all the earth did right in creating and destroying this vessel of wrath, Pharaoh.

The case of Pharaoh *establishes* the principle and illustrates the doctrine of Reprobation. If God actually reprobated Pharaoh, we may justly conclude that He reprobates all others whom He did not predestinate to be conformed to the image of His Son. This inference the apostle Paul manifestly draws from the fate of Pharaoh, for in Romans 9, after referring to God's purpose in raising up Pharaoh, he continues, *"therefore".* The case of Pharaoh is introduced to prove the doctrine of Reprobation as the counterpart of the doctrine of Election.

In conclusion, we would say that in forming Pharaoh God displayed neither justice nor injustice, but only His bare sovereignty. As the potter is sovereign in forming vessels, so God is sovereign in forming moral agents.

V. 18. *"Therefore hath He mercy on whom He will have mercy, and whom He will He hardeneth".* The "therefore" announces the general conclusion which the apostle draws from all he had said in the three preceding verses in denying that God was unrighteous in loving Jacob and hating Esau, and specifically it applies the principle exemplified in God's dealings with Pharaoh. It traces everything back to the sovereign will of the Creator. He loves one and hates another, He exercises mercy toward some and hardens others, without reference to anything save His own sovereign will.

That which is most repellant to the carnal mind in the above verse is the reference to *hardening*—"Whom He will He hardeneth"— and it is just here that so many commentators and expositors have adulterated the truth. The most common view is that the apostle is speaking of nothing more than *judicial* hardening, i.e., a *forsaking* by God *because* these subjects of His displeasure had *first* rejected His truth and forsaken Him. Those who contend for this interpretation appeal to such scriptures as Rom. 1:19-26—"God gave them up", that is (see context) those who "knew God" yet glorified Him not as God (v. 21). Appeal is also made to 2 Thess. 2:10-12. But it is to be noted that the word "harden" *does not occur* in either of these passages. But further. We submit that Rom. 9:18 has no reference whatever to *judicial* "hardening". The apostle is not there speaking of those who had already turned their backs on God's truth, but instead, he is dealing with *God's sovereignty,* God's sovereignty as seen not only in showing *mercy to whom He wills,* but also in *hardening whom He pleases.* The exact words are "Whom *He will"*—not "all who have rejected His truth"—"He hardeneth", and this, coming immediately after the mention of Pharaoh, clearly fixes their meaning. The case of Pharaoh is plain enough, though man by his glosses has done *his* best to *hide* the truth.

V. 18. *"Therefore hath He mercy on whom He will have mercy, and whom He will He hardeneth".* This affirmation of God's sovereign "hardening" of sinners' hearts—in contradistinction from judicial hardening—is not alone. Mark the language of John 12:37-40, "But though He had done so many miracles before them, yet they believed not on Him: that the saying of Isaiah the prophet might be fulfilled, which he spake, Lord, who hath believed our report? and to whom hath the arm of the Lord been revealed? *Therefore they could not believe* (why?), because that Isaiah said again, *He hath* blinded their eyes, and hardened their hearts (why? Because they had refused to believe on Christ? This is the popular belief, but mark the answer of Scripture) *that they should not* see with their eyes, nor understand with their heart, and be converted, and I should heal them." Now, reader, it is just a question as to whether or not you will believe what God has revealed in His Word. It is not a matter of prolonged searching or profound study, but a childlike spirit which is needed, in order to understand this doctrine.

V. 19. *"Thou wilt say then unto me, Why doth He yet find fault? For who hath resisted His will?"* Is not this the very objection which is urged today? The force of the apostle's questions here seems to be this: Since everything is dependent on God's will, which is irreversible, and since this will of God, according to which He can do everything as sovereign—since He can have mercy on whom He wills to have mercy, and can refuse mercy and inflict punishment on whom He chooses to do so—why does He not will to have mercy on all, so as to make them obedient, and thus put finding of fault out of court? Now it should be particularly noted that the apostle does not repudiate the ground on which the objection rests. He does not say God *does not* find fault. Nor does he say, *Men may* resist His will. Furthermore; he does not explain away the objection by saying: You have altogether misapprehended my meaning when I said 'Whom He wills He treats kindly, and whom He wills He treats severely'. But he says, "first, this is an objection you have *no right* to make; and then, This is an objection you have *no reason* to make" (vide Dr. Brown). The objection was utterly inadmissible, for it was a replying *against* God. It was to complain about, argue against, what *God* had done!

V. 19. *"Thou wilt say then unto me, Why doth He yet find fault? For who hath resisted His will?"* The language which the apostle here puts into the mouth of the objector is so plain and pointed, that misunderstanding ought to be impossible. Why doth He yet *find fault?* Now, reader, what can these words mean? Formulate *your own* reply before considering ours. Can the force of the apostle's question be any other than this: If it is true that God has "mercy" *on whom He wills,* and also "hardens" *whom He wills,* then what becomes of human responsibility? In such a case men are nothing better than *puppets,* and if this be true then it would be *unjust* for God to "find fault" with His helpless creatures. Mark the word "then"—Thou wilt say *then* unto me—he states the (false) *inference* or *conclusion* which the objector draws from what the apostle had been saying. And mark, my reader, the apostle readily saw the doctrine he had formulated *would* raise *this* very objection, and unless what *we* have written throughout this book provokes, in some at least, (*all* whose carnal minds are not subdued by divine grace) the *same* objection, then it must be either because we have not presented the doctrine which is set forth in Rom. 9, or else because human nature has *changed* since the apostle's day. Consider now the remainder of the verse (19). The apostle *repeats* the *same* objection in a slightly different form—repeats it so that his meaning may not be *mis*understood—namely, "For who hath resisted His will?" It is clear then that the subject under immediate discussion relates to God's "will", i.e., His sovereign ways, which *confirms* what we have said above upon vs. 17 and 18, where we contended that it is *not* judicial hardening which is in view (that is, hardening because of previous rejection of the truth), but *sovereign* "hardening", that is, the "hardening" of a fallen and sinful creature for no other reason than that which inheres in the sovereign will of God. And hence the question, "Who hath resisted His *will?*" What then does the apostle say in reply to these objections?

V. 20. *"Nay but, O man, who art thou that repliest against God? Shall the thing formed say to him that formed it, Why hast thou made me thus?"* The apostle, then, did not say the objection was pointless and groundless, instead, he rebukes the objector for his *impiety.* He reminds him that he is merely a "man", a creature, and that as such it is most unseemly and impertinent for *him* to "reply (argue, or reason) against God". Furthermore, he reminds him that he is nothing more than a "thing formed", and therefore, it is madness and blasphemy to rise up against the Former Himself. Ere leaving this verse it should be pointed out that its closing words, "Why hast thou made me *thus*" help us to determine, unmistakably, the precise subject under discussion. In the light of the immediate context what can be the force of the "thus"? What, but as in the case of Esau, why hast thou made me an object of "hatred"? What, but as in

the case of Pharaoh, Why hast thou made me simply to
"harden" me? What other meaning *can, fairly,* be assigned
to it?

It is highly important to keep clearly before us that the
apostle's object throughout this passage is to treat of God's
sovereignty in dealing with, on the one hand, those whom He
loves—vessels unto honor and vessels of mercy, and *also,*
on the other hand, with those whom He "hates" and "hardens"—vessels unto dishonour and vessels of wrath.

Vv. 21-23. *"Hath not the potter power over the clay, of
the same lump, to make one vessel unto honour, and another
unto dishonour? What if God, willing to shew His wrath,
and to make His power known, endured with much longsuffering the vessels of wrath fitted to destruction: And
that He might make known the riches of His glory on the
vessels of mercy, which He had afore prepared unto glory."*
In these verses the apostle furnishes a full and final reply
to the objections raised in v. 19. First, he asks, "Hath not
the potter power over the clay?" etc. It is to be noted the
word here translated "power" is a different one in the Greek
from the one rendered "power" in v. 22 where it can only
signify His *might;* but here in v. 21, the "power" spoken of
must refer to the Creator's *rights* or sovereign *prerogatives;*
that this is so, appears from the fact that the *same* Greek
word is employed in John 1:12—"As many as received Him,
to them gave He power to become the sons of God"—
which, as is well known, means the right or privilege to become the sons of God. The R. V. employs "right" both
in John 1:12 and Rom. 9:21.

V. 21. *"Hath not the potter power over the clay of the
same lump, to make one vessel unto honour, and another unto dishonour?"* That the "potter" here is God Himself is certain from the previous verse, where the apostle asks "Who
art thou that repliest against *God?"* and then, speaking in
the terms of the figure he was about to use, continues, "Shall
the *thing formed* say to Him that formed it" etc. Some
there are who would rob these words of their force by arguing that while the human potter makes certain vessels to
be used for less honorable purposes than others, nevertheless, they are designed to fill some useful place. But the
apostle does not here say, Hath not the potter power over the

clay of the same lump, to make one vessel unto an honorable use and another to a less honorable use, but he speaks of some "vessels" being made "unto *dis*honour". It is true, of course, that God's *wisdom* will yet be fully vindicated, inasmuch as the destruction of the reprobate *will* promote His glory—in what way the next verse tells us.

Ere passing to the next verse let us summarize the teaching of this and the two previous ones. In v. 19 two questions are asked, "Thou wilt say then unto me, Why doth He yet find fault? For who hath resisted His will?" To those questions a threefold answer is returned. First, in v. 20 the apostle denies the creature the right to sit in judgment upon the ways of the Creator—"Nay but, O man who art thou that repliest against God? Shall the thing formed say to Him that formed it, Why hast Thou made me thus?" The apostle insists that the rectitude of God's will *must not* be questioned. Whatever *He* does *must be* right. Second, in v. 21 the apostle declares that the Creator has the right to dispose of His creatures as He sees fit—"Hath not the Potter power over the clay, of the same lump, to make one vessel unto honor, and another unto dishonor?" It should be carefully noted that the word for "power" here is exousia—an entirely different word from the one translated "power" in the following verse ("to make known His power"), where it is dunaton. In the words "Hath not the Potter power over the clay?" it must be God's power *justly exercised*, which is in view—the exercise of God's rights *consistently with His justice,*—because the mere assertion of His omnipotency would be no such answer as God would return to the questions asked in v. 19. Third, in vv. 22, 23, the apostle gives the reasons *why* God proceeds differently with one of His creatures from another: on the one hand, it is to "shew His wrath" and to "make His power known"; on the other hand, it is to "make known the riches of His glory."

"Hath not the potter power over the clay of the same lump, to make one vessel unto honour, and another unto dishonour?" Certainly God has *the right* to do this because He is the Creator. Does He *exercise* this right? Yes, as vs. 13 and 17 clearly show us—"For this same purpose *have I* raised thee (Pharaoh) up".

V. 22. "*What if God, willing to shew His wrath, and to*

*make His power known, endured with much longsuffering
the vessels of wrath fitted to destruction".* Here the apostle
tells us in the second place, *why* God acts thus, i.e., differently with different ones—having mercy on some and hardening others, making one vessel "unto honour" and another
"unto dishonour". Observe, that here in v. 22 the apostle
first mentions "vessels of wrath", before he refers in v. 23
to the "vessels of mercy". Why is this? The answer to
this question is of first importance: we reply, Because it is
the "vessels *of wrath*" who are the subjects in view before
the objector in v. 19. Two reasons are given *why* God
makes some "vessels unto dishonour": first, to "shew His
wrath", and secondly "to make His power known"—both
of which were exemplified in the case of Pharaoh.

One point in the above verse requires separate consideration—"Vessels of wrath *fitted* to destruction". The usual
explanation which is given of these words is that the vessels
of wrath *fit themselves* to destruction, that is, fit themselves
by virtue of their wickedness; and it is argued that there
is no need for *God* to "fit them to destruction", because they
are already fitted by their own depravity, and that this *must*
be the real meaning of this expression. Now if by "destruction" we understand *punishment,* it is perfectly true that the
non-elect *do* "fit themselves", for every one will be judged
"according to his works"; and further, we freely grant that
subjectively the non-elect *do* fit themselves for destruction.
But the point to be decided is, Is *this* what the apostle is here
referring to? And, without hesitation, we reply it is not.
Go back to vs. 11-13: did Esau *fit himself* to be an object of
God's hatred, or was he not such *before* he was born?
Again; did Pharaoh *fit himself* for destruction, or did not
God harden his heart *before* the plagues were sent upon
Egypt?—see Ex. 4:21!

Rom. 9:22 is clearly a continuation in thought of v. 21,
and v. 21 is part of the apostle's reply to the questions raised
in v. 20: therefore, to fairly follow out the figure, it *must* be
God Himself who "fits" unto destruction the vessels of
wrath. Should it be asked *how* God does this, the answer,
necessarily, is, *objectively,*—He fits the non-elect unto destruction by His fore-ordinating decrees. Should it be asked
why God does this, the answer must be, To promote His

own glory, i.e., the glory of His justice, power and wrath. "The sum of the apostle's answer here is, that the grand object of God, both in the election and the reprobation of men, is that which is paramount to all things else in the creation of men, namely, His own glory" (Rob't Haldane).

V. 23. *"And that He might make known the riches of His glory on the vessels of mercy, which He had afore prepared unto glory."* The only point in this verse which demands attention is the fact that the "vessels of mercy" are here said to be *"afore* prepared unto glory". Many have pointed out that the previous verse does not say the vessels of wrath were *afore* prepared unto destruction, and from this omission they have concluded that we must understand the reference there to the non-elect *fitting themselves* in time, rather than God ordaining them for destruction from all eternity. But this conclusion by no means follows. We need to look back to v. 21 and note the figure which is there employed. "Clay" is *inanimate* matter, corrupt, decomposed, and therefore a *fit* substance to represent *fallen* humanity. As then the apostle is contemplating God's sovereign dealings with humanity *in view of the Fall,* He does not say the vessels of wrath were "afore" prepared unto destruction, for the obvious and sufficient reason that, it was not until *after* the Fall that they became *(in themselves)* what is here symbolized by the "clay". All that is necessary to refute the erroneous conclusion referred to above, is to point out that what is said of the vessels of wrath is not that they are *fit for* destruction (which is the word that would have been used if the reference had been to them *fitting themselves* by their own wickedness), but *fitted to* destruction; which, in the light of the whole context, must mean a *sovereign ordination* to destruction by the Creator. We quote here the pointed words of Calvin on this passage—"There are vessels prepared for destruction, that is, given up and appointed to destruction; they are also vessels of wrath, that is, *made and formed for this end,* that they may be examples of God's vengeance and displeasure. Though in the second clause the apostle asserts more expressly, that it is God who prepared the elect for glory, as he had simply said before that the reprobate are vessels prepared for destruction, there is yet no doubt but that the preparation of both is connected with the secret

counsel of God. Paul might have otherwise said, that the
reprobate gave up or cast themselves into destruction, but
he intimates here, that before they are born they are des-
tined to their lot". With this we are in hearty accord. Rom.
9:22 *does not* say the vessels of wrath *fitted themselves,*
nor does it say they are *fit for* destruction, instead, it declares they are "fitted *to* destruction", and the context shows
plainly it is *God* who thus "fits" them—objectively by His
eternal decrees.

Though Romans 9 contains the *fullest* setting forth of the
doctrine of Reprobation, there are still other passages which
refer to it, one or two more of which we will now briefly
notice :—

"What then? That which Israel seeketh for, that he ob-
obtained not, but the election obtained it, and the rest were
hardened" (Rom. 11:7 R. V.). Here we have two distinct
and clearly defined classes which are set in sharp antithesis :
the "election" and "the rest"; the one "obtained", the other
is "hardened". On this verse we quote from the comments
of John Bunyan of immortal memory :—"These are solemn
words : they sever between men and men—the election and
the rest, the chosen and the left, the embraced and the refused. By 'rest' here must needs be understood those *not
elect,* because set the one in opposition to the other, and
if not elect, whom then but reprobate?"

Writing to the saints at Thessalonica the apostle declared
"For God hath not appointed us to wrath, but to obtain
salvation by our Lord Jesus Christ" (1 Thess. 5:9). Now
surely it is patent to any impartial mind that this statement
is quite pointless if God has not "appointed" *any* to wrath.
To say that God "hath not appointed *us* to wrath", clearly
implies that there *are* some whom He *has* "appointed *to*
wrath", and were it not that the minds of so many professing Christians are so blinded by prejudice, they could
not fail to clearly see this.

"A Stone of stumbling, and a Rock or offence, even to
them who stumble at the Word, being disobedient, where-
unto also they *were appointed*" (1 Pet. 2:8). The "where-
unto" manifestly points back to the stumbling at the Word,
and their disobedience. Here, then, God expressly affirms
that there *are* some who have been "appointed" (it is the

same Greek word as in 1 Thess. 5:9) unto disobedience. Our business is not to *reason* about it, but to *bow* to Holy Scripture. Our first duty is not to *understand,* but to *believe* what God has said.

"But these, as natural brute beasts, *made to be taken and destroyed,* speak evil of the things that they understand not; and shall utterly perish in their own corruption" (2 Pet. 2:12). Here, again, every effort is made to escape the plain teaching of this solemn passage. We are told that it is the "brute beasts" who are "made to be taken and destroyed", and not the persons here likened to them. All that is needed to refute such sophistry is to inquire *wherein* lies the point of *analogy* between the "these" (men) and the "brute beasts"? What is the force of the "as"—but "these *as* brute beasts"? Clearly, it is that "these" men *as* brute beasts, are the ones who, like animals, are "made to be taken and destroyed": the closing words confirming this by *reiterating* the same sentiment—"and shall utterly perish in their own corruption."

"For there are certain men crept in unawares, who were before of old *ordained to this condemnation;* ungodly men, turning the grace of our God into lasciviousness, and denying the only Lord God, and our Lord Jesus Christ" (Jude 4). Attempts have been made to escape the obvious force of this verse by substituting a different translation. The R.V. gives: "But there are certain men crept in privily, even they who were of old *written of beforehand* unto this condemnation." But this altered rendering by no means gets rid of that which is so distasteful to our sensibilities. The question arises, *Where* were these "of old *written of* beforehand"? Certainly not in the Old Testament, for nowhere is there any reference *there* to wicked men creeping into *Christian assemblies.* If *"written of"* be the best translation of "prographo", the reference can only be to the book of the Divine *decrees.* So whichever alternative be selected there can be no evading the fact that certain men are *"before of old"* marked out *by* God "unto condemnation."

"And all that dwell on the earth shall worship him (viz. the Antichrist), every one whose name hath *not* been written from the foundation of the world in the Book of Life of the Lamb that hath been slain" (Rev. 13:8, R. V. compare Rev.

17:8). Here, then, is a positive statement affirming that there *are* those whose names *were not* written in the Book of Life. Because of this they shall render allegiance to and bow down before the Antichrist.

Here, then, are no less than ten passages which most plainly imply or expressly teach the fact of reprobation. They affirm that the wicked are made *for* the Day of Evil; that God fashions some vessels unto *dis*-honor; and by His eternal decree (objectively) fits them unto destruction; that they are like brute beasts, made to be taken and destroyed, being of old ordained unto this condemnation. Therefore in the face of these scriptures we unhesitatingly affirm (after nearly twenty years careful and prayerful study of the subject) that the Word of God unquestionably teaches both Predestination and Reprobation, or to use the words of Calvin, "Eternal Election is God's predestination of some to salvation, and others to destruction".

Having thus stated the doctrine of Reprobation, as it is presented in Holy Writ, let us now mention one or two important considerations to guard it against abuse and prevent the reader from making any unwarranted deductions:—

First, the doctrine of Reprobation does not mean that God purposed to take innocent creatures, make them wicked, and then damn them. Scripture says, "God hath made man upright, but they have sought out many inventions" (Eccl. 7:29). God has not created *sinful* creatures in order to destroy them, for God is not to be charged with the sin of His creatures. The responsibility and criminality is man's.

God's decree of Reprobation contemplated Adam's race as fallen, sinful, corrupt, guilty. From it God purposed to save a few as the monuments of His sovereign grace; the others He determined to destroy as the exemplification of His justice and severity. In determining to destroy these others, God did them no wrong. They had already fallen in Adam, their legal representative; they are therefore born with a sinful nature, and in their sins He leaves them. Nor can they complain. This is as *they* wish; they have no desire for holiness; they *love* darkness rather than light. Where, then, is there any injustice if God "gives them up to *their own* hearts' lusts" (Psa. 81:12)!

Second, the doctrine of Reprobation does not mean that

God refuses to save those who earnestly seek salvation. The fact is that the reprobate have no longing *for* the Saviour: they see in Him no beauty that they should desire Him. They will not come to Christ—why then should God force them to? He turns away *none* who *do* come—where then is the injustice of God fore-determining their *just* doom? None will be punished but for their iniquities; where then, is the supposed tyrannical cruelty of the Divine procedure? Remember that God is the Creator of the wicked, not of their wickedness; He is the Author of their being, but not the Infuser of their sin.

God does not (as we have been slanderously reported to affirm) compel the wicked to sin, as the rider spurs on an unwilling horse. God only says in effect that awful word, "Let them alone" (Matt. 15:14). He needs only to slacken the reins of providential restraint, and withhold the influence of saving grace, and apostate man will only too soon and too surely, of his own accord, fall by his iniquities. Thus the decree of reprobation neither interferes with the bent of man's own fallen nature, nor serves to render him the less inexcusable.

Third, the decree of Reprobation in nowise conflicts with God's goodness. Though the non-elect are not the objects of His goodness in the same way or to the same extent as the elect are, yet are they not wholly excluded from a participation of it. They enjoy the good things of Providence (temporal blessings) in common with God's own children, and very often to a higher degree. But how do they improve them? Does the (temporal) goodness of God lead them to repent? Nay, verily, they do but *"despise* His goodness, and forbearance, and longsuffering, and after their hardness and impenitency of heart treasure up unto themselves wrath against the day of wrath" (Rom. 2:4, 5). On what righteous ground, then, can they murmur against not being the objects of His benevolence in the endless ages yet to come? Moreover, if it did not clash with God's mercy and kindness to leave the entire body of the fallen angels (2 Pet. 2:4) under the guilt of their apostacy; still less can it clash with the Divine perfections to leave some of fallen mankind in their sins and punish them for them.

Finally, let us interpose this necessary caution: It is utterly impossible for any of us, during the present life, to ascertain who *are* among the reprobate. *We* must not now so judge any man, no matter how wicked he may be. The vilest sinner, may, for all we know, be included in the election of *grace* and be one day quickened by the Spirit of grace. Our marching orders are plain, and woe be unto us if we disregard them—"Preach the Gospel to *every* creature". When we have done so our skirts are clear. If men refuse to heed, their blood is on their own heads; nevertheless "we are unto God a sweet savour of Christ, in them that are saved, and in them that perish. To the one we are a savor of death unto death; and to the other we are a savor of life unto life" (2 Cor. 2:15, 16).

We must now consider a number of passages which are often quoted with the purpose of showing that God *has not* fitted certain vessels to destruction or ordained certain ones to condemnation. First, we cite Ezek. 18:31—"Why will ye die, O house of Israel?" On this passage we cannot do better than quote from the comments of Augustas Toplady: —"This is a passage very frequently, but very idly, insisted upon by Arminians, as if it were a hammer which would at one stroke crush the whole fabric to powder. But it so happens that the "death" here alluded to is neither spiritual nor eternal death: as is abundantly evident from the whole tenor of the chapter. The death intended by the prophet is a *political* death; a death of national prosperity, tranquillity, and security. The sense of the question is precisely this: What is it that makes you in love with captivity, banishment, and civil ruin? Abstainance from the worship of images might, as a people, exempt you from these calamities, and once more render you a respectable nation. Are the miseries of public devastation so alluring as to attract your determined pursuit? Why will ye die? die as the house of Israel, and considered as a political body? Thus did the prophet argue the case, at the same time adding—"For I have no pleasure in the death of him that dieth saith the Lord God, wherefore, turn yourselves, and live ye." This imports: First, the national captivity of the Jews added nothing to the happiness of God. Second, if the Jews turned from idolatry, and flung away their images, they should not die in a foreign, hostile country, but live peaceably in their own land and enjoy their liberties as an independent people." To the above we may add: *political* death *must* be what is in view in Ezek. 18:31, 32 for the simple but sufficient reason that they were *already* spiritually dead!

Matt. 25:41 is often quoted to show that God *has not* fitted certain vessels to destruction—"Depart from Me, ye cursed, into everlasting fire, prepared for the Devil and his angels." This is, in fact, one of the principal verses relied upon to disprove the doctrine of Reprobation. But we submit that the emphatic word here is *not* "for" but "Devil." This verse (see context) sets forth the *severity* of the judgment which awaits the lost. In other words, the above scripture expresses the *awfulness* of the everlasting fire rather than *the subjects* of it—if the fire be "prepared for *the Devil* and his angels" then how intolerable it will be! If the place of eternal torment into which the damned shall be cast is *the same* as that in which God's *arch-enemy* will suffer, how *dreadful* must that place be!

Again: if God has chosen only certain ones to salvation, why are we told that God "now commandeth all men everywhere to repent" (Acts 17:30)? That God commandeth "all men" to repent is but the enforcing of His righteous claims as the moral Governor of the world. How could He do less, seeing that all men everywhere have sinned against Him? Furthermore; that God commandeth all men everywhere to repent argues the universality of creature responsibility. But this scripture does not declare that it is God's pleasure to "give repentance" (Acts 5:31) to all men everywhere. That the apostle Paul did not believe God gave repentance to every soul is clear from his words in 2 Tim. 2:25—"In meekness instructing those that oppose themselves; *if* God *peradventure* will give them repentance to the acknowledging of the truth."

Again, we are asked, if God has "ordained" only certain ones unto eternal life, then why do we read that He "will have *all men* to be saved, and come to the knowledge of the truth" (1 Tim. 2:4)? The reply is, that the words "all" and "all men", like the term "world," are often used in a general and relative sense. Let the reader carefully examine the following passages: Mark 1:5; John 6:45; 8:2; Acts 21:28; 22:15; 2 Cor. 3:2 etc., and he will find full proof of our assertion. I Tim. 2:4 *cannot* teach that God *wills* the salvation of all mankind, or otherwise all mankind *would* be saved—"What His soul desireth *even that He doeth*" (Job 23:13)!

Again; we are asked, Does not Scripture declare, again and again, that God is no "respecter of persons"? We answer, it certainly does, and God's electing grace *proves* it. The seven sons of Jesse, though older and physically superior to David, are passed by, while the young shepherd-boy is exalted to Israel's throne. The scribes and lawyers pass unnoticed, and ignorant fishermen are chosen to be the apostles of the Lamb. Divine truth is hidden from the wise and prudent and is revealed to babes instead. The great majority of the wise and noble are ignored, while the weak, the base, the despised, are called and saved. Harlots and publicans are sweetly compelled to come in to the gospel feast, while self-righteous Pharisees are suffered to perish in their immaculate morality. Truly, God *is* "no respecter" of persons or He would not have saved *me*.

That the Doctrine of Reprobation is a "hard saying" to the carnal mind is readily acknowledged—yet, is it any "harder" than that of *eternal* punishment? That it is clearly taught in Scripture we have sought to demonstrate, and it is not for us to pick and choose from the truths revealed in God's Word. Let those who are inclined to receive those doctrines which commend themselves to *their* judgment, and who reject those which they *cannot* fully understand, remember those scathing words of our Lord's, "O fools, and slow of heart to believe *all* that the prophets have spoken" (Luke 24:25): fools because slow of heart; slow of heart, not dull of head!

Once more we would avail ourself of the language of Calvin: "But, as I have hitherto only recited such things as are delivered without any obscurity or ambiguity in the Scriptures, let persons who hesitate not to brand with ignominy those Oracles of heaven, beware what kind of opposition they make. For, if they pretend ignorance, with a desire to be commended for their modesty, what greater instance of pride can be conceived, than to oppose one little word to the authority of God! as, 'It appears otherwise to me,' or 'I would rather not meddle with this subject.' But if they openly censure, what will they gain by their puny attempts against heaven? Their petulance, indeed, is no novelty; *for in all ages there have been impious and profane men, who have virulently opposed this doctrine.* But they shall feel the truth of what the Spirit long ago declared by the mouth of David, that God 'is clear when He judgeth' (Psa. 51:4). David obliquely hints at the madness of men who display such excessive presumption amidst their insignificance, as not only to dispute against God, but to arrogate to themselves the power of condemning Him. In the meantime, he briefly suggests, that God is unaffected by all the blasphemies which they discharge against heaven, but that He dissipates the mists of calumny, and illustriously displays His righteousness; our faith, also, being founded on the Divine Word, and therefore, superior to all the world, from its exaltation looks down with contempt upon those mists" (John Calvin).

In closing this chapter we propose to quote from the writings of some of the standard theologians since the days of the Reformation, not that we would buttress our own statements by an appeal to human authority, however venerable or ancient, but in order to show that what we have advanced in these pages is no novelty of the twentieth century, no heresy of the 'latter days' but, instead, a doctrine which has been definitely formulated and commonly taught by many of the most pious and scholarly students of Holy Writ.

"Predestination we call the decree of God, by which He has determined in Himself, what He would have to become of every individual of mankind. For they are not all created with a similar destiny: but eternal life is foreordained for some, and eternal damnation for others. Every man, therefore, being created for one or the other of these ends, we say, he is predestinated either to life or to death"—from John Calvin's "Institutes" (1536 A. D.) Book III, Chapter XXI entitled "Eternal Election, or God's Predestination of Some to Salvation and of Others to Destruction."

We ask our readers to mark well the above language. A perusal of it should show that what the present writer has advanced in this chapter *is not* "Hyper-Calvinism" but *real* Calvinism, pure and simple. Our purpose in making this remark is to show that those who, not acquainted with Calvin's writings, in their *ignorance* condemn as ultra-Calvinism that which is simply a reiteration of what Calvin himself taught—a reiteration because that prince of theologians as well as his humble debtor have both found this doctrine in the Word of God itself.

Martin Luther is his most excellent work "De Servo Arbitrio" (Free will a Slave), wrote: "All things whatsoever arise from, and depend upon, the Divine appointments, whereby it was preordained who should receive the Word of Life, and who should disbelieve it, who should be delivered from their sins, and who should be hardened in them, who should be justified and who should be condemned. This is the very truth which razes the doctrine of freewill from its foundations, to wit, that God's eternal love of some men and hatred of others is immutable and cannot be reversed."

John Fox, whose Book of Martyrs was once the best known work in the English language (alas that it is not so today, when Roman Catholicism is sweeping upon us like a great destructive tidal wave!), wrote:—"Predestination is the eternal decreement of God, purposed before in Himself, what should befall all men, either to salvation, or damnation".

The "Larger Westminster Catechism" (1688)—adopted by the General Assembly of the Presbyterian Church—declares, "God, by an eternal and immutable decree, out of His mere love, for the praise of His glorious grace, to be manifested in due time, hath elected some angels to glory, and in Christ hath chosen some men to eternal life, and the means thereof; and also, according to His sovereign power, and the unsearchable counsel of His own will (whereby He extendeth or withholdeth favor as He pleases), hath passed by, and *fore-ordained the rest to dishonour and wrath,* to be for their sin inflicted, to the praise of the glory of His justice".

John Bunyan, author of "The Pilgrim's Progress," wrote a whole volume on "Reprobation". From it we make one brief extract:—"Reprobation is before the person cometh into the world, or hath done good or evil. This is evidenced by Rom. 9:11. Here you find twain in their mother's womb, and both receiving their destiny, not only *before* they had done good or evil, but before they were in a capacity to do it, they being yet unborn—their destiny, I say, the one unto, the other not unto the blessing of eternal life; the one elect, the other reprobate; the one chosen, the other refused". In his "Sighs from Hell", John Bunyan also wrote: "They that do continue to reject and slight the Word of God are such, for the most part, as are *ordained to be damned*".

Commenting upon Rom. 9:22, "What if God willing to shew His wrath, and to make His power known, endured with much longsuffering the vessels of wrath fitted to destruction" Jonathan Edwards (Vol. 4, p. 306—1743 A.D.) says, "How awful doth the majesty of God appear in the dreadfulness of His anger! This we may learn to be one end of the damnation of the wicked."

Augustus Toplady, author of "Rock of Ages" and other sublime hymns, wrote: "God, from all eternity decreed to leave some of Adam's fallen posterity in their sins, and to exclude them from the participation of Christ and His benefits". And again; "We, with the Scriptures, assert: That there is a predestination of some particular persons to life, for the praise of the glory of Divine grace; and also a predestination of other particular persons *to death* for the glory of Divine justice—which death of punishment they shall inevitably undergo, and that justly, on account of their sins".

George Whitefield, that stalwart of the eighteenth century, used by God in blessing to so many, wrote: "Without doubt, the doctrine of election and reprobation must stand or fall together. . . . I frankly acknowledge I believe the doctrine of Reprobation, that God intends to give saving grace, through Jesus Christ, only to a certain number; and that the rest of mankind, after the fall of Adam, being justly *left of God to continue in sin,* will at last suffer that eternal death which is its proper wages".

"Fitted to destruction" (Rom. 9:22). After declaring this phrase admits of two interpretations, Dr. Hodge—perhaps the best known and most widely read commentator on Romans—says, "The other interpretation assumes that the reference is to God and that the Greek word for 'fitted' has its full participle force; *prepared* (by God) *for destruction.*" This, says Dr. Hodge, "Is adopted not only by *the majority* of Augustinians, but also by *many* Lutherans".

Were it necessary we are prepared to give quotations from the writings of Wycliffe, Huss, Ridley, Hooper, Cranmer, Ussher, John Trapp, Thomas Goodwin, Thomas Manton (Chaplain to Cromwell), John Owen, Witsius, John Gill (predecessor of Spurgeon), and a host of others. We mention this simply to show that many of the most eminent saints in bye-gone days, the men most widely used of God, held and taught this doctrine which is so bitterly hated in these last days, when men will no longer "endure sound doctrine"; hated by men of lofty pretensions, but who, notwithstanding their boasted orthodoxy and much advertised piety, are not worthy to unfasten the shoes of the faithful and fearless servants of God of other days.

"O the depth of the riches both of the wisdom and knowledge of God! How unsearchable are His judgments and His ways past finding out! For who hath known the mind of the Lord? or who hath been His counsellor? or who hath first given to Him, and it shall be recompensed unto him again? For of Him, and through Him, and to Him, are all things: to whom be glory *forever, Amen*" (Rom. 11:33-36).*

---

*"Of Him"—His will is the origin of all existence; "through" or "by Him"—He is the Creator and Controller of all; "to Him"—all things promote His glory in their final end.

VI

THE SOVEREIGNTY OF GOD IN OPERATION

"For of Him, and thro' Him, and to Him, *are all things:* to whom be glory for ever. Amen" (Romans 11:36).

HAS God fore-ordained everything that comes to pass? Has He decreed that what is, was to have been? In the final analysis this is only another way of asking, Is God now *governing* the world and everyone and everything in it? If God *is* governing the world, then is He governing it according to a definite purpose, or aimlessly and at random? If He is governing it according to some purpose, then when was that purpose made? Is God continually changing His purpose and making a new one every day, or was His purpose formed from the beginning? Are God's actions, like ours, regulated by the change of circumstances, or are they the outcome of His eternal purpose? If God formed a purpose before man was created, then is that purpose going to be executed according to His original designs and is He now working toward that end? What saith the Scriptures? They declare God is One "who worketh *all things* after the counsel of His own will" (Eph. 1:11).

Few who read this book are likely to call into question the statement that God knows and foreknows *all things,* but perhaps many would hesitate to go further than this. Yet is it not self-evident that if God *foreknows* all things, He has also *fore-ordained* all things? Is it not clear that God foreknows what will be *because He has decreed what shall be?* God's foreknowledge is not the *cause* of events, rather are events the effects of His eternal purpose. When God has decreed a thing *shall* be, He knows it *will* be. In the nature of things there cannot be anything known as what shall be, unless it is *certain* to be, and there is nothing certain to be unless God has *ordained* it shall be. Take the Crucifixion as an illustration. On this point the teaching of Scripture is as clear as a sunbeam. Christ as the Lamb whose blood was to be shed, was "foreordained before the foundation of the world" (1 Pet. 1:20). Having then "ordained" the slaying of the Lamb, God *knew* He would be "led to the slaughter", and therefore made it known accordingly through Isaiah the prophet. The Lord Jesus was not "delivered" up by God fore-knowing it before it took place, but by His fixed counsel and fore-ordination (Acts 2:23). Fore-knowledge of future events then is founded upon God's decrees, hence if God foreknows everything that is to be, it is because He has determined in Himself from all eternity everything which will be—"Known unto God are all His works from the beginning of the world" (Acts 15:18), which shows that God *has a plan*, that God did not begin His work at random or without a knowledge of how His plan would succeed.

God created all things. This truth no one, who bows to the testimony of Holy Writ, will question; nor would any such be prepared to argue that the work of creation was an *accidental* work. God first formed the purpose to create, and then put forth the creative act in fulfilment of that purpose. All real Christians will readily adopt the words of the Psalmist and say, "O Lord, how manifold are Thy works! *in wisdom* hast Thou made them all." Will any who endorse what we have just said, deny that God purposed to *govern* the world which He created? Surely the creation of the world was not *the end* of God's purpose concerning it. Surely He did not determine simply to create the world and place man in it, and then leave both to their fortunes. It must be apparent that God has some great end or ends in view, worthy of His infinite perfections, and that He is now governing the world so as to accomplish these ends—"The counsel of the Lord standeth for ever, the thoughts of His heart to all generations" (Ps. 33:11).

"Remember the former things of old: for I am God, and there is none else; I am God, and there is none like Me, declaring the end from the beginning, and from ancient times the things that are not yet done, saying, My counsel shall stand, and I will do all My pleasure" (Isa. 46:9, 10). Many other passages might be adduced to show that God has many counsels concerning this world and concerning man, and that all these counsels will most surely be realized. It is only when they are thus regarded that we can intelligently appreciate the prophecies of Scripture. In prophecy the mighty God has condescended to take us into the secret chamber of His eternal counsels, and make known to us what He has purposed to do in the future. The hundreds of prophecies which are found in the Old and New Testaments are not so much predictions of what *will* come to pass, as they are *revelations to us of what God has purposed SHALL come to pass.* Do we know from prophecy that this present age, like all preceding ones, is to end with a full demonstration of man's failure; do we know that there is to be a universal turning away from the truth, a general apostasy; do we know that the Anti-christ is to be manifested, and that he will succeed in deceiving the whole world; do we know that Anti-christ's career will be cut short, and an end made of man's miserable attempts to govern himself, by the return of God's Son; then it is all because these and a hundred other things are included among God's eternal decrees, now made known to us in the sure Word of Prophecy, and because it is infallibly certain that *all* God has purposed *"must* shortly come to pass" (Rev. 1:1).

What then was the great purpose for which this world and the human race were created? The answer of Scripture is, "The Lord hath made all things *for Himself"* (Pro. 16:4). And again, "Thou hast created all things, and *for Thy pleasure* they are and were created" (Rev. 4:11). The great end of creation was the manifestation of God's glory. The heavens declare the glory of God and the firmament sheweth His handiwork; but it was by *man,* originally made in His own image and likeness, that God designed chiefly to manifest His glory. But how was the great Creator to be glorified by man? Before his creation, God foresaw the fall of Adam and the consequent ruin of his race, therefore He could not have designed that man should glorify Him by continuing in a state of innocency. Accordingly, we are taught that Christ was "fore-ordained before the foundation of the world" to be the Saviour of fallen men. The redemption of sinners by Christ was no mere after-thought of God: it was no expediency to meet an unlooked-for calamity. No; it was a Divine *pro-vision,* and therefore when man fell, he found mercy walking hand in hand with justice.

From all eternity God designed that our world should be the stage on which He would display His manifold grace and wisdom in the redemption of lost sinners: "To the intent that now unto the principalities and powers in heavenly places might be known by the Church the manifold wisdom of God, *according to the eternal purpose* which He purposed in Christ Jesus our Lord" (Eph. 3:11). For the accomplishment of this glorious design God has governed the world from the beginning, and will continue it to the end. It has been well said, "We can never understand the providence of God over our world, unless we regard it as a complicated machine having ten thousand parts, directed in all its operations to one glorious end—*the display of the manifold wisdom of God in the salvation of the Church,*" i.e., the "called out" ones. Everything else down here is subordinated to this central purpose. It was the apprehension of this basic truth that the apostle, moved by the Holy Spirit, was led to write, "Wherefore I endure all things *for the elect's sake,* that *they* may also obtain the salvation which is in Christ Jesus with eternal glory" (2 Tim. 2:10). What we would now contemplate is *the operation* of God's sovereignty in the government of this world.

In regard to the operation of God's government over the *material* world little needs now be said. In previous chapters we have shown that inanimate matter and all irrational creatures are absolutely subject to their Creator's pleasure. While we freely admit that the material world appears to be governed by laws that are stable and more or less uniform in their operations, yet Scripture, history, and observation, compel us to recognise the fact that God suspends these laws and acts apart from them whenever it pleaseth Him to do so. In sending His blessings or judgments upon His creatures He may cause the sun itself to stand still, and the stars in their courses to fight for His people (Judges 5:20); He may send or withhold "the early and the latter rains" according to the dictates of His own infinite wisdom; He may smite with plague or bless with health; in short, being God, being absolute Sovereign, He is bound and tied by no laws of Nature, but governs the material world as seemeth Him best.

But what of God's government of *the human family?* What does Scripture reveal in regard to *the modus operandi* of the operations of His governmental administration over mankind? To what extent and by what influences does God control the sons of men? We shall divide our answer to this question into two parts and consider first God's method of dealing with the righteous, His elect; and then His method of dealing with the wicked.

GOD'S METHOD OF DEALING WITH THE RIGHTEOUS:

1 God exerts upon His own elect a *quickening* influence or power.

By nature they are spiritually dead, dead in trespasses and sins, and their first need is spiritual life, for "Except a man be born again, *he cannot* see the kingdom of God" (John 3:3). In the new birth God brings us from death unto life (John 5:24). He imparts to us His own nature (2 Pet. 1:4). He delivers us from the power of darkness and translates us into the kingdom of His dear Son (Col. 1:13). Now, manifestly, we could not do this ourselves, for we were "without strength" (Rom. 5:6), hence it is written, "we are *His workmanship* created in Christ Jesus" (Eph. 2:10).

In the new birth we are made partakers of the Divine nature: a principle, a "seed," a life, is communicated to us which is "born of the Spirit," and therefore *"is* spirit;" is born of the Holy Spirit, and therefore *is holy*. Apart from this Divine and holy nature which is imparted to us at the new birth, it is utterly impossible for any man to generate a spiritual impulse, form a spiritual concept, think a spiritual thought, understand spiritual things, still less engage in spiritual works. "Without holiness no man shall see the Lord," but the natural man has no desire for holiness, and the provision that God has made he does not want. Will then a man pray for, seek for, strive after, that which he dislikes? Surely not. If then a man *does* "follow after" that which by nature he cordially dislikes, if he does now love the One he once hated, it is because a miraculous change has taken place within him; a power outside of himself has operated upon him, a nature entirely different from his old one has been imparted to him, and hence it is written, "Therefore if any man be in Christ, *he is a new creation:* old things are passed away, behold all things are become new" (2 Cor. 5:17). Such an one as we have just described has passed from death unto life, has been turned from darkness to light, and from the power of Satan unto God (Acts

26:18). In no other way can the great change be accounted for.

The new birth is very, very much more than simply shedding a few tears due to a temporary remorse over sin. It is far more than changing our course of life, the leaving off of bad habits and the substituting of good ones. It is something different from the mere cherishing and practising of noble ideals. It goes infinitely deeper than coming forward to take some popular evangelist by the hand, signing a pledge-card, or "joining the church." The new birth is no mere turning over a new leaf, but is the inception and reception of a new life. It is no mere reformation but a complete transformation. In short, the new birth is a miracle, the result of the supernatural operation of God. It is radical, revolutionary, lasting.

Here then is the first thing, in time, which God does in His own elect. He lays hold of those who are spiritually dead and quickens them into newness of life. He takes up one who was shapen in iniquity and conceived in sin, and conforms him to the image of His Son. He seizes a captive of the Devil and makes him a member of the household of faith. He picks up a beggar and makes him joint-heir with Christ. He comes to one who is full of enmity against Him, and gives him a new heart that is full of love for Him. He stoops to one who by nature is a rebel, and works in him both to will and to do of His good pleasure. By His irresistible power He transforms a sinner into a saint, an enemy into a friend, a slave of the Devil into a child of God. Surely then we are moved to say,

> "When all Thy mercies O my God
> My wondering soul surveys,
> Transported with the view I'm lost
> In wonder, love and praise."

2 God exerts upon His own elect an *energising* influence or power.

The apostle prayed to God for the Ephesian saints that the eyes of their understanding might be enlightened in order that, among other things, they might know "what is the exceeding greatness of His power *to usward who believe*" (Eph. 1:18), and that they might be "strengthened with might by His Spirit in the inner man" (3:16). It is thus that the children of God are enabled to fight the good fight of faith, and battle with the adverse forces which constantly war against them. In themselves they have no strength: they are but "sheep," and sheep are one of the most defenceless animals there is; but the promise is sure—"He giveth power to the faint, and to them that have no might He increaseth strength" (Is. 40:29).

It is this energising power that God exerts upon and within the righteous which enables them to serve Him acceptably. Said the prophet of old, "But truly I am full of power *by the Spirit of the Lord*" (Micah 3:8). And said our Lord to His apostles, "Ye shall *receive power* after that the Holy Spirit is come upon you" (Acts 1:8), and thus it proved, for of these same men we read subsequently, "And with great power gave the apostles witness of the resurrection of the Lord Jesus: and great grace was upon them all" (Acts 4:33). So it was, too, with the apostle Paul, "And my speech and my preaching was not with enticing words of man's wisdom, but in demonstration of the Spirit and of power" (1 Cor. 2:4). But the scope of this power is not confined to service, for we read in 2 Pet. 1:3, "According as His Divine power hath given unto us *all things that pertain unto life and godliness,* through the knowledge of Him that hath called us to glory and virtue." Hence it is that the various graces of the Christian character, "love, joy, peace, long-suffering, gentleness, goodness, faith, meekness, temperance," are ascribed directly to God Himself, being denominated "the fruit *of the Spirit*" (Gal. 5:22). Compare 2 Cor. 8:16.

3 God exerts upon His own elect a *directing* influence or power.

Of old He led His people across the wilderness, and directing their steps by a pillar of cloud by day and a pillar of fire by night; and today He still directs His saints, though now from within rather than from without. "For this God *is our God* for ever and ever: He will be *our Guide* even unto death" (Ps. 48:14), but He "guides" us by working in us both to will and to do of His good pleasure. That He does so guide us is clear from the words of the apostle in Eph. 2:10—"For we are His workmanship, created in Christ

Jesus unto good works, *which God hath before ordained that we should walk in them.*" Thus all ground for boasting is removed, and God gets all the glory, for with the prophet we have to say, "Lord, Thou wilt ordain peace for us: *for Thou also hast wrought all our works in us*" (Isa. 26:12). How true then that "A man's heart deviseth his way: but the Lord *directeth his steps*" (Pro. 16:9)! Compare Psa. 65:4, Ezek. 36:27.

4   God exerts upon His own elect a *preserving* influence or power.

Many are the scriptures which set forth this blessed truth. "He preserveth the souls of His saints; He delivereth them out of the hand of the wicked" (Ps. 97:10). "For the Lord loveth judgment, and forsaketh not His saints; they are *preserved for ever:* but the seed of the wicked shall be cut off" (Ps. 37:28). "The Lord preserveth *all* them that love Him: but all the wicked will He destroy" (Ps. 145:20). It is needless to multiply texts or to raise an argument at this point respecting the believer's responsibility and faithfulness —we can no more "persevere" *without* God preserving us, than we can breathe when God ceases to give us breath; we are *"kept by the power of God* through faith unto salvation ready to be revealed in the last time" (1 Pet. 1:5). Compare 1 Chron. 18:6. It remains for us now to consider,

GOD'S METHOD OF DEALING WITH THE WICKED:

In contemplating God's governmental dealings with the non-elect we find that He exerts upon them a fourfold influence or power. We adopt the clear-cut divisions suggested by Dr. Rice:

1   God exerts upon the wicked a *restraining* influence by which they are *prevented* from doing what they are naturally inclined to do.

A striking example of this is seen in Abimelech king of Gerar. Abraham came down to Gerar and fearful lest he might be slain on account of his wife he instructed her to pose as his sister. Regarding her as an unmarried woman, Abimelech sent and took Sarah unto himself; and then we learn how God put forth His power to protect her honor—

"And God said unto him in a dream, Yea, I know that thou didst this in the integrity of thy heart; *for I also withheld thee from sinning against Me:* therefore *suffered I thee not to touch her*" (Gen. 20:6). Had not God interposed, Abimelech would have grievously wronged Sarah, but the Lord restrained him and allowed him not to carry out the intentions of his heart.

A similar instance is found in connection with Joseph and his brethren's treatment of Him. Owing to Jacob's partiality for Joseph, his brethren "hated him," and when they thought they had him in their power, "they conspired against him to *slay* him" (Gen. 37:18). But God did not allow them to carry out their evil designs. First He moved Reuben to deliver him out of their hands, and next he caused Judah to suggest that Joseph should be sold to the passing Ishmaelites, who carried him down into Egypt. That it was *God* who thus restrained them is clear from the words of Joseph himself, when some years later he made known himself to his brethren: said he, "So now it was not you that sent me hither, *but God*" (Gen. 45:8)!

The restraining influence which God exerts upon the wicked was strikingly exemplified in the person of Balaam, the prophet hired by Balak to curse the Israelites. One cannot read the inspired narrative without discovering that, left to himself, Balaam had readily and certainly accepted the offer of Balak. How evidently God restrained the impulses of his heart is seen from his own acknowledgment—"How shall I curse, whom God hath not cursed? or how shall I defy, whom the Lord hath not defied? Behold I have *received commandment* to bless: and He hath blessed; and I cannot reverse it" (Num. 23:8, 20).

Not only does God exert a restraining influence upon wicked individuals, but He does so upon whole peoples as well. A remarkable illustration of this is found in Ex. 34:24—"For I will cast out the nations before thee, and enlarge thy borders: *neither shall any man desire thy land,* when thou shalt go up to appear before the Lord thy God thrice in the year." Three times every male Israelite, at the command of God, left his home and inheritance and journeyed to Jerusalem to keep the Feasts of the Lord; and in the above scripture we learn He promised them that, while they were at Jerusalem, He would guard their unprotected homes by *restraining* the covetous designs and desires of their heathen neighbors.

2 God exerts upon the wicked a *softening* influence disposing them contrary to their natural inclinations to do that which will promote *His* cause.

Above, we referred to Joseph's history as an illustration of God exerting a *restraining* influence upon the wicked, let us note now his experiences in Egypt as exemplifying our assertion that God also exerts a *softening* influence upon the unrighteous. We are told that while he was in the house of Potiphar, "The Lord was with Joseph, and his master saw the Lord was with him," and in consequence, "Joseph found favor in his sight and he made him over-seer over his house" (Gen. 39:3, 4). Later, when Joseph was unjustly cast into prison, we are told, "But the Lord was with Joseph, and shewed him mercy, and *gave him favor in the sight of the keeper of the prison*" (Gen. 39:21), and in consequence the prison-keeper shewed him much kindness and honor. Finally, after his release from prison, we learn from Acts 7:10 that the Lord *"gave him favor and wisdom in the sight of Pharaoh king of Egypt;* and he made him governor over Egypt and all his house."

An equally striking evidence of God's power to melt the hearts of his enemies, was seen in Pharaoh's daughter's treatment of the infant Moses. The incident is well known. Pharaoh had issued an edict commanding the destruction of every male child of the Israelites. A certain Levite had a son born to him who for three months was kept hidden by his mother. No longer able to conceal the infant Moses, she placed him in an ark of bulrushes, and laid him by the river's brink. The ark was discovered by none less than the king's daughter who had come down to the river to bathe, but instead of heeding her father's wicked decree and casting the child into the river, we are told that *"she had compassion on him"* (Ex. 2:6)! Accordingly, the young life was spared and later Moses became the adopted son of this princess!

God has access to the hearts of all men and He softens or hardens them according to His sovereign purpose. The pro-

fane Esau swore vengeance upon his brother for the decep-
tion which he had practiced upon his father, yet when next
he met Jacob, instead of slaying him we are told that Esau
"fell on his neck and kissed him" (Gen. 32:4)! Ahab, the
weak and wicked consort of Jezebel, was highly enraged
against Elijah the prophet, at whose word the heavens had
been shut up for three years and a half: so angry was he
against the one whom he regarded as his enemy that, we
are told he searched for him in every nation and kingdom,
and when he could not be found "he took an oath" (1 Kings
18:10). Yet, when they met, instead of killing the prophet,
Ahab meekly obeyed Elijah's behest and "sent unto all the
children of Israel and gathered the prophets together unto
Mount Carmel" (v. 20). Again; Esther the poor Jewess is
about to enter the presence-chamber of the august Medo-
Persian monarch which, said she, "is not according to the
law" (Est. 4:16). She went in expecting to "perish," but
we are told *"She obtained favor in his sight,* and the king
held out to Esther the golden scepter" (5:2). Yet again; the
boy Daniel is a captive in a foreign court. The king "appointed" a daily provision of meat and drink for Daniel and
his fellows. But Daniel purposed in his heart that he would
not defile himself with the allotted portion, and accordingly
made known his purpose to his master, the prince of the
eunuchs. What happened? His master was a heathen, and
"feared" the king. Did he turn then upon Daniel and angrily
demand that his orders be promptly carried out? No; for
we read, *"Now God had brought Daniel into favor and ten-
der love with the prince of the eunuchs"* (Dan. 1:9)!

"The king's heart is in the hand of the Lord, as the rivers
of water: He turneth it whithersoever He will" (Prov. 21:1).
A remarkable illustration of this is seen in Cyrus, the heathen king of Persia. God's people were in captivity, but the
predicted end of their captivity was almost reached. Mean-
while the Temple at Jerusalem lay in ruins, and, as we have
said, the Jews were in bondage in a distant land. What hope
was there then that the Lord's house would be re-built?
Mark now what God did, "Now in the first year of Cyrus
king of Persia, that the word of the Lord by the mouth of
Jeremiah might be fulfilled, *the Lord stirred up the spirit of
Cyrus* king of Persia, that he made a proclamation through-

out all his kingdom, and put it in writing, saying, Thus saith Cyrus king of Persia, The Lord God of heaven hath given me all the kingdoms of the earth; and He hath charged me to build Him a house at Jerusalem, which is in Judah" (Ezra 1:1, 2). Cyrus, be it remembered, was a pagan, and as secular history bears witness, a very wicked man, yet the Lord moved him to issue this edict, that His Word through Jeremiah seventy years before might be fulfilled. A similar and further illustration is found in Ezra 7:27, where we find Ezra returning thanks for what God had caused king Artaxerxes to do in completing and beautifying the house which Cyrus had commanded to be erected—"Blessed be the Lord God of our fathers *which hath put such a thing as this in the king's heart, to beautify* the house of the Lord which is in Jerusalem" (Ezra 7:27).

3   God exerts upon the wicked a *directing* influence so that good is made to result from their intended evil.

Once more we revert to the history of Joseph as a case in point.   In selling Joseph to the Ishmaelites, his brethren were actuated by cruel and heartless motives.   Their object was to make away with him, and the passing of these travelling traders furnished an easy way out for them.   To them the act was nothing more than the enslaving of a noble youth for the sake of gain.   But now observe how God was secretly working and over-ruling their wicked actions.   Providence so ordered it that these Ishmaelites passed by just in time to prevent Joseph being murdered, for his brethren had already taken counsel together to put him to death.   Further; these Ishmaelites were journeying to Egypt, which was the very country to which *God* had purposed to send Joseph, and He *ordained* they should purchase Joseph just when they did. That the hand of God was in this incident, that it was something more than a fortunate co-incidence, is clear from the words of Joseph to his brethren at a later date, *"God sent me* before you to preserve you a posterity in the earth, and to save your lives by a great deliverance" (Gen. 45:7).

Another equally striking illustration of *God directing the wicked* is found in Isaiah 10:5-7—"O Assyrian, the rod of Mine anger, and the staff in their hand is Mine indignation. *I will send him* against a hypocritical nation, and against the

people of My wrath will I give him a charge, to take the
spoil, and to take the prey, and to tread them down like the
mire of the streets. *Howbeit he meaneth not so, neither doth
his heart think so;* but it is in his heart to destroy and cut off
nations not a few." Assyria's king had determined to be a
world-conqueror, to "cut off nations not a few." But God
directed and *controlled* his military lust and ambition, and
caused him to confine his attention to the conquering of the
insignificant nation of Israel. Such a task was not in the
proud king's heart—"he meant it not so"—but *God* gave him
this charge and he could do nothing but fulfill it. Compare
also Judges 7:22.

The supreme example of the controlling, directing influence, which God exerts upon the wicked, is *the Cross of
Christ* with all its attending circumstances. If ever the *superintending* providence of God was witnessed, it was there.
From all eternity God had predestined every detail of that
event of all events. Nothing was left to chance or the ca-
price of man. God had decreed when and where and how
His blessed Son was to die. Much of what He had purposed
concerning the Crucifixion had been made known through
the Old Testament prophets, and in the accurate and literal
fulfillment of these prophecies we have clear proof, full demonstration, of the controlling and directing influence which
God exerts upon the wicked. Not a thing occurred except as
God had ordained, and *all* that He had ordained took place
exactly as He purposed. Had it been decreed (and made
known in Scripture) that the Saviour should be betrayed by
one of His own disciples—by His "familiar friend"—see Ps.
41:9 and compare Matt. 26:50—then the apostle Judas is
the one who sold Him. Had it been decreed that the betrayer should receive for his awful perfidy thirty pieces of silver,
then are the chief priests moved to offer him this very sum.
Had it been decreed that this betrayal sum should be put to
a particular use, namely, purchase the potter's field, then the
hand of God directs Judas to return the money to the chief
priests and so guided their "counsel" (Matt. 27:7) that they
did this very thing. Had it been decreed that there should be
those who bore "false witness" against our Lord (Ps. 35:
11), then accordingly such were raised up. Had it been decreed that the Lord of glory should be "spat upon and

scourged" (Is. 50:6), then there were not found wanting those who were vile enough to do so. Had it been decreed that the Saviour should be "numbered with the transgressors," then unknown to himself, Pilate, directed by God, gave orders for His crucifixion along with two thieves. Had it been decreed that vinegar and gall should be given Him to drink while He hung upon the Cross, then this decree of God was executed to the very letter. Had it been decreed that the heartless soldiers should gamble for His garments, then sure enough they did this very thing. Had it been decreed that not a bone of Him should be broken (Ps. 34:20), then the controlling hand of God which suffered the Roman soldier to break the legs of the thieves, prevented him from doing the same with our Lord. Ah! there were not enough soldiers in all the Roman legions, there were not sufficient demons in all the hierarchies of Satan, to break one bone in the body of Christ. And why? Because the Almighty Sovereign had decreed that not a bone *should be* broken. Do we need to extend this paragraph any farther? Does not the accurate and literal fulfillment of all that Scripture had predicted in connection with the Crucifixion, demonstrate beyond all controversy that an Almighty power was *directing* and *superintending* everything that was done on that Day of days?

4 God also *hardens* the hearts of wicked men and *blinds* their minds.

"*God* hardens men's hearts! *God* blinds men's minds!" Yes, so Scripture represents Him. In developing this theme of the sovereignty of God in Operation we recognise that we have now reached its most solemn aspect of all, and that here especially, we need to keep very close indeed to the words of Holy Writ. God forbid that we should go one fraction *further* than His Word goes; but may He give us grace to go *as far as* His Word goes. It is true that secret things belong unto the Lord, but it is also true that those things which are revealed in Scripture belong unto us and to our children.

"*He* turned their heart to *hate* His people, to deal *subtly* with His servants" (Ps. 105:25). The reference here is to the sojourn of the descendants of Jacob in the land of Egypt when, after the death of the Pharaoh who had welcomed the old patriarch and his family, there "arose up a new king who knew not Joseph;" and in his days the children of Israel had "increased greatly" so that they outnumbered the Egyptians; then it was that God "turned their heart to hate His people."

The consequence of the Egyptians' "hatred" is well known: they brought them into cruel bondage and placed them under merciless taskmasters, until their lot became unendurable. Helpless and wretched the Israelites cried unto Jehovah, and in response, He appointed Moses to be their deliverer. God revealed Himself unto His chosen servant, gave him a number of miraculous signs which he was to exhibit at the Egyptian court, and then bade him go to Pharaoh, and demand that the Israelites should be allowed to go a three days' journey into the wilderness, that they might worship the Lord. But before Moses started out on his journey God warned him concerning Pharaoh, *"I will harden his heart* that he shall not let the people go" (Ex. 4:21). If it be asked, *Why* did God harden Pharaoh's heart? the answer furnished by Scripture itself is, In order that God might show forth *His power* in him (Rom. 9:17); in other words, it was so that the Lord might demonstrate that it was just as easy for Him to overthrow this haughty and powerful monarch as it was for Him to crush a worm. If it should be pressed further, Why did God *select such a method* of displaying His power? then the answer must be, that being sovereign God reserves to Himself the right to act as He pleases.

Not only are we told that God hardened the heart of Pharaoh so that he would not let the Israelites go, but after God had plagued his land so severely that he reluctantly gave a qualified permission, and after that the first-born of all the Egyptians had been slain, and Israel had actually left the land of bondage, God told Moses, "And I, behold, *I will harden the hearts of the Egyptians,* and they shall follow them: and I will get Me honor upon Pharaoh, upon his chariots, and upon his horsemen. And the Egyptians shall know that I am the Lord, when I have gotten Me honor upon Pharaoh, upon his chariots, and upon his horsemen" (Ex. 14:17, 18).

The same thing happened subsequently in connection with Sihon king of Heshbon, through whose territory Israel had

to pass on their way to the promised Land. When review-
ing their history, Moses told the people, "But Sihon king
of Heshbon would not let us pass by him: *for the Lord thy
God hardened his spirit, and made his heart obstinate,* that
He might deliver him into thy hand" (Deut. 2:30)!

So it was also after that Israel had entered Canaan. We
read, "There was not a city that made peace with the children of Israel, save the Hivites the inhabitants of Gibeon:
all other they took in battle. *For it was of the Lord to
harden their hearts, that they should come against Israel* in
battle, that He might destroy them utterly, and that they
might have no favor, but that He might destroy them, as
the Lord commanded Moses" (Josh. 11:19, 20). From
other scriptures we learn why God purposed to "destroy
utterly" the Canaanites—it was because of their awful wickedness and corruption.

Nor is the revelation of this solemn truth confined to the
Old Testament. In John 12:37-40 we read, "But though He
had done so many miracles before them, yet they believed not
on Him: *that* (in order that) *the saying of Isaiah the prophet might be fulfilled,* which he spake, Lord, who hath believed our report? and to whom hath the arm of the Lord
been revealed? *Therefore they could not believe,* because
that Isaiah said again, *HE hath blinded their eyes, and hardened their heart; that they should not* see with their eyes,
nor understand with their heart, and be converted, and
I should heal them." It needs to be carefully noted here
that these whose eyes God "blinded" and whose heart He
"hardened," were men who had deliberately scorned the
Light and rejected the testimony of God's own Son.

Similarly we read in 2 Thess. 2:11, 12, "And for this cause
God shall send them strong delusion, that they should believe
a lie: that they all might be damned who believed not the
truth, but had pleasure in unrighteousness". The fulfillment
of this scripture is yet future. What God did unto the Jews
of old He is yet going to do unto Christendom. Just as the
Jews of Christ's day despised His testimony, and in consequence, were "blinded," so a guilty Christendom which has
rejected the Truth shall yet have sent them from God a
"strong delusion" that they may believe a lie.

Is God really governing the world? Is He exercising rule

over the human family? What is the *modus operandi* of His governmental administration over mankind? To what extent and by what means does He control the sons of men? *How* does God exercise an influence upon the wicked, seeing their hearts are at enmity against Him? These are some of the questions we have sought to answer from Scripture in the previous sections of this chapter. Upon His own elect God exerts a quickening, an energising, a directing, and a preserving power. Upon the wicked God exerts a restraining, softening, directing, and hardening and blinding power, according to the dictates of His own infinite wisdom and unto the outworking of His own eternal purpose. God's decrees *are* being executed. What He has ordained is being accomplished. *Man's wickedness is bounded.* The limits of evil-doing and of evil-doers has been Divinely defined and cannot be exceeded. Though many are in ignorance of it, all men, good and bad, are under the jurisdiction of and are absolutely subject to the administration of the Supreme Sovereign.—"Alleluia: for the Lord God omnipotent reigneth" (Rev. 19:6)—reigneth over all.

VII

GOD'S SOVEREIGNTY AND THE HUMAN WILL

"It is God which worketh in you *both to will and to do* of His good pleasure" (Phil. 2:13).

CONCERNING the nature and the power of fallen man's will, the greatest confusion prevails today, and the most erroneous views are held, even by many of God's children. The popular idea now prevailing, and which is taught from the great majority of pulpits, is that man has a "free will", and that salvation comes to the sinner through his *will* co-operating with the Holy Spirit. To deny the "free will" of man, i.e. his power to choose that which is good, his native ability to accept Christ, is to bring one into disfavor at once, even before most of those who profess to be orthodox. And yet Scripture emphatically says, *"It is not of him that willeth, nor of him that runneth, but of God that showeth mercy"* (Rom. 9:16). Which shall we believe: God, or the preachers?

But some one may reply, Did not Joshua say to Israel, "Choose you this day whom ye will serve"? Yes, he did; but why not complete his sentence?—*"whether* the gods that your fathers served which were on the other side of the flood, *or* the gods of the Amorites, in whose land ye dwell" (Josh. 24:15)! But why attempt to pit scripture *against* scripture? The Word of God never contradicts itself, and the Word expressly declares, "There is *none that seeketh* after God" (Rom. 3:11). Did not Christ say to the men of His day, "Ye *will not* come to Me, that ye might have life" (John 5:40)? Yes, but some *did* "come" to Him, some *did* receive Him. True and who were they? John 1:12, 13 tells us: "But as many as received Him, to them gave He power to become the sons of God, to them that believe on His name: which *were born,* not of blood, *nor of the will* of the flesh, nor of the will of man, but of God"!

But does not Scripture say, "Whosoever will may come"? It does, but does this signify that everybody has the will *to* come? What of those who *won't* come? "Whosoever will may come" no more implies that fallen man has the power (in himself) *to* come, than "Stretch forth thine hand" implied that the man with the withered arm had ability (in himself) to comply. In and of himself the natural man has power to reject Christ; but in and of himself he has not the power to receive Christ. And why? Because he has a mind that is "enmity against" Him (Rom. 8:7); because he has a heart that hates Him (John 15:18). Man chooses that which is according to his nature, and therefore before he will ever choose or prefer that which is divine and spiritual, a new nature must be imparted to him; in other words, he *must* be born again.

Should it be asked, But does not the Holy Spirit *overcome* a man's enmity and hatred when He convicts the sinner of his sins and his need of Christ; and does not the Spirit of God produce such conviction in many that perish? Such language betrays confusion of thought: were such a man's enmity *really* "overcome", then he *would* readily turn to Christ; that he does not come to the Saviour, demonstrates that his enmity is not overcome. But that many are, through the preaching of the Word, convicted by the Holy Spirit, who nevertheless die in unbelief, is solemnly true. Yet, it is a fact which must not be lost sight of that, the Holy Spirit does *something more* in each of God's elect than He does in the non-elect: He works in them "both to will and to do of God's good pleasure" (Phil. 2:13).

In reply to what we have said above, Arminians would answer, No; the Spirit's work of conviction is the same both in the converted and in the unconverted, that which distinguishes the one class from the other is that the former *yielded* to His strivings, whereas the latter *resist* them. But if this *were* the case, then the Christian would *make himself* to "differ", whereas the Scripture attributes the "differing" to God's discriminating grace (1 Cor. 4:7). Again; if such *were* the case, then the Christian would have ground for boasting and self-glorying over *his* co-operation with the Spirit; but this would flatly contradict Eph. 2:8, "For by grace are ye saved through faith; and that *not of yourselves:* it is the gift of God".

Let us appeal to the actual experience of the Christian reader. Was there not a time (may the remembrance of it bow each of us into the dust) when you were unwilling to come to Christ? There was. Since then you *have* come to Him. Are you now prepared to give Him *all* the glory for that (Psa. 115:1)? Do you not acknowledge you came to Christ because the Holy Spirit brought you from unwillingness to willingness? You do. Then is it not also a patent fact that the Holy Spirit has not done in many others what He *has* in you! Granting that many others have heard the Gospel, been shown their need of Christ, yet, they are still unwilling to come to Him. Thus He *has* wrought more in you, than in them. Do you answer, Yet I remember well the time when the Great Issue was presented to me, and my consciousness testifies that *my* will acted and that I yielded to the claims of Christ upon me. Quite true. But *before* you "yielded", the Holy Spirit overcame the native enmity of your mind against God, and this "enmity" He does not overcome in all. Should it be said, That is because they are unwilling for their enmity to be overcome. Ah, none are thus "willing" till He has put forth His *all-mighty* power and wrought a miracle of grace in the heart.

But let us now inquire, *What is* the human Will? Is it a self-determining agent, or is it, in turn, determined by something else? Is it sovereign or servant? Is the will superior to every other faculty of our being so that it governs them, or is it moved by their impulses and subject to their pleasure? Does the will rule the mind, or does the mind control the will? Is the will free to do as it pleases, or is it under the necessity of rendering obedience to something outside of itself? "Does the will stand apart from the other great faculties or powers of the soul, *a man within a man,* who can reverse the man and fly against the man and split him into segments, as a glass snake breaks in pieces? Or, is the will connected with the other faculties, as the tail of the serpent is with his body, and that again with his head, so that where the head goes, the whole creature goes, and, as a man *thinketh* in his *heart,* so is he? First thought, then heart (desire or aversion), and then act. Is it this way, the dog wags the tail? Or, is it the will, the tail, wags the dog? Is the will the first and chief thing in the man, or is it the last thing—to be kept subordinate, and in its place beneath the other faculties? and, is the true philosophy of moral action and its process that of Gen. 3:6: 'And when the woman saw that the tree was good for food' (sense-perception, intelligence), 'and a tree to be desired' (affections), 'she took and ate thereof' (the will)." (G. S. Bishop). These are questions of more than academical interest. They are of practical importance. We believe that we do not go too far when we affirm that the answer returned to these questions is a fundamental test of doctrinal soundness.*

I. THE NATURE OF THE HUMAN WILL.

What is the Will? We answer, the will is the faculty of choice, the immediate cause of all action. Choice necessarily implies the refusal of one thing and the acceptance of another. The positive and the negative must both be present to the mind before there can be any choice. In every act of the will there is a preference—the desiring of one thing rather than another. Where there is no preference, but complete indifference, there is no volition. To will is to choose, and to choose is to decide between two or more alternatives. But there is something which *influences* the choice; something which *determines* the decision. Hence the will cannot be sovereign because it is the servant of that something. The will cannot be both sovereign and servant. It cannot be both cause and effect. The will *is not causative,* because, as we have said, something causes it *to choose,* therefore that something must be the causative agent. Choice itself is affected by certain considerations, is determined by various influences brought to bear *upon the individual himself,* hence, volition is the effect of these considerations and influences, and if the effect, it must be their *servant;* and if the will is their servant then it is not sovereign, and if the will is *not* sovereign, we certainly cannot predicate absolute "freedom" of it. Acts of the will cannot come to pass of themselves—to say they can, is to postulate an *uncaused* effect. Ex nihilo nihil fit—nothing cannot produce something.

In all ages, however, there have been those who contended

*Since writing the above we have read an article by the late J. N. Darby entitled, "Man's so-called freewill," that opens with these words: "This re-appearance of the doctrine of freewill serves to support that of the pretension of the natural man to be not irremediably fallen, for this is what such doctrine tends to. All who have never been deeply convicted of sin, all persons in whom this conviction is based on gross external sins, believe more or less in freewill."

for the absolute freedom or sovereignty of the human will. Men will argue that the will possesses a *self-determining* power. They say, for example, I can turn my eyes up or down, the mind is quite indifferent which I do, the will must decide. But this is a contradiction in terms. This case supposes that I choose one thing in preference to another, while I am in a state of complete indifference. Manifestly, both cannot be true. But it may be replied, the mind was quite indifferent until it came to have a preference. Exactly; and at that time the will was quiescent, too! But the moment indifference vanished, choice was made, and the fact that indifference gave place to preference, overthrows the argument that the will is capable of choosing between two equal things. As we have said, choice implies the acceptance of one alternative and the rejection of the other or others.

That which determines the will is that which causes it to choose. If the will is determined, then there must be a determiner. *What is it* that determines the will? We reply, The strongest motive power which is brought to bear upon it. What this motive power is, varies in different cases. With one it may be the logic of reason, with another the voice of conscience, with another the impulse of the emotions, with another the whisper of the Tempter, with another the power of the Holy Spirit; whichever of these presents the *strongest* motive power and exerts the *greatest* influence *upon the individual himself,* is that which impels the will to act. In other words, the action of the will is determined by that condition of mind (which in turn is influenced by the world, the flesh, and the Devil, as well as by God), which has the greatest degree of tendency to excite volition. To illustrate what we have just said let us analyze a simple example—

On a certain Lord's day afternoon a friend of ours was suffering from a severe headache. He was anxious to visit the sick, but feared that if he did so his own condition would grow worse, and as the consequence, be unable to attend the preaching of the Gospel that evening. Two alternatives confronted him: to visit the sick that afternoon and risk being sick himself, or, to take a rest that afternoon (and visit the sick the next day), and probably arise refreshed and fit for the evening service. Now what was it that decided our

friend in choosing between these two alternatives? The *will?*
Not at all. True, that in the end, the will made a choice, but
the will itself was *moved* to make the choice. In the above
case certain considerations presented strong motives for
selecting either alternative; these motives were balanced the
one against the other *by the individual himself,* i. e., his
heart and mind, and the one alternative being supported by
stronger motives than the other, decision was formed accordingly, *and then* the will acted. On the one side, our
friend felt impelled by a sense of duty to visit the sick; he
was moved with compassion to do so, and thus a strong motive was presented to his mind. On the other hand, his
judgment reminded him that he was feeling far from well
himself, that he badly needed a rest, that if he visited the
sick his own condition would probably be made worse, and
in such case he would be prevented from attending the
preaching of the Gospel that night; furthermore, he knew
that on the morrow, the Lord willing, he could visit the sick,
and this being so, he concluded he ought to rest that afternoon. Here then were two sets of alternatives presented
to our Christian brother: on the one side was a sense of
duty plus his own sympathy, on the other side was a sense
of his own need plus a real concern for God's glory, for he
felt that he *ought* to attend the preaching of the Gospel that
night. The latter prevailed. Spiritual considerations out-
weighed his sense of duty. Having formed his decision the
will acted accordingly, and he retired to rest. An analysis
of the above case shows that the mind or reasoning faculty
was directed by spiritual considerations, and the mind regulated and controlled the will. Hence we say that, if the will
is *controlled,* it is neither sovereign nor free, but is the servant of the mind.

It is only as we see the real nature of freedom and mark
that the will is subject to the motives brought to bear upon
it, that we are able to discern there is no conflict between two
statements of Holy Writ which concern our blessed Lord.
In Matt. 4:1 we read, "Then was Jesus *led up* of the Spirit
into the wilderness to be tempted of the Devil;" but in Mark
1:12, 13 we are told, "And immediately the Spirit *driveth*
Him into the wilderness. And He was there in the wilderness forty days, tempted of Satan". It is utterly impossible

to harmonize these two statements by the Arminian conception of the will. But really there is no difficulty. That Christ was "driven", implies it was by a forcible motive or powerful impulse, such as was not to be resisted or refused; that He was "led" denotes His freedom in going. Putting the two together we learn, that He was *driven, with a voluntary condescension thereto.* So, there is the liberty of man's will and the victorious efficacy of God's grace united together: a sinner may be "drawn" and yet "come" to Christ —the "drawing" presenting to him the irresistible motive, the "coming" signifying the response of his will—as Christ was "driven" and "led" by the Spirit into the wilderness.

Human philosophy insists that it is the will which governs the man, but the Word of God teaches that it is the *heart* which is the dominating center of our being. Many scriptures might be quoted in substantiation of this. "Keep thy heart with all diligence; for *out of it* are the issues of life" (Prov. 4:23). "For from within, *out of the heart of men, proceed* evil thoughts, adulteries, fornications, murders," etc. (Mark 7:21). Here our Lord traces these sinful acts back to their source, and declares that their fountain is the "heart," and not the will! Again; "This people draweth nigh unto Me with their lips, but *their heart* is far from Me" (Matt. 15:8). If further proof were required we might call attention to the fact that the word "heart" is found in the Bible more than three times oftener than is the word "will," even though nearly half of the references to the latter refer to *God's* will!

When we affirm that it is the *heart* and not the will which governs the man, we are not merely striving about words, but insisting on a distinction that is of vital importance. Here is an individual before whom two alternatives are placed; which will he choose? We answer, the one which is most agreeable to himself, i.e., his "heart"—the innermost core of his being. Before the sinner is set a life of virtue and piety, and a life of sinful indulgence; which will he follow? The latter. Why? Because this is his choice. But does that prove the will is sovereign? Not at all. Go back from effect to cause. *Why* does the sinner choose a life of sinful indulgence? Because he *prefers* it—and he *does* prefer it, all arguments to the contrary notwithstanding, though of course he does not enjoy the *effects* of such a course. And why does he prefer it? Because his *heart* is sinful. The same alternatives, in like manner, confront the Christian, and he chooses and strives after a life of piety and virtue. Why? Because God has given him a *new heart* or nature. Hence we say it is not *the will* which makes the sinner impervious to all appeals to "forsake his way," but his corrupt and evil *heart*. He will not come to Christ, *because* he does not want to, and he does not want to because his *heart* hates Him and loves sin: see Jer. 17:9!

In defining the will we have said above, that "the will is the faculty of choice, the immediate cause of all action." We say the *immediate* cause, for the will is not the primary cause of any action, any more than the hand is. Just as the hand is controlled by the muscles and nerves of the arm, and the arm by the brain; so the will is the servant of the mind, and the mind, in turn, is affected by various influences and motives which are brought to bear upon it. But, it may be asked, Does not Scripture make its appeal to man's *will?* Is it not written, "And whosoever *will*, let him take the water of life freely" (Rev. 22:17)? And did not our Lord say, "ye *will not* come to Me that ye might have life" (John 5:40)? We answer; the appeal of Scripture is not always made to man's "will"; other of his faculties are also addressed. For example: "He that hath *ears* to hear, let him hear." "*Hear* and your soul shall live." "*Look* unto Me and be ye saved." "*Believe* on the Lord Jesus Christ and thou shalt be saved." "Come now and let us *reason* together," "with *the heart* man believeth unto righteousness," etc., etc.

2 THE BONDAGE OF THE HUMAN WILL.

In any treatise that proposes to deal with the human will, its nature and functions, respect should be had to the will in three different men, namely, unfallen Adam, the sinner, and the Lord Jesus Christ. In unfallen Adam the will was *free,* free in *both* directions, free toward good and free toward evil. Adam was created in a state of *innocency,* but not in a state of holiness, as is so often assumed and asserted. Adam's will was therefore in a condition of moral equipoise:

that is to say, in Adam there was no constraining *bias* in him toward either good or evil, and as such, Adam differed radically from all his descendants, as well as from "the Man Christ Jesus." But with the sinner it is far otherwise. The sinner is born with a will that is *not* in a condition of moral equipoise, because in him there is a heart that is "deceitful above all things and desperately wicked," and this gives him *a bias toward evil*. So, too, with the Lord Jesus it was far otherwise: He also differed radically from unfallen Adam. The Lord Jesus Christ *could not sin* because He was "the Holy One of God." Before He was born into this world it was said to Mary, "The Holy Spirit shall come upon thee, and the power of the Highest shall overshadow thee: therefore also *that Holy Thing* which shall be born of thee shall be called the Son of God" (Luke 1 :35). Speaking reverently then, we say, that the will of the Son of Man was *not* in a condition of moral equipoise, that is, capable of turning toward either good or evil. The will of the Lord Jesus was *biased toward that which is good* because, side by side with His sinless, holy, perfect humanity, was His eternal Deity. Now in contradistinction from the will of the Lord Jesus which was biased toward good, and Adam's will which, before his fall, was in a condition of moral equipoise—capable of turning toward either good or evil—the *sinner's* will is *biased toward evil,* and therefore is free in one direction only, namely, in the direction of evil. The sinner's will is *enslaved* because it is in bondage to and is the servant of a depraved heart.

In what does the sinner's freedom consist? This question is naturally suggested by what we have just said above. The sinner is 'free' in the sense of being unforced *from without.* God never *forces* the sinner to sin. But the sinner is not free to do *either* good or evil, because an evil heart within is ever inclining him toward sin. Let us illustrate what we have in mind. I hold in my hand a book. I release it; what happens? It falls. In which direction? Downwards; always downwards. Why? Because, answering the law of gravity, its own weight sinks it. Suppose I desire that book to occupy a position three feet higher; then what? I must lift it; a power outside of that book must raise it. Such is the relationship which fallen man sustains toward God. Whilst

Divine power upholds him, he is preserved from plunging still deeper into sin; let that power be withdrawn, and he falls—his own weight (of sin) drags him down. God does not push him down, anymore than I did that book. Let all Divine restraint be removed, and every man is capable of becoming, would become, a Cain, a Pharaoh, a Judas. How then is the sinner to move heavenwards? By an act of his own will? Not so. A power outside of himself must grasp hold of him and lift him every inch of the way. The sinner *is* free, but free in one direction only—free to fall, free to sin. As the Word expresses it: "For when ye were the servants of sin, ye were *free from* righteousness" (Rom. 6:20). The sinner is free to do as he pleases, always as he pleases (except as he is restrained by God), but his pleasure is to sin.

In the opening paragraph of this chapter we insisted that a proper conception of the nature and function of the will is of practical importance, nay, that it constitutes a fundamental test of theological orthodoxy or doctrinal soundness. We wish to amplify this statement and attempt to demonstrate its accuracy. The freedom or bondage of the will was the dividing line between Augustinianism and Pelagianism, and in more recent times between Calvinism and Arminianism. Reduced to simple terms, this means, that the difference involved was the affirmation or denial of the total depravity of man. In taking the affirmative we shall now consider,

3   THE IMPOTENCY OF THE HUMAN WILL.

Does it lie within the province of man's will to accept or reject the Lord Jesus Christ as Saviour? Granted that the Gospel is preached to the sinner, that the Holy Spirit convicts him of his lost condition, does it, in the final analysis, lie within the power of his own will to resist or to yield himself up to God? The answer to this question defines our conception of human depravity. That man is a fallen creature all professing Christians will allow, but what many of them mean by "fallen" is often difficult to determine. The general impression seems to be that man is now mortal, that he is no longer in the condition in which he left the hands of his Cre-

ator, that he is liable to disease, that he inherits evil tenden-
cies; but, that if he employs his powers to the best of his
ability, somehow he will be happy at last. O, how far short
of the sad truth! Infirmities, sickness, even corporeal death,
are but trifles in comparison with the moral and spiritual
effects of the Fall! It is only by consulting the Holy Scriptures that we are able to obtain some conception of the extent of that terrible calamity.

When we say that man is totally depraved, we mean that
the entrance of sin into the human constitution has affected
every part and faculty of man's being. Total depravity
means that man is, in spirit and soul and body, the slave of
sin and the captive of the Devil—walking "according to the
prince of the power of the air, the spirit that now worketh
in the children of disobedience" (Eph. 2:2). This statement
ought not to need arguing: it is a common fact of human experience. Man is *unable* to realize his own aspirations and
materialize his own ideals. He *cannot* do the things that he
would. There is a moral inability which paralyzes him.
This is proof positive that he is no free man, but instead, the
slave of sin and Satan. "Ye are of your father the Devil,
and the lusts (desires) of your father ye will do" (John
8:44). Sin is more than an act or a series of acts; it is a
state or condition: it is that which lies behind and produces
the acts. Sin has penetrated and permeated the whole of
man's make-up. It has blinded the understanding, corrupted
the heart, and alienated the mind from God. *And the will
has not escaped.* The will is under the dominion of sin and
Satan. Therefore, the will is not free. In short, the affections love as they do and the will chooses as it does because
of the state of *the heart,* and because the heart is deceitful
above all things and desperately wicked "There is *none* that
seeketh after God" (Rom. 3:11).

We repeat our question; Does it lie within the power of
the sinner's will to yield himself up to God? Let us attempt
an answer by asking several others: Can water (of itself)
rise above its own level? Can a clean thing come out of an
unclean? Can the will reverse the whole tendency and strain
of human nature? Can that which is under the dominion of
sin originate that which is pure and holy? Manifestly not.
If ever the will of a fallen and depraved creature is to move

Godwards, a Divine power must be brought to bear upon it which will overcome the influences of sin that pull in a counter direction. This is only another way of saying, "No man can come to Me, except the Father which hath sent Me, *draw him*" (John 6:44). In other words, God's people must be *made willing* in the day of His power (Ps. 110:3). As said Mr. Darby, "If Christ came to save that which is *lost,* free will has no place. Not that God prevents men from receiving Christ—far from it. But even when God uses all possible inducements, all that is capable of exerting influence in the heart of man, it only serves to show that man will have none of it, that so corrupt is his heart, and so decided his will not to submit to God (however much it may be the devil who encourages him to sin) that nothing can induce him to receive the Lord, and to give up sin. If by the words, 'freedom of man,' they mean that no one forces him to reject the Lord, this liberty fully exists. But if it is said that, on account of the dominion of sin, of which he is the slave, and that voluntarily, he cannot escape from his condition, and make choice of the good—even while acknowledging it to be good, and approving of it—*then he has no liberty whatever* (italics ours). He is not subject to the law, neither indeed can be; hence, they that are in the flesh cannot please God."

The will is not sovereign; it is a servant, because influenced and controlled by the other faculties of man's being. The sinner is not a free agent because he is a slave of sin—this was clearly implied in our Lord's words, "If the Son shall therefore *make you free,* ye shall be free indeed" (John 8:36). Man is a rational being and as such responsible and accountable to God, but to affirm that he is a *free* moral agent *is to deny that he is totally depraved*—i.e., depraved in will as in everything else. Because man's will is governed by his mind and heart, and because these have been vitiated and corrupted by sin, then it follows that if ever man is to turn or move in a Godward direction, God Himself must work in him "both *to will and to do* of His good pleasure" (Phil. 2:13). Man's boasted freedom is in truth "the bondage of corruption"; he "*serves* divers lusts and pleasures." Said a deeply taught servant of God, "Man is impotent as to his will. He has no will favorable to God. I believe in free will; but then it is *a will only free to act according to nature* (italics ours). A dove has no will to eat carrion; a raven no will to eat the clean food of the dove. Put the nature of the dove into the raven and it will eat the food of the dove. Satan could have no will for holiness. We speak it with reverence, God could have no will for evil. The sinner in his sinful nature could never have a will according to God. For this he must be born again" (J. Denham Smith). This is just what we have contended for throughout this chapter— *the will is regulated by the nature.*

Among the "decrees" of the Council of Trent (1563), which is the avowed standard of Popery, we find the following:—

"If any one shall affirm, that man's free-will, moved and excited by God, does not, by consenting, co-operate with God, the mover and exciter, so as to *prepare* and *dispose* itself for the *attainment* of justification; if moreover, anyone shall say, that the human will cannot refuse complying, if it *pleases;* but that it is unactive, and merely passive; let such an one *be accursed"!*

"If anyone shall affirm, that since the fall of Adam, man's free-will is *lost* and extinguished; or, that it is a thing titular, yea a name, without a thing, and a fiction introducted by Satan into the Church; let such an one *be accursed"!*

Thus, those who today insist on the free-will of the natural man believe precisely what Rome teaches on the subject! That Roman Catholics and Arminians walk hand in hand may be seen from others of the decrees issued by the Council of Trent:—"If any one shall affirm that a regenerate and justified man is bound to believe that he is certainly in the number of the elect (which, 1 Thess. 1:4, 5 plainly teaches. A.W.P.) let such an one be accursed"! "If any one shall affirm with positive and absolute certainty, that he shall surely have the gift of perseverance to the end (which John 10:28-30 assuredly guarantees, A.W.P.); let him be accursed"!

In order for any sinner to be saved three things were indispensable: God the Father had to *purpose* his salvation, God the Son had to *purchase* it, God the Spirit has to *apply* it. God does more than "propose" to us: were He *only* to "invite", every last one of us would be lost. This is strikingly illustrated in the Old Testament. In Ezra 1:

1-3 we read, "Now in the first year of Cyrus king of Persia, that the word of the Lord by the mouth of Jeremiah might be fulfilled, the Lord stirred up the spirit of Cyrus king of Persia, that he made a proclamation throughout all his kingdom, and put it also in writing saying, Thus saith Cyrus king of Persia, the Lord God of heaven hath given me all the kingdoms of the earth, and He hath charged me to build Him an house at Jerusalem, which is in Judah. Who is there among you of all His people? his God be with him, and let him go up to Jerusalem which is in Judah, and build the house of the Lord God of Israel." Here was an *"offer"* made, made to a people in captivity, affording them opportunity to leave and return to Jerusalem—God's dwelling-place. Did *all* Israel eagerly respond to this offer? No indeed. The vast majority were content to remain in the enemy's land. Only an insignificant "remnant" availed themselves of this overture of mercy! And *why* did *they?* Hear the answer of Scripture: "Then rose up the chief of the fathers of Judah and Benjamin, and the priests, and the Levites, with all whose spirit *God had stirred up,* to go up to build the house of the Lord which is in Jerusalem" (Ezra 1:5)! In like manner, *God* "stirs up" the spirits of His elect when the effectual call comes to them, and not till then do they have any *willingness to* respond to the Divine proclamation.

The superficial work of many of the professional evangelists of the last fifty years is largely responsible for the erroneous views now current upon the *bondage* of the natural man, encouraged by the laziness of those in the pew in their failure to *"prove* all things" (1 Thess. 5:21). The average evangelical pulpit conveys the impression that it lies wholly in the power of the sinner whether or not he shall be saved. It is said that "God has done His part, now man must do his." Alas, what *can* a lifeless man do, and man by nature is *"dead* in trespasses and sins" (Eph. 2:1)! If this were really believed, there would be more dependence upon the Holy Spirit to come in with His miracle-working power, and less confidence in *our* attempts to "win men for Christ."

When addressing the unsaved, preachers often draw an analogy between God's sending of the Gospel to the sinner, and a sick man in bed, with some healing medicine on a table by his side: all he needs to do is reach forth his hand and take it. But in order for this illustration to be in any wise true to the picture which Scripture gives us of the fallen and depraved sinner, the sick man in bed must be described as one who is blind (Eph. 4:18) so that he cannot see the medicine, his hand paralyzed (Rom. 5:6) so that he is unable to reach forth for it, and his heart not only devoid of all confidence in the medicine but filled with hatred against the physician himself (John 15:18). O what superficial views of man's desperate plight are now entertained! Christ came here not to help those who were willing to help themselves, but to do for His people what they were incapable of doing for themselves: "To open the blind eyes, to bring out the prisoners from the prison, and them that sit in darkness out of the prison house" (Isa. 42:7).

Now in conclusion let us anticipate and dispose of the usual and inevitable objection—*Why preach the Gospel if man is powerless to respond?* Why bid the sinner come to Christ if sin has so enslaved him that he has no power in himself *to* come? Reply:—We do not preach the Gospel *because we* believe that men are free moral agents, and therefore capable of receiving Christ, but we preach it *because we are commanded to do so* (Mark 16:15); and though to them that perish it is *foolishness,* yet, "unto us which are saved it is *the power of God*" (1 Cor. 1:18). "The foolishness of God is wiser than men; and the weakness of God is stronger than men" (1 Cor. 1:25). The sinner is dead in trespasses and sins (Eph. 2:1), and a dead man is utterly incapable of willing anything, hence it is that "they that are in the flesh (the unregenerate) cannot please God" (Rom. 8:8).

To fleshly wisdom it appears the height of folly to preach the Gospel to those that are *dead,* and therefore *beyond* the reach of doing anything themselves. Yes, but God's ways are different from ours. It pleases God "by the *foolishness of preaching* to save them that believe" (1 Cor. 1:21). Man may deem it folly to prophesy to *"dead bones"* and to say unto them, "O, ye dry bones, hear the Word of the Lord" (Ezek. 37:4). Ah! but then it is the Word *of the Lord,* and the words He speaks "they are spirit, *and they are life"*

(John 6:63). Wise men standing by the grave of Lazarus might pronounce it an evidence of insanity when the Lord addressed a *dead* man with the words, "Lazarus, Come forth." Ah! but He who thus spake was and is Himself the Resurrection and the Life, and at *His* word even the dead live! We go forth to preach the Gospel, then, not because we believe that sinners have within themselves the power to receive the Saviour it proclaims, but because the Gospel itself *is the power of God unto* salvation to everyone that believeth, and because we know that "as many as were ordained to eternal life" (Acts 13:48), *shall* believe (John 6:37; 10:16—note the "shall's"!) in God's appointed time, for it is written, "Thy people *shall* be willing in the day of *Thy* power" (Ps. 110:3)!

What we have set forth in this chapter is not a product of "modern thought"; no indeed, it is at direct variance with it. It is those of the past few generations who have *departed* so far from the teachings of their scripturally-instructed fathers. In the thirty-nine Articles of the Church of England we read, "The condition of man after the fall of Adam is such, that he cannot turn and prepare himself by his own natural strength and good works to faith, and calling upon God: Wherefore we have *no power* to do good works, pleasant and acceptable to God, without the grace of God by Christ preventing us (being before-hand with us), that we may have a good will, and working with us, when we have that good will" (Article 10). In the Westminster Catechism of Faith (adopted by the Presbyterians) we read, "The sinfulness of that state whereinto man fell, consisteth in the guilt of Adam's first sin, the wont of that righteousness wherein he was created, and the corruption of his nature, whereby he is *utterly indisposed,* disabled, and made opposite unto all that is spiritually good, and *wholly* inclined to all evil, and that continually" (Answer to question 25). So in the Baptists' Philadelphian Confession of Faith, 1742, we read, "Man, by his fall into a state of sin, hath wholly lost *all ability of will* to any spiritual good accompanying salvation; so as a natural man, being altogether averse from good, and dead in sin, is not able by his own strength to convert himself, or to prepare himself thereunto" (Chapter 9).

VIII

GOD'S SOVEREIGNTY AND HUMAN RESPONSIBILITY

"So then every one of us
shall give account of himself to God" (Romans 14:12).

IN our last chapter we considered at some length the
much debated and difficult question of the human will.
We have shown that the will of the natural man is neither
sovereign nor free but, instead, a servant and slave. We
have argued that a right conception of the sinner's will—
its *servitude*— is essential to a just estimate of his depravity
and ruin. The utter corruption and degradation of human
nature is something which man hates to acknowledge, and
which he will hotly and insistently deny, until he is "taught
of God." Much, very much, of the unsound doctrine which
we now hear on every hand is the direct and logical outcome
of man's repudiation of God's expressed estimate of human
depravity. Men are claiming that they are "increased with
goods, and have need of nothing," and know not that they
are "wretched and miserable, and poor, and blind, and
naked" (Rev. 3:17). They prate about the 'Ascent of Man,'
and deny his Fall. They put darkness for light and light
for darkness. They boast of the 'free moral agency' of man
when, in fact, he is in bondage to sin and enslaved by Satan
—"taken captive by him *at his will"* (2 Tim. 2:26). But if
the natural man is *not* a 'free moral agent,' does it also follow that he is not *accountable?*

'Free moral agency' is an expression of human invention
and, as we have said before, to talk of the freedom of the
natural man is to flatly repudiate his spiritual ruin. Nowhere
does Scripture speak of the freedom or moral ability of the
sinner, on the contrary, it insists on his moral and spiritual
inability.

This is, admittedly, the most difficult branch of our subject. Those who have ever devoted much study to this
theme have uniformly recognized that the harmonizing of
God's Sovereignty with Man's Responsibility is the gordian
knot of theology.

The main difficulty encountered is to define *the relationship* between God's sovereignty and man's responsibility.

143

Many have summarily disposed of the difficulty by denying its existence. A certain class of theologians, in their anxiety to maintain man's responsibility, have magnified it beyond all due proportions, until God's sovereignty has been lost sight of, and in not a few instances flatly denied. Others have acknowledged that the Scriptures present *both* the sovereignty of God and the responsibility of man, but affirm that in our present finite condition and with our limited knowledge it is *impossible* to reconcile the two truths, though it is the bounden duty of the believer to receive both. The present writer believes that it has been too readily *assumed* that the Scriptures themselves do not reveal the several points which show the conciliation of God's sovereignty and man's responsibility. While perhaps the Word of God does not clear up all the mystery (and this is said with reserve), it *does* throw much light upon the problem, and it seems to us *more honoring* to God and His Word to prayerfully search the Scriptures for the completer solution of the difficulty, and even though others have thus far searched in vain, that ought only to drive *us* more and more to our knees. God has been pleased to reveal many things out of His Word during the last century which were hidden from earlier students. Who then dare affirm that there is not much to be learned yet respecting our present inquiry!

As we have said above, our chief difficulty is to determine *the meeting-point* of God's sovereignty and man's responsibility. To many it has seemed that for God to *assert* His sovereignty, for Him to *put forth His power* and exert a direct influence upon man, for Him to do anything more than warn or invite, would be to interfere with man's freedom, destroy his responsibility, and reduce him to a machine. It is sad indeed to find one like the late Dr. Pierson —whose writings are generally so scriptural and helpful —saying, "It is a tremendous thought that even God Himself cannot control my moral frame, or constrain my moral choice. He cannot prevent me defying and denying Him, and would not exercise His power in such directions if He could, and could not if He would" (A Spiritual Clinique). It is sadder still to discover that many other respected and loved brethren are giving expression to the same sentiments. Sad, because directly at variance with the Holy Scriptures.

It is our desire to face honestly the difficulties involved, and to examine them carefully in what light God has been pleased to grant us. The chief difficulties might be expressed thus: first, How is it possible for God to so bring His power to bear upon men that they are *prevented* from doing what they desire to do, and *impelled* to do other things they do not desire to do, and yet to preserve their responsibility? Second, How can the sinner be held responsible *for* the doing of what he is *unable* to do? And how can he be justly condemned for *not doing* what he *could not* do? Third, How is it possible for God to *decree* that men *shall* commit certain sins, hold them *responsible* in the committal of them, and adjudge them guilty *because* they committed them? Fourth, How can the sinner be held responsible to receive Christ, and be damned for rejecting Him, when God had foreordained him to condemnation? We shall now deal with these several problems in the above order. May the Holy Spirit Himself be our Teacher, so that in His light we may see light.

I. HOW IS IT POSSIBLE FOR GOD TO SO BRING HIS POWER TO BEAR UPON MEN THAT THEY ARE PREVENTED FROM DOING WHAT THEY DESIRE TO DO, AND IMPELLED TO DO OTHER THINGS THEY DO NOT DESIRE TO DO, AND YET TO PRESERVE THEIR RESPONSIBILITY?

It would seem that if God put forth His power and exerted a direct influence upon men their freedom would be interfered with. It would appear that if God did *anything more* than warn and invite men their responsibility would be infringed upon. We are told that God must not coerce man, still less compel him, or otherwise he would be reduced to a machine. This sounds very plausible; it appears to be good philosophy, and based upon sound reasoning; it has been almost universally accepted as an axiom in ethics; *nevertheless, it is refuted by Scripture!*

Let us turn first to Gen. 20:6—"And God said unto him in a dream, Yea, I know that thou didst this in the integrity of thy heart; for I also *withheld thee* from sinning against Me: therefore suffered I thee not to touch her." It is argued, almost universally, that God *must not* interfere with man's liberty, that he *must not* coerce or compel him, lest he be reduced to a machine. But the above scripture proves, unmistakably proves, that it is *not* impossible for God to exert His power upon man without destroying his responsibility. Here is a case where God *did* exert His power, restrict man's freedom, and *prevent* him from doing that which he otherwise would have done.

Ere turning from this scripture, let us note how it throws light upon the case of the first man. Would-be philosophers, who sought to be wise above that which was written, have argued that God *could not* have prevented Adam's fall without reducing him to a mere automaton. They tell us, constantly, that God must not coerce or compel His creatures, otherwise He would destroy their accountability. But the answer to all such philosophisings is, that Scripture records a number of instances where we are expressly told God *did prevent* certain of His creatures from sinning both against Himself and against His people, in view of which all men's reasonings are utterly worthless. If God could "withhold" Abimelech from sinning against Him, then why was He *unable* to do the same with Adam? Should someone ask, Then *why did not* God do so? we might return the question by asking, Why did not God "withhold" Satan from falling? or, Why did not God "withhold" the Kaiser from starting the recent War? The usual reply is, as we have said, God *could not* without interfering with man's "freedom" and reducing him to a machine. But the case of Abimelech proves conclusively that such a reply is untenable and erroneous— we might add *wicked* and *blasphemous,* for who are we to *limit* the Most High! How dare any finite creature take it upon him to say what the Almighty can and *cannot* do? Should we be pressed further as to *why* God refused to exercise His power and *prevent* Adam's fall, we should say, Because Adam's fall better served His own wise and blessed purpose—among other things, it provided an opportunity to demonstrate that where sin had abounded grace could much more abound. But we might ask further; Why did God place in the garden the tree of the knowledge of good and evil, when He *foresaw* that man would disobey His prohibition and eat of it; for mark, it *was* God and not Satan who made that tree. Should someone respond, Then is God the Author of Sin? We would have to ask, in turn, What is meant by "Author"? Plainly it was God's *will* that sin *should* enter this world, otherwise it *would not* have entered, for nothing happens save as God has eternally decreed. Moreover, there was more than a bare *permission,* for God only permits that which He has purposed. But we leave now the origin of sin, insisting once more, however, that God *could* have "withheld" Adam from sinning *without* destroying his responsibility.

The case of Abimelech does not stand alone. Another illustration of the same principle is seen in the history of *Balaam,* already noticed in the last chapter, but concerning which a further word is in place. Balak the Moabite sent for this heathen prophet to "curse" Israel. A handsome reward was offered for his services, and a careful reading of Numbers 22—24 will show that Balaam was willing, yea, anxious, to accept Balak's offer and thus sin against God and His people. But Divine power "withheld" him. Mark his own admission, "And Balaam said unto Balak, Lo, I am come unto thee: *have I now any power at all to say anything?* the word that *God* putteth in my mouth, that shall I speak" (Num. 22:38). Again, after Balak had remonstrated with Balaam, we read, "He answered and said, Must I not take heed to speak that which the Lord hath put in my mouth? . . . Behold, I have received commandment to bless: and He hath blessed; *and I cannot reverse it"* (23:12, 20). Surely these verses show us God's power, and Balaam's powerlessness: man's will frustrated, and God's will performed. But was Balaam's "freedom" or responsibility destroyed? Certainly not, as we shall yet seek to show.

One more illustration: "And the fear of the Lord fell upon all the kingdoms of the lands that were round about Judah, *so that they made no war against Jehoshaphat"* (2 Chron. 17:10). The implication here is clear. Had not the "fear of the Lord" *fallen upon* these kingdoms, they *would* have made war upon Judah. God's restraining power alone *prevented* them. Had their own will been allowed to act, "war" would have been the consequence. Thus we see that Scripture teaches that God "withholds" nations as well as individuals, and that when it pleaseth Him to do so He interposes and prevents war. Compare further Gen. 35:5.

The question which now demands our consideration is,

How is it possible for God to "withhold" men from sinning and yet not to interfere with their liberty and responsibility—a question which so many say is incapable of solution in our present finite condition. This question causes us to ask, In what does moral "freedom," *real moral freedom,* consist? We answer, *it is the being delivered from the BONDAGE of sin.* The more any soul is emancipated from the thraldom of sin, the more does he enter into a state of freedom—"If the Son therefore shall make you free, ye shall be *free indeed*" (John 8:36). In the above instances God "withheld" Abimelech, Balaam, and the heathen kingdoms *from sinning,* and therefore we affirm that He did not in anywise interfere with their real *freedom.* The nearer a soul approximates to sinlessness, the nearer does he approach to God's holiness. Scripture tells us that God *"cannot* lie," and that He *"cannot* be tempted," but is *He* any the less *free* because He cannot do that which is evil? Surely not. Then is it not evident that the more man is raised up to God, and the more he be "withheld" from sinning, the greater is his *real* freedom!

A pertinent example setting forth the *meeting-place* of God's sovereignty and man's responsibility, as it relates to the question of moral freedom, is found in connection with the giving to us of the Holy Scriptures. In the communication of His Word God was pleased to employ human instruments, and in the using of them He did not reduce them to mere mechanical amanuenses: "Knowing this first, that no prophecy of the Scripture is of any private interpretation (Greek: of its own origination). For the prophecy came not at any time by the will of man: but holy men of God spake *moved by the Holy Spirit"* (2 Pet. 1:20, 21). Here we have man's responsibility and God's sovereignty placed in juxtaposition. These holy men were "moved" (Greek: "borne along") by the Holy Spirit, yet was not their moral responsibility disturbed nor their "freedom" impaired. God enlightened their minds, enkindled their hearts, revealed to them His truth, and so *controlled* them that error on their part was, by Him, made impossible, as they communicated His mind and will to men. But what was it that might have, *would* have, caused error, had not God controlled as He did the instruments which He employed? The answer is SIN, the sin which was in them. But as we have seen, the holding in check of sin, the preventing of the exercise of the carnal mind in these "holy men," was not a *destroying* of their "freedom," rather was it the inducting of them into real freedom.

A final word should be added here concerning the nature of true *liberty*. There are three chief things concerning which men in general greatly err: misery and happiness, folly and wisdom, bondage and liberty. The world counts none miserable but the *afflicted,* and none happy but the *prosperous,* because they judge by the present ease of the flesh. Again; the world is pleased with a false show of wisdom (which is "foolishness" with God), neglecting that which makes wise unto salvation. As to liberty, men would be at their own disposal, and live as they please. They suppose the only true liberty is to be at the command and under the control of none above themselves, and live according to their heart's desire. But this is a thraldom and bondage of the worst kind. True liberty is not the power to live as we please, but to live as we *ought!* Hence, the only One Who has ever trod this earth since Adam's fall that has enjoyed perfect freedom was the Man Christ Jesus, the Holy Servant of God, Whose meat it ever was to do the will of the Father.

We now turn to consider the question.

II. How can the sinner be held responsible FOR the doing of what he is UNABLE to do? And how can he be justly condemned for NOT DOING what he COULD NOT do?

As a *creature* the natural man is responsible to love, obey, and serve God; as a *sinner* he is responsible to repent and believe the Gospel. But at the outset we are confronted with the fact that the natural man is *unable* to love and serve God, and that the sinner, of himself, *cannot* repent and believe. First, let us prove what we have just said. We begin by quoting and considering John 6:44, *"No man can come to Me, except the Father which hath sent Me draw him".* The heart of the natural man (every man) is so "desperately wicked" that if he is left to himself he will never 'come to Christ.' This statement would not be questioned if the full

force of the words "Coming to Christ" were properly apprehended. We shall therefore digress a little at this point to
define and consider what is implied and involved in the
words "No man can *come to Me*"—cf. John 5:40, "Ye will
not *come to Me* that ye might have life."

For the sinner to come to Christ that he might have life,
is for him to realize the awful danger of his situation; is for
him to see that the sword of Divine justice is suspended over
his head; is to awaken to the fact that there is but a step betwixt him and death, and that after death is the "judgment;" and in consequence of this discovery, is for him to
be *in real earnest* to escape, and in *such* earnestness that he
shall *flee* from the wrath to come, *cry* unto God for mercy,
and *agonize* to enter in at the "strait gate."

To come to Christ for life, is for the sinner to feel and
acknowledge that he is utterly destitute of any claim upon
God's favor; is to see himself as "without strength," lost
and undone; is to admit that he is deserving of nothing but
eternal death, thus taking side with God against himself; it is
for him to cast himself into the dust before God, and humbly
sue for Divine mercy.

To come to Christ for life, is for the sinner to abandon
his own righteousness and be ready to be made the righteousness of God in Christ; it is to disown his own wisdom
and be guided by His; it is to repudiate his own will and be
ruled by His; it is to unreservedly receive the Lord Jesus as
his Saviour and Lord, as his All in all.

Such, in part and in brief, is what is *implied and involved*
in "Coming to Christ." But is the sinner willing to take *such*
an attitude before God? No; for in the first place, he *does
not realize* the danger of his situation, and in consequence is
not in real earnest after his escape; instead, men are for the
most part *at ease,* and apart from the operations of the Holy
Spirit whenever they *are* disturbed by the alarms of conscience or the dispensations of providence, they flee to any
other refuge but Christ. In the second place, they will not
acknowledge that all their righteousnesses are as filthy rags
but, like the Pharisee, will thank God they are not as the
Publican. And in the third place, they are not ready to receive Christ as their Saviour and Lord, for they are *unwilling* to part with their *idols:* they had rather hazard their

soul's eternal welfare than give them up. Hence we say that, left to himself, the natural man is so depraved at heart that he *cannot* come to Christ.

The words of our Lord quoted above by no means stand alone. Quite a number of Scriptures set forth the moral and spiritual *inability* of the natural man. In Joshua 24:19 we read, "And Joshua said unto the people, *Ye cannot serve the Lord:* for He is a holy God." To the Pharisees Christ said, "Why do ye not understand My speech? Even because *ye cannot hear* My word" (John 8:43). And again: "The carnal mind is enmity against God: for it is not subject to the law of God, *neither indeed can be.* So then they that are in the flesh *cannot* please God" (Rom. 8:7, 8).

But now the question returns, How can God hold the sinner responsible for failing to do what he is *unable* to do? This necessitates a careful definition of terms. Just what is meant by "unable" and "cannot"?

Now let it be clearly understood that, when we speak of the sinner's *inability,* we do not mean that *if* men *desired* to come to Christ they lack the necessary power to carry out their desire. No; the fact is that the sinner's inability or absence of power is itself *due* to *lack of willingness* to come to Christ, and this lack of willingness is the fruit of a depraved heart. It is of first importance that we distinguish between *natural* inability and moral and spiritual inability. For example, we read, "But Ahijah *could not see;* for his eyes were set by reason of his age" (1 Kings 14:4); and again, "The men rowed hard to bring it to the land; but *they could not:* for the sea wrought, and was tempestuous against them" (Jonah 1:13). In both of these passages the words "could not" refer to *natural inability.* But when we read, "And when his brethren saw that their father loved him (Joseph) more than all his brethren, they hated him, *and could not* speak peaceably unto him" (Gen. 37:4), it is clearly *moral inability* that is in view. They did not lack the *natural* ability to "speak peaceably unto him", for they were not *dumb.* Why then was it that they "could not speak peaceably unto him"? The answer is given in the same verse: it was because "they *hated* him." Again; in 2 Pet. 2:14 we read of a certain class of wicked men "having eyes full of adultery, and that *cannot cease from sin.*" Here

again it is *moral inability* that is in view. Why is it that
these men "cannot cease from sin"? The answer is, Because
their eyes were full of adultery. So of Rom. 8:8—"They
that are in the flesh *cannot* please God": here it is *spiritual
inability*. Why is it that the natural man "cannot please
God"? Because he is *"alienated* from the life of God"
(Eph. 4:18). No man can choose that from which his heart
is *averse*—"O generation of vipers *how can ye,* being evil,
speak good things?" (Matt. 12:34). "No man *can come
to Me,* except the Father which hath sent Me draw him"
(John 6:44). Here again it is *moral and spiritual inability*
which is before us. Why is it the sinner cannot come to
Christ unless he is "drawn"? The answer is, Because his
wicked heart *loves sin* and *hates Christ.*

We trust we have made it clear that the Scriptures distinguish sharply between natural inability and moral and
spiritual inability. Surely all can see the difference between
the blindness of Bartimeus, who was ardently desirous of
receiving his sight, and the Pharisees, whose eyes were
closed, "lest at any time they should see with their eyes,
and hear with their ears, and should understand with their
heart, and should be converted" (Matt. 13:15). But should
it be said, The natural man *could* come to Christ if he *wished*
to do so, we answer, Ah! but in that IF lies the hinge of the
whole matter. The inability of the sinner consists of *the
want* of moral power *to wish* and will so as to actually perform.

What we have contended for above is of first importance.
Upon the distinction between the sinner's natural Ability,
and his moral and spiritual Inability, rests his *Responsibility.*
The depravity of the human heart does not destroy man's
accountability to God; so far from this being the case the
very moral inability of the sinner only serves to *increase his
guilt.* This is easily proven by a reference to the scriptures
cited above. We read that Joseph's brethren "could not
speak peaceably unto him," and why? It was because they
"hated" Him. But was this moral inability of theirs any
excuse? Surely not: in this very moral inability consisted
the greatness of their sin. So of those concerning whom it
is said, "They cannot cease from sin" (2 Pet. 2:14), and

why? Because "their eyes were full of adultery," but that only made their case worse. It was a real fact that they could not cease from sin, yet this did not excuse them—it only made their sin the greater.

Should some sinner here object, I cannot help being born into this world with a depraved heart, and therefore I am not responsible for my moral and spiritual inability which accrue from it, the reply would be, Responsibility and Culpability lie in the *indulgence* of the depraved propensities, the *free* indulgence, for God does not force any *to sin.* Men might pity me, but they certainly would not excuse me if I gave vent to a fiery temper, and then sought to extenuate myself on the ground of having *inherited* that temper from my parents. Their own common sense is sufficient to guide their judgment in such a case as this. They would argue I was responsible to restrain my temper. Why then cavil against this same principle in the case supposed above? "Out of *thine own mouth* will I judge thee thou wicked servant" surely applies here! What would the reader say to a man who had robbed him, and who later argued in defence, "I cannot help being a thief, that is my nature"? Surely the reply would be, Then the penitentiary is the proper place for that man. What then shall be said to the one who argues that he cannot help following the bent of his sinful heart? Surely, that the Lake of Fire is where *such an one* must go. Did ever murderer plead that he hated his victim so much that he *could not* go near him *without* slaying him. Would not that only magnify the enormity of his crime! Then what of the one who loves sin so much that he is "at enmity against *God"!*

The *fact* of man's responsibility is almost universally acknowledged. It is inherent in man's moral nature. It is not only taught in Scripture but witnessed to by the natural conscience. The *basis* or ground of human responsibility is human *ability.* What is implied by this general term "ability" must now be defined. Perhaps a concrete example will be more easily grasped by the average reader than an abstract argument.

Suppose a man owed me $100 and could find plenty of money for his own pleasures but none for me, yet pleaded that he was *unable* to pay me. What would I say? I would say that the only ability that was lacking was *an honest heart*. But would it not be an unfair construction of my words if a friend of my dishonest debtor should say I had stated that an honest heart was that which *constituted the ability* to pay the debt? No; I would reply: the ability of my debtor lies in the power of his hand to write me a check, *and this he has,* but what is lacking is *an honest principle.* It is his power to write me a check which makes him responsible to do so, and the fact that he lacks an honest heart does not destroy his accountability.*

Now, in like manner, the sinner while altogether lacking in moral and spiritual ability *does,* nevertheless, possess *natural* ability, and this it is which renders him accountable unto God. Men have the same *natural* faculties to love God with as they have to hate Him with, the same hearts to believe with which they disbelieve, and it is *their failure* to love and believe which constitutes their guilt. An idiot or an infant is not personally responsible to God, because *lacking* in *natural* ability. But the normal man who is endowed with rationality, who is gifted with a conscience that is capable of distinguishing between right and wrong, *who is able to weigh eternal issues* IS a responsible being, and it is because he *does* possess these very faculties that he will yet have to "give account of himself to God" (Rom. 14:12).

We say again that the above distinction between the natural ability and the moral and spiritual inability of the sinner is of prime importance. By nature he possesses natural ability but *lacks* moral and spiritual ability. The fact that he *does not possess* the latter, does not *destroy* his responsibility, because his responsibility rests upon the fact that he *does* possess the former. Let me illustrate again. Here are two men guilty of theft: the first is an idiot, the second perfectly sane but the offspring of criminal parents. No just judge would sentence the former; but every right-minded judge would the latter. Even though the second of these thieves possessed a vitiated moral nature inherited from criminal parents, that would not *excuse* him, providing he

---

*The terms of this example are suggested by an illustration used by the late Andrew Fuller.

was a normal *rational* being. Here then is *the ground of human accountability*—the possession of rationality plus the gift of conscience. It is because the sinner *is endowed* with these natural faculties that he is a *responsible* creature; because he *does not use* his natural powers for God's glory, constitutes his *guilt*.

How can it remain consistent with His mercy that God should require the debt of obedience from him that is not able to pay? In addition to what has been said above, it should be pointed out that God has not lost His *right*, even though man has lost his *power*. The creature's impotence does not cancel his obligation. A drunken servant is a servant still, and it is contrary to all sound reasoning to argue that his master loses his rights through his servant's default. Moreover, it is of first importance that we should ever bear in mind that God contracted with us in Adam, who was our federal head and representative, and in him, God gave us a power which we lost through our first parent's fall; but though our power be gone, nevertheless, God may justly demand His due of obedience and of service.

We turn now to ponder,

III. How is it possible for God to DECREE that men SHOULD commit certain sins, hold them RESPONSIBLE in the committal of them, and adjudge them GUILTY because they committed them?

Let us now consider the extreme case of Judas. We hold that it is clear from Scripture that God *decreed* from all eternity that Judas should betray the Lord Jesus. If anyone should challenge this statement we refer him to the prophecy of Zechariah, through whom God declared that His Son should be sold for "Thirty pieces of silver" (Zech. 11:12). As we have said in earlier pages, in prophecy God makes known what *will be,* and in making known what will be, He is but revealing to us what He has ordained *shall be.* That Judas was the one through whom the prophecy of Zechariah was fulfilled needs not to be argued. But now the question we have to face is, Was Judas a *responsible agent in* fulfilling this decree of God? We reply that he was. Responsibility attaches mainly to the *motive* and *intention* of the one committing the act. This is recognised on every hand. Human law distinguishes between a blow inflicted by accident (without evil design), and a blow delivered with 'malice aforethought.' Apply then this same principle to the case of Judas. What was the *design* of his heart when he bargained with the priests? Manifestly he had no conscious desire to *fulfil* any decree of God, though unknown to himself he was actually doing so. On the contrary, *his intention* was evil only, and therefore, though God had decreed and directed his act, nevertheless, *his own evil intention* rendered him justly *guilty* as he afterwards acknowledged himself—"I have *betrayed* innocent blood." It was the same with the Crucifixion of Christ. Scripture plainly declares that He was "delivered up *by the determinate counsel* and foreknowledge of God" (Acts 2:23), and that though "the kings of the earth stood up, and the rulers were gathered together against the Lord, and against His Christ" yet, notwithstanding, it was but "for to do whatsoever Thy hand and Thy counsel *determined before to be done*" (Acts 4:26, 28); which verses teach very much more than a bare *permission* by God, declaring, as they do, that the Crucifixion and all its details had been *decreed by God*. Yet, nevertheless, it was by *"wicked hands,"* not merely "human hands", that our Lord was "crucified and slain" (Acts 2:23). "Wicked" because the *intention* of His crucifiers was only evil.

But it might be objected that, if God had decreed that Judas *should* betray Christ, and that the Jews and Gentiles *should* crucify Him, they could not do otherwise, and therefore, they were not responsible for their intentions. The answer is, God had decreed that they should perform the *acts* they did, but in the actual perpetration of these deeds *they* were justly *guilty,* because *their own purposes* in the doing of them was evil only. Let it be emphatically said that God does not *produce* the sinful dispositions of any of His creatures, though He does *restrain* and *direct* them to the accomplishing of His own purposes. Hence He is neither the Author nor the Approver of sin. This distinction was expressed thus by Augustine: "That men sin proceeds from themselves; that in sinning they perform this or that action, is from the power of God who divideth the darkness according to His pleasure." Thus it is written, "A man's heart deviseth his way: but the Lord *directeth his steps"* (Prov. 16:9). What we would here insist upon is, that God's decrees are not the *necessitating cause* of the sins of men, but the foredetermined and prescribed *boundings* and *directings* of men's sinful acts. In connection with the betrayal of Christ, God did not decree that He should be sold by one of His creatures and then take up a good man, instill an evil desire into his heart and thus *force* him to perform the terrible deed *in order to execute* His decree. No; not so do the Scriptures represent it. Instead, God decreed the act and selected the one who was to perform the act, but He did not *make him evil* in order that he *should* perform the deed; on the contrary, the betrayer was a "devil" at the time the Lord Jesus chose him as one of the twelve (John 6:70), and in the *exercise* and *manifestation* of his *own* devilry God simply *directed* his actions, actions which were perfectly *agreeable* to his *own* vile heart, and performed with the most wicked *intentions*. Thus it was with the Crucifixion.

IV. HOW CAN THE SINNER BE HELD RESPONSIBLE TO RE-
CEIVE CHRIST, AND BE DAMNED FOR REJECTING HIM,
WHEN GOD FOREORDAINED HIM TO CONDEMNA-
TION?

Really, this question has been covered in what has been said under the other queries, but for the benefit of those who are exercised upon this point we give it a separate, though brief, examination. In considering the above difficulty the following points should be carefully weighed:

In the first place, no sinner, while he is in this world, knows for certain, nor can he know, that *he* is a "vessel of wrath fitted to destruction". This belongs to the hidden counsels of God, to which he has not access. God's *secret* will is no business of his; God's *revealed* will (in the Word) is the standard of human responsibility.* And God's *re-vealed* will is plain. Each sinner is among those whom God now "commandeth to repent" (Acts 17:30). Each sinner who hears the Gospel is "commanded" to believe (1 John 3:23). And all who *do* truly repent and believe are saved. Therefore, is every sinner *responsible* to repent and believe.

In the second place, it is the *duty* of every sinner to search the Scriptures which "are able to make wise unto salvation" (2 Tim. 3:15). It is the sinner's "duty" because the Son of God has *commanded* him to search the Scriptures (John 5:39). If he searches them with a heart that is seeking after God, then does he put himself in the way where God is accustomed to meet with sinners. Upon this point the Puritan Manton has written very helpfully.

"I cannot say to every one that ploweth, infallibly, that he shall have a good crop; but this I can say to him, It is God's use to bless the diligent and provident. I cannot say to every one that desireth posterity, Marry, and you shall have children; I cannot say infallibly to him that goeth forth to battle for his country's good that he shall have victory and success; but I can say, as Joab, (1 Chron. 19:13) 'Be of good courage, and let us behave ourselves valiantly for our people and the cities of our God, and let the Lord do what is good in His sight'. I cannot say infallibly you shall have grace; but I can say to every one, *Let him use the means, and leave the success of his labor and his own salvation to the will and good pleasure of God*. I cannot say this infallibly, for there is no obligation upon God. And still this work is made the fruit of God's will and mere arbitrary dispensation —'Of His own will begat He us by the Word of Truth' (James 1:18). Let us do what God hath commanded, and let God do what He will. And I need not say so; for the whole world in all their actings are and should be guided by this principle. Let us do our duty, and refer the success to God, Whose ordinary practice it is to meet with the creature that seeketh after Him; yea, He is with us already; this earnest importunity in the use of means proceeding from the earnest impression of His grace. And therefore, since He is beforehand with us, and hath not showed any backwardness to our good, we have no reason to despair of His goodness and mercy, but rather to hope for the best" (Vol. XXI, page 312).

God has been pleased to give to men the Holy Scriptures which "testify" of the Saviour, and make known the way of salvation. Every sinner has the same *natural* faculties for the reading of the Bible as he has for the reading of the newspaper; and if he is illiterate or blind so that he is unable to read, he has the same mouth with which to ask a friend to read the Bible to him, as he has to enquire concerning other matters. If, then, God has given to men His Word, and in that Word has made known the way of salvation, and if men are commanded to search those Scriptures which are able to make them wise unto salvation, and they *refuse* to do so, then is it plain that they are *justly* censureable, that their blood lies on *their own heads,* and that God *can righteously* cast them into the Lake of Fire.

In the third place, should it be objected, Admitting all you have said above, Is it not still a fact that each of the non-elect is *unable* to repent and believe? The reply is, Yes. Of every sinner it is a fact that, of himself, he *cannot* come to Christ. And from God's side the "cannot" is absolute. But we are now dealing with the *responsibility* of the sinner (the sinner foreordained to condemnation, though *he* knows it not), and from the *human side* the inability of the sinner is a *moral* one, as previously pointed out. Moreover, it needs to be borne in mind that in addition to the *moral* inability of the sinner there is a *voluntary* inability, too. The sinner must be regarded not only as impotent to do good, but as *delighting* in evil. From the *human* side, then, the "cannot" is a *will not;* it is a *voluntary* impotence. Man's impotence lies in his obstinacy. Hence, is everyone left "without excuse", And hence, is God "clear" when He judgeth (Psa. 51:4), and righteous in damning all who *"love* darkness rather than light".

That God *does* require what is beyond our own power to render is clear from many scriptures. God gave *the Law* to Israel at Sinai and demanded a full compliance with it, and solemnly pointed out what would be the consequences of their disobedience (see Deut. 28). But will any readers be so foolish as to affirm that Israel *were* capable of fully obeying the Law! If they do, we would refer them to Romans 8:3 where we are expressly told, "For what the law *could not do,* in that it was weak through the flesh, God sending His own Son in the likeness of sinful flesh, and for sin, condemned sin in the flesh".

Come now to the New Testament. Take such passages as Matt. 5:48, "Be ye therefore perfect, even as your Father

which is in heaven is perfect". I Cor. 15:34, "Awake to
righteousness and sin not". I John 2:1, "My little children,
these things I write unto you, that ye sin not". Will any
reader say he *is* capable in himself of complying with *these*
demands of God? If so, it is useless for us to argue with
him.

But now the question arises, Why has God demanded
of man that which he is *incapable* of performing? The first
answer is, Because God refuses to lower His standard to
the level of our sinful infirmities. Being perfect, God must
set a perfect standard before us. Still we must ask, if man
is incapable of measuring up to God's standard, *wherein*
lies his *responsibility?* Difficult as seems the problem it is
nevertheless capable of a simple and satisfactory solution.

Man is responsible to (1st) *acknowledge* before God his
inability, and (2nd) to *cry* unto Him for enabling grace.
Surely this will be admitted by every Christian reader. It
is my bounden duty to own before God my ignorance, my
weakness, my sinfulness, my impotence *to* comply with His
holy and just requirements. It is also my bounden duty, as
well as blessed privilege, to earnestly beseech God to give
me the wisdom, strength, grace, which will *enable* me to do
that which is pleasing in His sight; to ask Him to *work in
me* "both to will and to do of His good pleasure" (Phil. 2:
13).

In like manner, the sinner, every sinner, is *responsible* to
call upon the Lord. Of himself he can neither repent nor
believe. He can neither come to Christ, nor turn from his
sins. God *tells* him so; and his first duty is to "set to his seal
that God is true". His second duty is to *cry* unto God for
His enabling power—to ask God in mercy to overcome his
enmity, and "draw" him to Christ; to bestow upon him the
gifts of repentance and faith. If *he will* do so, sincerely
from the heart, then most surely *God will* respond to his
appeal, for it is written—"For whosoever shall call upon the
name of the Lord shall be saved" (Rom. 10:13).

Suppose, I had slipped on the icy pavement, late at night,
and had broken my hip. I am *unable* to arise; if I remain
on the ground, I must freeze to death. What, then, ought
I to do? If I am determined to perish, I shall lie there silent
—but I shall be to blame for such a course. If I am anxious

to be rescued, I shall lift up my voice and *cry for help*. So the sinner, though *unable* of himself to rise and take the first step toward Christ, *is* responsible to *cry to God*, and if he does (from the heart), there is a Deliverer to hand. God is "not far from every one of us" (Acts 17:27); yea, "He is a very *present* help in trouble" (Psa. 46:1). But if the sinner *refuses* to cry unto the Lord, if he is determined to perish, then his blood is on his own head, and his "damnation is just" (Rom. 3:8).

A brief word now concerning the *extent* of human responsibility.

It is obvious that the *measure* of human responsibility *varies* in different cases, and is greater or less with particular individuals. The standard of measurement was given in the Saviour's words, "For unto whomsoever much is given, of him shall much be required" (Luke 12:48). Surely God did not require as much from those living in Old Testament times as He does from those who have been born during the Christian dispensation. Surely God will not require as much from those who lived during the 'dark ages,' when the Scriptures were accessible to but a few, as He will from those of this generation, when practically every family in the land own a copy of His Word for themselves. In the same way, God will not demand from the heathen what He will from those in christendom. The heathen will not perish because they have not believed in Christ, but because they failed to live up to the light which they did have—the testimony of God in nature and conscience.

To sum up. The *fact* of man's responsibility rests upon his natural ability, is witnessed to by conscience, and is insisted on throughout the Scriptures. The *ground* of man's responsibility is that he is a rational creature capable of weighing eternal issues, and that he possesses a written Revelation from God, in which his relationship with and duty toward his Creator is plainly defined. The *measure* of responsibility varies in different individuals, being determined by the degree of light each has enjoyed from God. The *problem* of human responsibility receives at least a partial solution in the Holy Scriptures, and it is our solemn obligation as well as privilege to search them prayerfully and carefully for further light, looking to the Holy Spirit to guide us "into *all* truth." It is written, "The *meek* will He guide in judgment: and the *meek* will He teach His way" (Ps. 25: 9).

In conclusion it remains to point out that it is the responsibility of every man to use the means which God has placed to his hand. An attitude of fatalistic inertia, because I know that God has irrevocably decreed whatsoever comes to pass, is to make a sinful and hurtful use of what God has revealed for the comfort of my heart. The same God who has decreed that a certain end shall be accomplished, has also decreed that that end shall be attained through and as the result of His own appointed means. God does not disdain the use of means, nor must I. For example: God has decreed that "while the earth remaineth, seed-time and harvest. . . shall not cease" (Gen. 8:22); but that does not mean man's ploughing of the ground and sowing of the seed are needless. No; God moves men *to do* those very things, blesses their labours, and so fulfills His own ordination. In like manner, God has, from the beginning, chosen a people unto salvation; but that does not mean there is no need for evangelists to preach the Gospel, or for sinners to believe it; it is *by* such means that His eternal counsels are effectuated.

To argue that, because God has irrevocably determined the eternal destiny of every man, relieves us of all responsibility for any concern about our souls, or any diligent use of the means to salvation, would be on a par with refusing to perform my *temporal* duties because God has fixed my earthly lot. And that He *has* is clear from Acts 17:26, Job 7:1; 14:5, etc. If then the foreordination of God may consist with the respective activities of man in present concerns, why not in the future? What God has joined together we must not cut asunder. Whether we can or cannot see the link which unites the one to the other, our duty is plain: "The secret things belong unto the Lord our God: but those things which are revealed belong unto us and to our children forever, *that we may do* all the words of this law" (Deut. 29:29).

In Acts 27:22 God made known that He had ordained the temporal preservation of all who accompanied Paul in the ship; yet the apostle did not hesitate to say, "Except these abide in the ship, ye cannot be saved" (v. 31); God appointed that means for the execution of what He had decreed. From 2 Kings 20 we learn that God was absolutely resolved to add fifteen years to Hezekiah's life, yet *he* must take a lump of figs and lay it on his boil! Paul knew that he was eternally secure in the hand of Christ (John 10: 28), yet he "kept under his body" (1 Cor. 9:26). The apostle John assured those to whom he wrote, "Ye *shall* abide in Him", yet in the very next verse he exhorted them, "And now, little children, *abide* in Him" (1 John 2:27, 28). It is only by taking heed to this vital principle, that we are responsible *to use* the means of God's appointing, that we shall be enabled to preserve the *balance* of Truth, and be saved from a paralyzing fatalism.

IX

GOD'S SOVEREIGNTY AND PRAYER

"If we ask anything according to *His* will,
He heareth us" (I John 5:14).

THROUGHOUT this book it has been our chief aim to exalt the Creator and abase the creature. The well-nigh universal tendency, now, is to magnify man and dishonor and degrade God. On every hand it will be found that, when spiritual things are under discussion, the human side and element is pressed and stressed, and the Divine side, if not altogether ignored, is relegated to the background. This holds, true of very much of the modern teaching about prayer. In the great majority of the books written and in the sermons preached upon prayer, the human element fills the scene almost entirely: it is the conditions which *we* must meet, the promises *we* must "claim", the things *we* must do, in order to get our requests granted; and *God's* claims, *God's* rights, *God's* glory are disregarded.

As a fair sample of what is being given out today we subjoin a brief editorial which appeared recently in one of the leading religious weeklies entitled "Prayer, or Fate?"

"God in His sovereignty has ordained that human destinies may be changed and moulded by the will of man. This is at the heart of the truth that prayer changes things, meaning that God changes things when men pray. Some one has strikingly expressed it this way: 'There are certain things that will happen in a man's life whether he prays or not. There are other things that will happen if he prays, and will not happen if he does not pray'. A Christian worker was impressed by these sentences as he entered a business office, and he prayed that the Lord would open the way to speak to some one about Christ, reflecting that things would be changed because he prayed. Then his mind turned to other things and the prayer was forgotten. The opportunity came to speak to the business man on whom he was calling, but he did not grasp it, and was on his way out when he remembered his prayer of a half hour before, and God's answer. He promptly returned and had a talk with the business man, who, though a church-member, had never in his life been asked whether he was saved. Let us give ourselves to prayer, and open the way for God to change things. Let us beware lest we become virtual fatalists by failing to exercise our God-given wills in praying".

The above illustrates what is now being taught on the subject of prayer, and the deplorable thing is that scarcely a voice is lifted in protest. To say that "human destinies *may be changed* and moulded *by the will of man"* is rank infidelity—that is the only proper term for it. Should any one challenge this classification, we would ask them whether they can find an infidel anywhere who would dissent from such a statement, and we are confident that such an one could not be found. To say that *"God* has *ordained* that human destinies may be changed and moulded by the will of man", is absolutely untrue. "Human destiny" is settled *not* by "the will of man," but by the will of God. That which determines human destiny is whether or not a man has been born again, for it is written, "Except a man be born again he cannot see the kingdom of God". And as to *whose* will, whether God's or man's, is responsible for the new birth is settled, unequivocally, by John 1:13—"Which were born, not of blood, nor of the will of the flesh, *nor of the will of man,* but OF GOD". To say that "human destiny" may be *changed* by the will of man, is to make the creature's will *supreme,* and that is, virtually, to *dethrone God.* But what saith the Scriptures? Let the Book answer: "The Lord killeth, and maketh alive: *He* bringeth down to the grave, and bringeth up. The Lord maketh poor, and maketh rich: *He* bringeth low, and lifteth up. *He* raiseth up the poor out of the dust, and lifteth up the beggar from the dunghill, to set them among princes, and to make them inherit the throne of glory" (1 Sam. 2:6-8).

Turning back to the Editorial here under review, we are next told, "This is at the heart of the truth that prayer changes things, meaning that God changes things when men pray." Almost everywhere we go today one comes across a motto-card bearing the inscription "Prayer Changes Things". As to what these words are designed to signify is evident from the current literature on prayer—*we* are to persuade God to *change* His purpose. Concerning this we shall have more to say below.

Again, the Editor tells us, "Some one has strikingly expressed it this way: 'There are certain things that will happen in a man's life whether he prays or not. There are other things that will happen if he prays, and will not happen if he does not pray'." That things happen whether a man prays or not is exemplified daily in the lives of the unregenerate, most of whom never pray at all. That 'other things will happen if he prays' is in need of qualification. If a believer prays in faith and asks for those things which are according to God's will, he will most certainly obtain that for which he has asked. Again, that other things will happen if he prays, is also true in respect to the subjective benefits derived from prayer: God will become more real to him and His promises more precious. That other things 'will not happen if he does not pray' is true so far as his own life is concerned—a prayerless life means a life lived out of communion with God and all that is involved by this. But to affirm that God will not and cannot bring to pass His eternal purpose unless we pray, is utterly erroneous, for the same God who has decreed the end has also decreed that His end shall be reached through His appointed means, and one of these is prayer. The God who has determined to grant a blessing, also gives a spirit of supplication which first seeks the blessing.

The example cited in the above Editorial of the Christian Worker and the business man is a very unhappy one to say the least, for according to the terms of the illustration the Christian Worker's prayer was not answered by God at all, inasmuch as, apparently, the way was not opened to speak to the business man about his soul. But on leaving the office and recalling his prayer the Christian Worker (perhaps in the energy of the flesh) determined to answer the prayer *for himself,* and instead of leaving *the Lord* to "open the way" for him, took matters into his own hand.

We quote next from one of the latest books issued on Prayer. In it the author says, "The possibilities and necessity of prayer, its power and results, are manifested in arresting and *changing the purposes of God* and in relieving the stroke of His power". Such an assertion as this is a horrible reflection upon the character of the Most High God, who "doeth according to His will in the army of heaven, and among the inhabitants of the earth: and *none can stay His hand,* or say unto Him, What doest Thou?" (Dan. 4: 35). There is *no need* whatever *for* God to change His designs or alter His purpose, for the all-sufficient reason that these were framed under the influence of perfect goodness and unerring wisdom. *Men* may have occasion to alter *their* purposes, for in their short-sightedness they are frequently unable to anticipate what may arise *after* their plans are formed. But not so with God, for He knows the end from the beginning. To affirm that God *changes* His purpose is either to impugn His goodness or to deny His eternal wisdom.

In the same book we are told, "The prayers of God's saints are the capital stock in heaven by which Christ carries on His great work upon earth. The great throes and mighty convulsions on earth are the results of these prayers. Earth is changed, revolutionized, angels move on more powerful, more rapid wing, and *God's policy is shaped* as the prayers are more numerous, more efficient". If possible, this is even worse, and we have no hesitation in denominating it as blasphemy. In the first place, it flatly denies Eph. 3:11, which speaks of God's having an *"eternal* purpose". If God's purpose is an eternal one, then His "policy" is *not* being "shaped" today. In the second place, it contradicts Eph. 1:11 which expressly declares that God "worketh *all* things after the counsel of *His own* will," therefore it follows that, "God's policy" is *not* being "shaped" by man's prayers. In the third place, such a statement as the above makes the will of the creature supreme, for if *our* prayers shape *God's* policy, then is the Most High subordinate to worms of the earth. Well might the Holy Spirit ask through the apostle, "For who hath known the mind of the Lord? *or who hath been His counsellor?*" (Rom. 11:34).

Such thoughts on prayer as we have been citing are due to low and inadequate conceptions of God Himself. It ought to be apparent that there could be little or no comfort in praying to a God that was like the chameleon, which changes its color every day. What encouragement is there to lift up our hearts to One who is in one mind yesterday and another today? What would be the use of petitioning an earthly monarch, if we knew he was so mutable as to grant a petition one day and deny it another? Is it not the very *unchangeableness* of God which is our greatest encouragement *to pray?* It is because He is *"without* variableness or shadow of turning" we are assured that if we ask anything according to His will we are most certain of being heard. Well did Luther remark, "Prayer is not overcoming God's reluctance, but laying hold of His willingness."

And this leads us to offer a few remarks concerning the *design* of prayer. *Why* has God appointed that we should pray? The vast majority of people would reply, In order that we may obtain from God the things which we need. While this *is* one of the purposes of prayer, it is by no means the chief one. Moreover, it considers prayer only from the *human* side, and prayer sadly needs to be viewed from the *Divine* side. Let us look, then, at some of the reasons why *God* has bidden us to pray.

First and foremost, prayer has been appointed that the Lord God Himself should be *honored.* God requires we should recognize that He is, indeed, "the *high* and *lofty* One that inhabiteth eternity" (Isa. 57:17). God requires that we shall own His *universal dominion:* in petitioning God for rain, Elijah did but confess His control over the elements; in praying to God to deliver a poor sinner from the wrath to come, we acknowledge that "salvation is of the Lord" (Jonah 2:9); in supplicating His blessing on the Gospel unto the uttermost parts of the earth, we declare His rulership over the whole world.

Again; God requires that we shall *worship* Him, and prayer, real prayer, is an act of worship. Prayer is an act of worship inasmuch as it is the prostrating of the soul before Him; inasmuch as it is a calling upon His great and holy name; inasmuch as it is the owning of His goodness, His power, His immutability, His grace, and inasmuch as it is the recognition of His sovereignty, owned by a submission to His will. It is highly significant to notice in this connection that the Temple was not termed by Christ the House of Sacrifice, but instead, the House of Prayer.

Again; prayer *redounds to God's glory,* for in prayer we do but acknowledge our dependency upon Him. When we humbly supplicate the Divine Being we cast ourselves upon His power and mercy. In seeking blessings from God we

own that He is the Author and Fountain of every good
and perfect gift. That prayer brings glory to God is further
seen from the fact that prayer calls faith into exercise, and
nothing from us is so honoring and pleasing to Him as the
confidence of our hearts.

In the second place, prayer is appointed by God *for our
spiritual blessing,* as a means for *our growth in grace.* When
seeking to learn the *design* of prayer, this should ever occupy
us *before* we regard prayer as a means for obtaining the supply of our need. Prayer is designed by God for our *humbling.* Prayer, real prayer, is a coming into the Presence
of God, and a sense of His awful majesty produces a realization of our nothingness and unworthiness. Again; prayer
is designed by God for *the exercise of our faith.* Faith is
begotten in the Word (Rom. 10:17), but it is exercised in
prayer; hence, we read of "the prayer of faith". Again;
prayer calls *love* into action. Concerning the hypocrite the
question is asked, "Will he delight himself in the Almighty?
Will he always call upon God?" (Job 27:10). But they
that love the Lord cannot be long away from Him, for
they *delight* in unburdening themselves to Him. Not only
does prayer call love into action, but through the direct an-
swers vouchsafed to our prayers, our love to God is increased—"I love the Lord, *because* He hath heard my voice
and my supplications" (Psa. 116:1). Again; prayer is designed by God to teach us the *value* of the blessings we have
sought from Him, and it causes us to rejoice the more
when He *has* bestowed upon us that for which we supplicate
Him.

Third, prayer is appointed by God for our seeking from
Him the things which we are in need of. But here a difficulty may present itself to those who have read carefully
the previous chapters of this book. If God has fore-ordained, before the foundation of the world, everything which
happens in time, what is the use of prayer? If it is true that
"of Him and through Him and to Him are *all things*"
(Rom. 11:36), then why pray? Ere replying directly to
these queries it should be pointed out how that there is just
as much reason to ask, What is the use of me coming to God
and telling Him what He already knows? wherein is the use
of me spreading before Him my need, seeing He is already

acquainted with it? as there is to object, What is the use of praying for anything when everything has been ordained beforehand by God? Prayer is not for the purpose of informing God, as if He were ignorant, (the Saviour expressly declared "for your Father knoweth what things ye have need of, before ye ask Him"—Matt. 6:8), but it is to acknowledge He *does* know what we are in need of. Prayer is not appointed for the furnishing of God with the knowledge of what we need, but it is designed as a confession to Him of *our sense* of the need. In this, as in everything, God's thoughts are not as ours. God requires that His gifts should be sought for. He designs to be *honored* by our asking, just as He is to be *thanked* by us after He has bestowed His blessing.

However, the question still returns on us, If God be the Predestinator of everything that comes to pass, and the Regulator of all events, then is not prayer a profitless exercise? A sufficient answer to these questions is, that God *bids* us to pray—"*Pray* without ceasing" (1 Thess. 5:17). And again, "men *ought* always to pray" (Luke 18:1). And further: Scripture declares that, "the prayer of faith shall save the sick", and, "the effectual fervent prayer of a righteous man availeth much" (Jas. 5:15, 16); while the Lord Jesus Christ—our perfect Example in all things—was pre-eminently a Man of Prayer. Thus, it is evident, that prayer is neither meaningless nor valueless. But still this does not *remove* the difficulty nor *answer* the question with which we started out. What then is the *relationship* between God's sovereignty and Christian prayer?

First of all, we would say with emphasis, that prayer is *not intended* to *change* God's purpose, nor is it to move Him to form fresh purposes. God has decreed that certain events *shall* come to pass, but He has also decreed that these events shall come to pass through the means He has appointed for their accomplishment. God has elected certain ones to be saved, but He has also decreed that these ones shall be saved *through* the preaching of the Gospel. The Gospel, then, is one of the appointed means for the working out of the eternal counsel of the Lord; and prayer is another. God has decreed the means as well as the end, and among the means is prayer. Even the prayers of His people are included in His eternal decrees. Therefore, instead of prayers being in vain, they are among the means through which God exercises His decrees. "If indeed all things happen by a blind chance, or a fatal necessity, prayers in that case could be of no moral efficacy, and of no use; but since they are regulated by the direction of Divine wisdom, prayers have a place in the order of events" (Haldane).

That prayers for the execution of the very things *decreed* by God are *not* meaningless, is clearly taught in the Scriptures. Elijah *knew* that God *was* about to give rain, but that did not prevent him from at once betaking himself to prayer, (Jas. 5:17, 18). Daniel "understood" by the writings of the prophets that the captivity was to last but seventy years, yet when these seventy years were almost ended, we are told that he "set his face unto the Lord God, *to seek* by prayer and supplications, with fasting and sackcloth and ashes" (Dan. 9:2, 3). God told the prophet Jeremiah "For I know the thoughts that I think toward you, saith the Lord, thoughts of peace, and not of evil, to give you an expected end"; but instead of adding, there is, therefore, no need for you to supplicate Me for these things, He said, "*Then* shall ye call upon Me, and ye shall go and pray unto Me, and I will hearken unto you" (Jer. 29:12).

Once more; in Ezek. 36 we read of the explicit, positive, and unconditional promises which God has made concerning the future restoration of Israel, yet in verse 37 of this same chapter we are told, "Thus saith the Lord God; *I will yet for this be enquired of* by the house of Israel, to do it for them"! Here then is *the* design of prayer: not that God's will may be *altered,* but that it may be *accomplished* in His own good time and way. It is because God *has* promised certain things, that we can ask for them with the full assurance of faith. It is God's purpose that His will shall be brought about by His own appointed means, and that He may do His people good upon *His own* terms, and that is, by the 'means' and 'terms' of entreaty and supplication. Did not the Son of God *know* for certain that after His death and resurrection He *would be* exalted by the Father? Assuredly He did. Yet we find Him *asking for* this very thing: "O Father, glorify Thou Me with Thine Own Self with the glory which I had with Thee before the world was"

(John 17:5)! Did not He know that none of His people could perish? yet He besought the Father to "keep" them (John 17:11)!

Finally; it should be said that God's will is immutable, and cannot be altered by our cryings. When the mind of God is not toward a people to do them good, it cannot be turned to them by the most fervent and importunate prayers of those who have the greatest interest in Him—"Then said the Lord unto me, Though Moses and Samuel stood before Me, *yet My mind could not be* toward this people: cast them out of My sight, and let them go forth" (Jer. 15:1). The prayers of Moses to enter the promised land is a parallel case.

Our views respecting prayer need to be revised and brought into harmony with the teaching of Scripture on the subject. The prevailing idea seems to be, that I come to God and *ask* Him for something that I want, and that I *expect* Him to give me that which I have asked. But this is a most dishonoring and degrading conception. The popular belief reduces God to a servant, *our* servant: doing our bidding, performing our pleasure, granting our desires. No; prayer is a coming to God, telling Him my *need,* committing my way unto the Lord, and leaving Him to deal with it as seemeth *Him* best. *This* makes my will subject to His, instead of, as in the former case, seeking to bring His will into subjection to mine. No prayer is pleasing to God unless the spirit actuating it is, *"not* my will, but thine be done". "When God bestows blessings on a praying people, it is not for the sake of their prayers, as if He was inclined and turned by them; but it is for His own sake, and of His own sovereign will and pleasure. Should it be said, to what purpose then is prayer? it is answered, This is the way and means God has appointed, for the communication of the blessing of His goodness to His people. For though He has purposed, provided, and promised them, yet He will be sought unto, to give them, and it is a duty and privilege to ask. When they are blessed with a spirit of prayer, it forebodes well, and looks as if God intended to bestow the good things asked, which should be asked always with submission to the will of God, saying, *Not my will but Thine be done"* (John Gill).

The distinction just noted above is of great practical importance for our peace of heart. Perhaps the one thing that exercises Christians as much as anything else is that of *unanswered* prayers. They have asked God for something: so far as they are able to judge, they have asked in faith believing they would receive that for which they had supplicated the Lord: and they have asked earnestly and repeatedly, *but* the answer has not come. The result is that, in many cases, faith in the efficacy of prayer becomes weakened, until hope gives way to despair and the closet is altogether neglected. Is it not so?

Now will it surprise our readers when we say that *every* real prayer of faith that has ever been offered to God *has been* answered? Yet we unhesitatingly affirm it. But in saying this we must refer back to our definition of prayer. Let us repeat it. Prayer is a coming to God, telling Him my *need* (or the need of others), committing my way unto the Lord, and then leaving Him to deal with the case as seemeth Him best. This leaves God to answer the prayer in whatever way He sees fit, and often, His answer may be the very opposite of what would be most acceptable to the flesh; yet, if we have *really LEFT* our need in His hands, it will be His *answer,* nevertheless. Let us look at two examples.

In John 11 we read of the sickness of Lazarus. The Lord "loved" him, but He was absent from Bethany. The sisters sent a messenger unto the Lord acquainting Him of their brother's condition. And note particularly *how* their appeal was worded—"Lord, behold, he whom Thou lovest is sick." That was all. They did not ask Him to heal Lazarus. They did not request Him to hasten at once to Bethany. They simply spread their need before Him, committed the case into His hands, and left Him to act as *He* deemed best! And what was our Lord's reply? Did He respond to their appeal and answer their mute request? Certainly He did, though not, perhaps, in the way they had hoped. He answered by abiding "two days still in the same place where He was" (John 11:6), and allowing Lazarus to die! But in this instance, that was not all. Later, He journeyed to Bethany and raised Lazarus from the dead. Our purpose in referring here to this case, is to

illustrate the proper attitude for the believer to take before
God in the hour of need. The next example will emphasize, rather, God's method of responding to His needy child.
Turn to 2 Cor. 12. The apostle Paul had been accorded
an unheard-of privilege. He had been transported into
Paradise. His ears have listened to and his eyes have gazed
upon that which no other mortal had heard or seen this side
of death. The wondrous revelation was more than the apostle could endure. He was in danger of becoming "puffed
up" by his extra-ordinary experience. Therefore, a thorn in
the flesh, the messenger of Satan, was sent to buffet him lest
he be exalted above measure. And the apostle spreads his
need before the Lord; he thrice beseeches Him that this
thorn in the flesh should be *removed*. Was his prayer answered? Assuredly, though not in the manner he had desired. The "thorn" was not removed, but grace was given to
bear it. The burden was not lifted, but strength was vouchsafed to carry it.

Does someone object that it is our privilege to do more
than spread our need before God? Are we reminded that
God has, as it were, given us a blank cheque and invited
us to fill it in? Is it said that the promises of God are all-in-
clusive, and that we may *ask God for what we will?* If
so, we must call attention to the fact that it is necessary to
compare scripture with scripture if we are to learn the full
mind of God on any subject, and that as this is done we discover God has *qualified* the promises given to praying souls
by saying, "If we ask anything *according to His will* He
heareth us" (1 John 5:14). Real prayer is communion with
God, so that there will be common thoughts between His
mind and ours. What is needed is for Him to fill our hearts
with *His* thoughts, and then His desires will become *our*
desires flowing back to Him. Here then is the meeting-place
between God's sovereignty and Christian prayer: If we ask
anything according to *His will* He heareth us, and if we do
not so ask, He *does not* hear us; as saith the apostle James,
"Ye ask, and receive not, *because ye ask amiss,* that ye might
consume it upon *your* lusts" or desires (4:3)

But did not the Lord Jesus tell His disciples, "Verily,
verily, I say unto you, *Whatsoever* ye shall ask the Father
in My name, He will give it you" (John 16:23)? He did;

but this promise does not give praying souls *carte blanche.*
These words of our Lord are in perfect accord with those
of the apostle John—"If we ask anything according to
His will He heareth us." What is it to ask "in the name of
Christ"? Surely it is very much more than a prayer form-
ula, the mere concluding of our supplications with the *words*
"in the name of Christ." To apply to God for anything in
the name of Christ, it must needs be in keeping with what
Christ is! To ask God in the name of Christ is as though
Christ Himself were the suppliant. *We can only ask God
for what Christ would ask.* To ask in the name of Christ,
is therefore, to *set aside* our own wills, accepting God's!

Let us now amplify our definition of prayer. What is
prayer? Prayer is not so much an act as it is an *attitude*—
an attitude of *dependency*, dependency upon God. Prayer
is a confession of creature weakness, yea, of helplessness.
Prayer is the acknowledgment of our need and the spreading
of it before God. We do not say that this is *all* there is in
prayer, it is not: but it *is* the essential, the primary element in
prayer. We freely admit that we are quite unable to give a
complete definition of prayer within the compass of a brief
sentence, or in any number of words. Prayer is both an attitude *and* an act, a *human* act, and yet there is the *Divine*
element in it too, and it is this which makes an exhaustive
analysis impossible as well as impious to attempt. But admitting this, we do insist again, that prayer is fundamentally
an attitude of dependency upon God. Therefore, prayer is
the very opposite of *dictating* to God. Because prayer is
an attitude of dependency, the one who really prays is *submissive,* submissive to the Divine will; and submission to the
Divine will means, that we are content for the Lord to supply our need according to the dictates of His own sovereign
pleasure. And hence it is that we say, *every prayer* that is
offered to God in *this* spirit is sure of meeting with an answer or response from Him.

Here then is the reply to our opening question, and the
scriptural solution to the seeming difficulty. Prayer is not
the requesting of God to alter His purpose or for Him to
form a new one. Prayer is the taking of an attitude of dependency upon God, the spreading of our need before Him,

the asking for those things which are in accordance with His will, and therefore there is nothing whatever *inconsistent* between Divine sovereignty and Christian prayer.

In closing this chapter we would utter a word of caution to safeguard the reader against drawing a false conclusion from what has been said. We have not here sought to *epitomize* the whole teaching of Scripture on the subject of prayer, nor have we even attempted to discuss in general the *problem* of prayer; instead, we have confined ourselves, more or less, to a consideration of the *relationship* between God's Sovereignty and Christian Prayer. What we have written is intended chiefly as a *protest* against much of the modern teaching, which so stresses the *human* element in prayer, that the Divine side is almost entirely lost sight of.

In Jer. 10:23 we are told "It is not in man that walketh to direct his steps" (cf. Prov. 16:9) ; and yet in many of his prayers, man impiously presumes to direct the Lord as to *His* way, and as to what *He* ought to do : even implying that if only *he* had the direction of the affairs of the world and of the Church, *he* would soon have things very different from what they are. This cannot be denied : for anyone with any spiritual discernment at all could not fail to detect this spirit in many of our modern prayer-meetings where the flesh holds sway. How slow we all are to learn the lesson that the haughty creature needs to be brought down to his knees and humbled into the dust. *And this is where the very act of prayer is intended to put us.* But man (in his usual perversity) turns the footstool into a throne, from whence he would fain direct the Almighty as to what He *ought* to do! giving the onlooker the impression that if God had half the compassion that those who pray (?) have, all would quickly be put right! Such is the arrogance of the old nature even in a child of God.

Our main purpose in this chapter has been to emphasize the need for submitting, in prayer, *our wills to God's*. But it must also be added, that prayer is much more than a pious exercise, and far otherwise than a mechanical performance. Prayer is, indeed, a Divinely appointed means whereby we may obtain from God the things we ask, *providing* we ask for those things which are in accord with *His will*. These

pages will have been penned in vain unless they lead both
writer and reader to cry with a deeper earnestness than here-
tofore, "Lord, *teach us* to pray" (Luke 11:1).

X

OUR ATTITUDE TOWARD GOD'S SOVEREIGNTY

"Even so, Father: for so it seemed good in Thy sight" (Matt. 11:26).

I N the present chapter we shall consider, somewhat briefly, the practical application to ourselves of the great truth which we have pondered in its various ramifications in earlier pages. In chapter twelve we shall deal more in detail with the *value* of this doctrine, but here we would confine ourselves to a definition of what ought to be our *attitude toward* the sovereignty of God.

Every truth that is revealed to us in God's Word is there not only for our information but also for our inspiration. The Bible has been given to us not to gratify an idle curiosity but to edify the souls of its readers. The sovereignty of God is something more than an abstract principle which explains the *rationale* of the Divine government: it is designed as a motive for godly fear, it is made known to us for the promotion of righteous living, it is revealed in order to bring into subjection our rebellious hearts. A true *recognition* of God's sovereignty humbles as nothing else does or can humble, and brings the heart into lowly submission before God, causing us to relinquish our own self-will and making us delight in the perception and performance of the Divine will.

When we speak of the sovereignty of God we mean very much more than the *exercise* of God's governmental power, though, of course, that is included in the expression. As we have remarked in an earlier chapter, the sovereignty of God means the Godhood of God. In its fullest and deepest meaning the title of this book signifies the *Character* and *Being* of the One whose pleasure is performed and whose will is executed. To truly *recognize* the sovereignty of God is, therefore, to gaze upon the Sovereign Himself. It is to come into the presence of the august "Majesty on High." It is to have a sight of the thrice holy God in His excellent glory. The *effects* of such a sight may be learned from those scriptures which describe the experience of different ones who obtained a view of the Lord God.

Mark the experience of Job—the one of whom the Lord

179

Himself said, "There is none like him in the earth, a perfect and an upright man, one that feareth God, and escheweth evil" (Job 1:8). At the close of the book which bears his name we are shown Job in the Divine presence, and how does he carry himself when brought face to face with Jehovah? Hear what he says: "I have heard of Thee by the hearing of the ear; but now mine eye seeth Thee: Wherefore *I abhor* myself, and *repent* in dust and ashes" (Job 42:5, 6). Thus, a sight of God, God revealed in awesome majesty, caused Job to abhor himself, and not only so, but to *abase* himself before the Almighty.

Take note of Isaiah. In the sixth chapter of his prophecy a scene is brought before us which has few equals even in Scripture. The prophet beholds the Lord upon the Throne, a Throne, "high and lifted up." Above this Throne stood the seraphim with veiled faces, crying, "Holy, holy, holy, is the Lord of hosts." What is the *effect* of this sight upon the prophet? We read, *"Then* said I, Woe is me! for I am undone; because I am a man of unclean lips, and I dwell in the midst of a people of unclean lips: for mine eyes have seen the King, the Lord of hosts" (Is. 6:5). A sight of the Divine *King* humbled Isaiah into the dust, bringing him, as it did, to a realization of his own nothingness.

Once more. Look at the prophet Daniel. Toward the close of his life this man of God beheld the Lord in theophanic manifestation. He appeared to His servant in human form "clothed in linen" and with loins "girded with fine gold"—symbolic of holiness and Divine glory. We read that, "His body also was like the beryl, and His face as the appearance of lightning, and His eyes as lamps of fire, and His arms and His feet like in color to polished brass, and the voice of His words like the voice of a multitude." Daniel then tells the effect this vision had upon him and those who were with him—"And I Daniel alone saw the vision: for the men that were with me saw not the vision; but a great quaking fell upon them, so that they fled to hide themselves. Therefore I was left alone, and saw this great vision, *and there remained no strength in me:* for my comeliness was turned in me into corruption, and I retained no strength. Yet heard I the voice of His words: and when I heard the voice of His words, then was I in a deep sleep *on my face,* and my face toward the ground" (Dan. 10:6-9). Once more, then, we are shown that to obtain a sight of the Sovereign God is for creature strength to wither up, and results in man being humbled into the dust before his Maker. What then ought to be *our* attitude toward the Supreme Sovereign? We reply,

I ONE OF GODLY FEAR.

Why is it that, today, the masses are so utterly unconcerned about spiritual and eternal things, and that they are lovers of pleasure more than lovers of God? Why is it that even on the battlefields multitudes were so indifferent to their soul's welfare? Why is it that defiance of heaven is becoming more open, more blatant, more daring? The answer is, Because "There is no fear of God before their eyes" (Rom. 3:18). Again; why is it that the authority of the Scriptures has been lowered so sadly of late? Why is it that even among those who profess to be the Lord's people there is so little real subjection to His Word, and that its precepts are so lightly esteemed and so readily set aside? Ah! what needs to be stressed to-day is that God is *a God to be feared.*

"The *fear of the Lord* is the beginning of wisdom" (Pro. 1:7). Happy the soul that has been awed by a view of God's majesty, that has had a vision of God's awful greatness, His ineffable holiness, His perfect righteousness, His irresistible power, His sovereign grace. Does someone say, "But it is only the unsaved, those *outside* of Christ, who need to *fear* God"? Then the sufficient answer is that the saved, those who are *in Christ,* are admonished to work out their own salvation with "fear and trembling." Time was, when it was the general custom to speak of a believer as a "God-fearing man"—that such an appellation has become nearly extinct only serves to show whither we have drifted. Nevertheless, it still stands written, "Like as a father pitieth his children, so the Lord pitieth them that *fear* Him" (Ps. 103:13)!

When we speak of godly fear, of course, we do not mean a servile fear, such as prevails among the heathen in connection with their gods. No; we mean that spirit which Jehovah is pledged to bless, that spirit to which the prophet referred when he said, "To this man will I (the Lord) look, even to him that is poor and of a contrite spirit, *and trembleth at My Word*" (Is. 66:2). It was this the apostle had in view when he wrote, "Honor all men. Love the brotherhood. *Fear God*. Honor the king" (1 Pet. 2:17). And nothing will foster this godly fear like a recognition of the sovereign Majesty of God.

What ought to be our attitude toward the Sovereignty of God? We answer again,

2   ONE OF IMPLICIT OBEDIENCE.

A sight of God leads to a realization of our littleness and nothingness, and issues in a sense of dependency and of casting ourselves upon God. Or, again; a view of the Divine Majesty promotes the spirit of godly fear and this, in turn, begets an obedient walk. Here then is the Divine antidote for the native evil of our hearts. Naturally, man is filled with a sense of his own importance, with his greatness and self-sufficiency; in a word, with pride and rebellion. But, as we remarked, the great corrective is to behold the Mighty God, for this alone will really humble him. Man will glory either in himself or in God. Man will live either to serve and please himself, or he will seek to serve and please the Lord. None can serve two masters.

Irreverence begets disobedience. Said the haughty monarch of Egypt, "Who is the Lord that I should obey His voice to let Israel go? *I know not the Lord;* neither will I let Israel go" (Ex. 5:2). To Pharaoh, the God of the Hebrews was merely *a* god, one among many, a powerless entity who needed not to be feared or served. How sadly mistaken he was, and how bitterly he had to pay for his mistake, he soon discovered; but what we are here seeking to emphasize is that, Pharaoh's defiant spirit was the fruit of irreverence, and this irreverence was the consequence of *his ignorance* of the majesty and authority of the Divine Being.

Now if irreverence begets disobedience, true reverence will produce and promote obedience. To realize that the Holy Scriptures are a revelation from the Most High, communicating to us His mind and defining for us His will, is the first step toward practical godliness. To recognize that

the Bible is *God's* Word, and that its precepts are the precepts of the Almighty, will lead us to see what an awful
thing it is to despise and ignore them. To receive the Bible
as addressed to our own souls, given to us by the Creator
Himself, will cause us to cry with the Psalmist, *"Incline my
heart unto Thy testimonies.* . . . Order my steps in Thy
Word" (Ps. 119:36, 133). Once the sovereignty of the Author of the Word is apprehended, it will no longer be a matter of picking and choosing from the precepts and statutes
of that Word, selecting those which meet with *our* approval;
but it will be seen that nothing less than an unqualified and
whole-hearted submission becomes the creature.

What ought to be our attitude toward the Sovereignty of
God? We answer, once more,

3 ONE OF ENTIRE RESIGNATION.

A true recognition of God's Sovereignty will exclude all
murmuring. This is self-evident, yet the thought deserves
to be dwelt upon. It is natural to murmur against afflictions
and losses. It is natural to complain when we are deprived
of those things upon which we had set our hearts. We are
apt to regard our possessions as ours unconditionally. We
feel that when we have prosecuted our plans with prudence
and diligence that we are *entitled* to success; that when by
dint of hard work we have accumulated a 'competence,' we
deserve to keep and enjoy it; that when we are surrounded
by a happy family, no power may lawfully enter the charmed
circle and strike down a loved one; and if in any of these
cases disappointment, bankruptcy, death, actually comes, the
perverted instinct of the human heart is to cry out against
God. But in the one who, by grace, has recognised God's
sovereignty, such murmuring is silenced, and instead, there
is a bowing to the Divine will, and an acknowledgment that
He has not afflicted us as sorely as we *deserve*.

A true recognition of God's sovereignty will avow God's
perfect right to do with us as He wills. The one who bows
to the pleasure of the Almighty will acknowledge His absolute right to do with us as seemeth Him good. If He chooses to send poverty, sickness, domestic bereavements, even
while the heart is bleeding at every pore, it will say, Shall
not the Judge of all the earth do right! Often there will

be a struggle, for the carnal mind remains in the believer
to the end of his earthly pilgrimage. But though there may
be a conflict within his breast, nevertheless, to the one who
has really yielded himself to this blessed truth, there will
presently be heard that Voice saying, as of old it said to the
turbulent Gennesareth, "Peace be still"; and the tempestuous flood within will be quieted and the subdued soul will
lift a tearful but confident eye to heaven and say, "Thy will
be done."

A striking illustration of a soul bowing to the sovereign
will of God is furnished by the history of Eli the high priest
of Israel. In 1 Samuel 3 we learn how God revealed to
the young child Samuel that He was about to slay Eli's two
sons for their wickedness, and on the morrow Samuel com-
municates this message to the aged priest. It is difficult
to conceive of more appalling intelligence for the heart of a
pious parent. The announcement that his child is going to be
stricken down by sudden death is, under any circumstances,
a great trial to any father, but to learn that his two sons—in
the prime of their manhood, and utterly *unprepared* to die
—were to be cut off by a Divine judgment, must have been
overwhelming. Yet, what was the effect upon Eli when he
learned from Samuel the tragic tidings? What reply did he
make when he heard the awful news? "And he said, It is
the Lord: *let Him do what seemeth Him good*" (1 Sam. 3:
18). And not another word escaped him. Wonderful submission! Sublime resignation! Lovely exemplification of
the power of Divine grace to control the strongest affections
of the human heart and subdue the rebellious will, bringing
it into unrepining acquiescence to the sovereign pleasure of
Jehovah.

Another example, equally striking, is seen in the life of
Job. As is well known, Job was one that feared God and
eschewed evil. If ever there was one who might reasonably
expect Divine providence to smile upon him—we speak as
a man—it was Job. Yet, how fared it with him? For a
time, the lines fell unto him in pleasant places. The Lord
filled his quiver by giving him seven sons and three daughters. He prospered him in his temporal affairs until he
owned great possessions. But of a sudden, the sun of life
was hidden behind dark clouds. In a single day Job lost not

only his flocks and herds, but his sons and daughters as well.
News arrived that his cattle had been carried off by robbers,
and his children slain by a cyclone. And how did he receive
this intelligence? Hearken to his sublime words: *"The Lord
gave, and the Lord hath taken away."* He bowed to the
sovereign will of Jehovah. He traced his afflictions back
to their First Cause. He looked behind the Sabeans who
had stolen his cattle, and beyond the winds that had destroyed his children, and saw *the hand of God.* But not
only did Job *recognise* God's sovereignty, he *rejoiced* in it,
too. To the words, "The Lord gave, and the Lord hath
taken away," he added, *"Blessed be the name of the Lord"*
(Job 1:21). Again we say, Sweet submission! Sublime
resignation!

A true recognition of God's sovereignty causes us to hold
our every plan in abeyance to God's will. The writer well
recalls an incident which occurred in England over twenty
years ago. Queen Victoria was dead, and the date for the
coronation of her eldest son, Edward, had been set for April
1902. In all the announcements which were sent out, two
little letters were omitted—D. V.—Deo Volente: God willing. Plans were made and all arrangements completed for
the most imposing celebrations that England had ever witnessed. Kings and emperors from all parts of the earth had
received invitations to attend the royal ceremony. The
Prince's proclamations were printed and displayed, but, so
far as the writer is aware, the letters D. V. were not found
on a single one of them. A most imposing programme had
been arranged, and the late Queen's eldest son was to be
crowned Edward the Seventh at Westminster Abbey at a
certain hour on a fixed day. *And then God intervened,* and
all man's plans were frustrated. A still small voice was
heard to say, "You have reckoned without Me," and Prince
Edward was stricken down with appendicitis, and his coronation postponed for months!

As remarked, a true recognition of God's sovereignty
causes us to hold *our* plans in abeyance to God's will. It
makes us recognise that the Divine Potter has absolute power over the clay and moulds it according to his own imperial
pleasure. It causes us to heed that admonition—now, alas!
so generally disregarded—"Go to now, ye that say, Today or

tomorrow *we will* go into such a city, and continue there a
year, and buy and sell, and get gain: Whereas ye know not
what shall be on the morrow. For what is your life? It is
even a vapor, that appeareth for a little time, and then van-
isheth away. For that ye *ought* to say, *If the Lord will*, we
shall live, and do this, or that" (Jas. 4:13-15). Yes, it is to
the *Lord's will* we must bow. It is for *Him* to say where I
shall live—whether in America or Africa. It is for *Him*
to determine under what circumstances I shall live—whether
amid wealth or poverty, whether in health or sickness. It is
for *Him* to say how long I shall live—whether I shall be cut
down in youth like the flower of the field, or whether I shall
continue for three score and ten years. To *really* learn this
lesson is, by grace, to attain unto a high form in the school
of God, and even when we think we have learnt it, we discover, again and again, that we have to relearn it.

4   ONE OF DEEP THANKFULNESS AND JOY.

The *heart's* apprehension of this most blessed truth of the
sovereignty of God, produces something far different than a
sullen bowing to the inevitable. The philosophy of this
perishing world knows nothing better than to "make the
best of a bad job". But with the Christian it should be far
other wise. Not only should the recognition of God's supremacy beget within us godly fear, implicit obedience, and
entire resignation, but it should cause us to say with the
Psalmist, "Bless the Lord, O my soul: and all that is within
me, bless His holy name". Does not the apostle say, "Giving
thanks *always* for all things unto God and the Father in the
name of our Lord Jesus Christ" (Eph. 5:20)? Ah, it is at
this point the state of our souls is so often put to the test.
Alas, there is so much self-will in each of us. When things
go as *we* wish them, we appear to be very grateful to God;
but what of those occasions when things go contrary to our
plans and desires?

We take it for granted when the real Christian takes a
train-journey that, upon reaching his destination, he devoutly returns thanks unto God—which, of course, argues that
He controls everything; otherwise, we ought to thank the
engine-driver, the stoker, the signalmen etc. Or, if in business, at the close of a good week, gratitude is expressed

unto the Giver of every good (temporal) and of every perfect (spiritual) gift—which again, argues that *He* directs all customers to your shop. So far, so good. Such examples occasion no difficulty. But imagine the opposites. Suppose my train was delayed for hours, did I fret and fume; suppose another train ran into it, and I am injured! Or, suppose I have had a poor week in business, or that lightning struck my shop and set it on fire, or that burglars broke in and rifled it—then what: do I see the hand of God in *these* things?

Take the case of Job once more. When loss after loss came his way, what did he do? Bemoan his "bad luck"? Curse the robbers? Murmur against God? No; he bowed before Him in worship. Ah, dear reader, there is no real rest for your poor heart until you learn to see the hand of God in everything. But for that, *faith* must be in constant exercise. And what is faith? A blind credulity? A fatalistic acquiesence? No, far from it. Faith is a resting on the sure Word of the living God, and therefore says, "We *know* that all things work together for good to them that love God, to them who are the called according to His purpose" (Rom. 8:28); and therefore faith will give thanks "always for all things". Operative faith will "Rejoice in the Lord *alway*" (Phil. 4:4).

We turn now to mark how this recognition of God's sovereignty which is expressed in godly fear, implicit obedience, entire resignation, and deep thankfulness and joy was supremely and perfectly exemplified by the Lord Jesus Christ.

In all things the Lord Jesus has left us an example that we should follow His steps. But is this true in connection with the first point made above? Are the words "godly fear" ever linked with *His* peerless name? Remembering that 'godly fear' signifies not a servile terror, but rather a filial subjection and reverence, and remembering too that "the fear of the Lord is the beginning of wisdom," would it not rather be strange if no mention at all were made of 'godly fear' in connection with the One who was wisdom incarnate! What a wonderful and precious word is that of Heb. 5:7—"Who in the days of His flesh, having offered up prayers and supplications with strong crying and tears unto Him that was able to save Him from death, and having been heard *for His godly fear"* (R. V.). What was it but *'godly fear'* which caused the Lord Jesus to be "subject" unto Mary and Joseph in the days of His childhood? Was it not 'godly fear'—a filial subjection to and reverence for God—that we see displayed, when we read, "And He came to Nazareth where He had been brought up: and, *as His custom was,* He went into the synagogue on the Sabbath day" (Luke 4:16)? Was it not 'godly fear' which caused the incarnate Son to say, when tempted by Satan to fall down and worship him, "It is written, thou shalt worship *the Lord thy God* and Him only shalt thou serve"? Was it not 'godly fear' which moved Him to say to the cleansed leper, "Go thy way, shew thyself to the priest, and offer the gift that Moses *commanded"* (Matt. 8:4)? But why multiply illustrations?*

How perfect was the *obedience* that the Lord Jesus offered to God the Father! And in reflecting upon this let us not lose sight of that wondrous grace which caused Him, who was in the very form of God, to stoop so low as to take upon Him the form of a *Servant,* and thus be brought into the place where obedience was becoming. As the perfect Servant He yielded complete obedience to His Father. How absolute and entire that obedience was we may learn from the words, He "became *obedient unto death,* even the death of the Cross" (Phil. 2:8). That this was a conscious and intelligent obedience is clear from His own language—"Therefore doth My Father love Me, because I lay down My life, that I might take it again. No man taketh it from Me, but I lay it down of Myself. I have power to lay it down, and I have power to take it again. *This commandment* have I received from My Father" (John 10:17, 18).

And what shall we say of the absolute *resignation* of the Son to the Father's will—what, but, between Them there was entire oneness of accord. Said He, "For I came down from heaven, not to do Mine own will, but the will of Him that sent Me" (John 6:38), and how fully He substantiated that claim all know who have attentively followed His path as marked out in the Scriptures. Behold Him in Gethsemane! The bitter 'cup,' held in the Father's hand, is presented

---

*Note how Old Testament prophecy also declared that "the Spirit of the Lord" should "rest upon Him, the spirit of wisdom and understanding, the spirit of counsel and might, the spirit of knowledge and of *the fear of the Lord"* (Isaiah 11:1, 2).

to His view. Mark well His attitude. *Learn* of Him who was meek and lowly in heart. Remember that there in the Garden we see the Word become flesh—a perfect Man. His body is quivering at every nerve, in contemplation of the physical sufferings which await Him; His holy and sensitive nature is shrinking from the horrible indignities which shall be heaped upon Him; His heart is breaking at the awful "reproach" which is before Him; His spirit is greatly troubled as He foresees the terrible conflict with the Power of Darkness; and above all, and supremely, His soul is filled with horror at the thought of being separated from God Himself—thus and there He pours out His soul to the Father, and with strong crying and tears He sheds, as it were, great drops of blood. And now observe and listen. Still the beating of thy heart, and hearken to the words which fall from His blessed lips—"Father, if *Thou* be willing, remove this cup from Me: *nevertheless,* not My will, but *Thine* be done" (Luke 22:42). Here is submission personified. Here is resignation to the pleasure of a sovereign God superlatively exemplified. And He has left us an example that we should follow His steps. He who was God became man, and was tempted in all points like as we are—sin apart—to show us *how* to wear *our* creature nature!

Above we asked, What shall we say of Christ's absolute resignation to the Father's will? We answer further, This, —that here, as everywhere, He was unique, peerless. In all things He has the pre-eminence. In the Lord Jesus there was no rebellious will to be broken. In His heart there was nothing to be subdued. Was not this one reason why, in the language of prophecy, He said, "I am a worm, and no man" (Ps. 22:6)—*a worm has no power of resistance!* It was because in Him there *was* no resistance that He could say, "*My meat* is to do the will of Him that sent Me" (John 4:34). Yea, it was because He was in perfect accord with the Father in all things that He said, "*I delight* to do Thy will, O God; yea, Thy law is within My heart" (Ps. 40:8). Note the last clause here and behold *His* matchless excellency. God has to *put* His laws into *our* minds, and *write* them in *our* hearts (see Heb. 8:10), but His law was *already* in *Christ's* heart!

What a beautiful and striking illustration of Christ's

thankfulness and joy is found in Matt. 11. There we behold,
first, the failure in the faith of His forerunner (vv. 22, 23).
Next, we learn of the discontent of the people: satisfied neither with Christ's joyous message, nor with John's solemn
one (vv. 16-20). Third, we have the non-repentance of those
favoured cities in which our Lord's mightiest works were
done (vv. 21-24). And then we read, *"At that time* Jesus
answered and said, I *thank* Thee, O Father, Lord of heaven
and earth, because Thou *hast* hid these things from the wise
and prudent, and hast revealed them unto babes" (v. 25)!
Note the parallel passage in Luke 10:21 opens by saying, "In
that hour Jesus *rejoiced* in spirit, and said, I thank Thee"
etc. Ah, here was submission in its purest form. Here was
One by which the worlds were made, yet, in the days of His
humiliation, and in the face of His rejection, thankfully
and joyously bowing to the will of the "Lord of heaven and
earth".

What ought to be our attitude towards God's sovereignty?
Finally,

5 ONE OF ADORING WORSHIP.

It has been well said that "true worship is based upon
recognised GREATNESS, and greatness is superlatively
seen in Sovereignty, and at no other footstool will men
really worship" (J. B. Moody). In the presence of the Divine King upon His throne even the seraphim 'veil their
faces.'

Divine sovereignty is not the sovereignty of a tyrannical
Despot, but the exercised pleasure of One who is infinitely
wise and good! Because God is infinitely wise He *cannot*
err, and because He is infinitely righteous He *will not* do
wrong. Here then is the *preciousness* of this truth. The
mere fact itself that God's will is irresistible and irreversible
fills me with fear, but once I realise that God wills only that
which is good, my heart is made to rejoice.

Here then is the final answer to the question of this
chapter—What ought to be our attitude toward the sovereignty of God? The becoming attitude for us to take
is that of godly fear, implicit obedience, and unreserved
resignation and submission. But not only so: the recog-

nition of the sovereignty of God, and the realization that the Sovereign Himself is my *Father,* ought to overwhelm the heart and cause me to bow before Him in adoring worship. At all times I must say, "Even so, Father, for *so* it seemeth *good* in Thy sight." We conclude with an example which well illustrates our meaning.

Some two hundred years ago the saintly Madam Guyon, after ten years spent in a dungeon lying far below the surface of the ground, lit only by a candle at meal-times, wrote these words,

> "A little bird I am,
> Shut from the fields of air;
> Yet in my cage I sit and sing
> To Him who placed me there;
> Well pleased a prisoner to be,
> *Because, my God, it pleases Thee.*
>
> Nought have I else to do
> I sing the whole day long;
> And He whom most I love to please,
> Doth listen to my song;
> He caught and bound my wandering wing
> But still He bends to hear me sing.
>
> My cage confines me round;
> Abroad I cannot fly;
> But though my wing is closely bound,
> My heart's at liberty.
> My prison walls cannot control
> The flight, the freedom of the soul.
>
> Ah! it is good to soar
> These bolts and bars above,
> To Him *whose purpose I adore,*
> Whose Providence I love;
> And in Thy mighty will to find
> The joy, the freedom of the mind."

XI

DIFFICULTIES AND OBJECTIONS

*"Yet ye say, The way of the Lord is not equal.
Hear now, O house of Israel; Is not My way equal?
are not your ways unequal?"* (Ezekiel 18:25).

A CONVENIENT point has been reached when we may now examine, more definitely, some of the difficulties encountered and the objections which might be advanced against what we have written in previous pages. The author deemed it better to reserve these for a separate consideration, rather than deal with them as he went along, requiring as that would have done the breaking of the course of thought and destroying the strict unity of each chapter, or else cumbering our pages with numerous and lengthy footnotes.

That there *are* difficulties involved in an attempt to set forth the truth of God's sovereignty is readily acknowledged. The hardest thing of all, perhaps, is to maintain the *balance* of truth. It is largely a matter of *perspective*. That God is sovereign is explicitly declared in Scripture: that man is a responsible creature is also expressly affirmed in Holy Writ. To define the relationship of these two truths, to fix the dividing line betwixt them, to show exactly where they meet, to exhibit the perfect consistency of the one with the other, is the weightiest task of all. Many have openly declared that it is *impossible* for the finite mind to harmonize them. Others tell us it is not necessary or even wise to attempt it. But, as we have remarked in an earlier chapter, it seems to us more honoring to God to seek in His Word the solution to every problem. What is impossible to man is possible with God, and while we grant that the finite mind is limited in its reach, yet, we remember that the Scriptures are given to us that the man of God may be *"thoroughly* furnished," and if we approach their study in the spirit of humility and of expectancy, then, according unto our *faith* will it be unto us.

As remarked above, the hardest task in this connection is to preserve the balance of truth while insisting on *both* the sovereignty of God and the responsibility of the creature. To some of our readers it may appear that in pressing the sovereignty of God to the lengths we have, man is reduced

193

to a mere puppet. Hence, to guard against this, they would *modify* their definitions and statements relating to God's sovereignty, and thus seek to blunt the keen edge of what is so offensive to the carnal mind. Others, while refusing to weigh the evidence that we have adduced in support of our assertions, may raise objections which to their minds are sufficient to dispose of the whole subject. We would not waste time in the effort to refute objections made in a carping and contentious spirit, but we *are* desirous of meeting fairly the *difficulties* experienced by those who are anxious to obtain a fuller knowledge of the truth. Not that we deem ourselves able to give a satisfactory and final answer to every question that might be asked. Like the reader, the writer knows but "in part" and sees through a glass "darkly." All that we can do is to examine these difficulties in the light we now have, in dependence upon the Spirit of God that we may follow on to know the Lord better.

We propose now to retrace our steps and pursue the same order of thought as that followed up to this point. As a part of our *"definition"* of God's sovereignty we affirmed: "To say that God is sovereign is to declare that He is the Almighty, the Possessor of all power in heaven and earth, so that none can defeat His counsels, thwart His purpose, or resist His will. . . . The sovereignty of the God of Scripture is absolute, irresistible, infinite." To put it now in its strongest form, we insist that God does *as* He pleases, *only* as He pleases, *always* as He pleases: that whatever takes place in time is but the outworking of that which He decreed in eternity. In proof of this assertion we appeal to the following scriptures—"But our God is in the heavens: He hath done *whatsoever* He hath pleased" (Ps. 115:3). "For the Lord of hosts hath purposed, *and who shall disannul it?* and His hand is stretched out, and who shall turn it back?" (Is. 14:27). "And all the inhabitants of the earth are reputed as nothing: and He doeth according to His will in the army of heaven, and among the inhabitants of the earth: and *none* can stay His hand or say unto Him, What doest thou?" (Dan. 4:35). "For of Him, and through Him, and to Him, *are all things:* to whom be glory for ever. Amen" (Rom. 11:36).

The above declarations are so plain and positive that any

comments of ours upon them would simply be darkening counsel by words without knowledge. Such express statements as those just quoted, are so sweeping and so dogmatic that all controversy concerning the subject of which they treat ought for ever to be at an end. Yet, rather than receive them at their face value, every device of carnal ingenuity is resorted to so as to neutralize their force. For example, it has been asked, If what we see in the world today is but the outworking of God's eternal purpose, if God's counsel *is NOW* being accomplished, then why did our Lord teach His disciples to pray, "Thy will *be done on earth* as it is in heaven"? Is it not a clear implication from these words that God's will is *not* now being done on earth? The answer is very simple. The emphatic word in the above clause is "as." God's will *is* being done on earth today, if it is not, then our earth is not subject to God's rule, and if it is not subject to His rule then He is not, as Scripture proclaims Him to be, "The Lord of all the earth" (Josh. 3:13). But God's will is not being done on earth *as it is* in heaven. *How* is God's will "done in heaven"?—consciously and joyfully. How is it "done on earth"?—for the most part, unconsciously and sullenly. In heaven the angels perform the bidding of their Creator intelligently and gladly, but on earth the unsaved among men accomplish His will blindly and in ignorance. As we have said in earlier pages, when Judas betrayed the Lord Jesus and when Pilate sentenced Him to be crucified, they had no conscious intention of fulfilling God's decrees yet, nevertheless, unknown to themselves they *did* do so!

But again. It has been objected: If everything that happens on earth is the fulfilling of the Almighty's pleasure, if God has fore-ordained—before the foundation of the world —everything which comes to pass in human history, then why do we read in Gen. 6:6, "It *repented* the Lord that He had made man on the earth, and it *grieved* Him at His heart"? Does not this language intimate that the antediluvians had followed a course which their Maker had not marked out for them, and that in view of the fact they had "corrupted" their way upon the earth, the Lord *regretted* that He had ever brought such a creature into existence? Ere drawing such a conclusion let us note what is *involved* in such an inference. If the words "It repented the Lord that He had made man" are regarded in an *absolute* sense, then God's *omniscience* would be denied, for in such a case the course followed by man must have been *un*-foreseen by God in the day that He created him. Therefore it must be evident to every reverent soul that this language bears some other meaning. We submit that the words, "It *repented* the Lord" is an *accommodation* to our finite intelligence, and in saying this we are not seeking to escape a difficulty or *cut* a knot, but are advancing an interpretation which we shall seek to show is in perfect accord with the general trend of Scripture.

The Word of God is addressed to *men*, and therefore it speaks the language of men. Because we cannot rise to God's level He, in grace, comes down to ours and converses with us in our own speech. The apostle Paul tells us of how he was "caught up into Paradise and heard unspeakable words which it is not possible (margin) to utter" (2 Cor. 12:4) Those on earth could not understand the vernacular of heaven. The finite cannot comprehend the Infinite, hence the Almighty deigns to couch His revelation in terms we may understand. It is for this reason the Bible contains many anthropomorphisms—i.e., representations of God in the form of man. God is Spirit, yet the Scriptures speak of Him as having eyes, ears, nostrils, breath, hands etc., which is surely an accommodation of terms brought down to the level of human comprehension.

Again; we read in Gen. 18:20, 21, "And the Lord said, Because the cry of Sodom and Gomorrah is great, and because their sin is very grievous, I will go down now, *and see whether they have done* altogether according to the cry of it, which is come up unto Me; and if not, I will know." Now, manifestly, this is an anthropologism—God, speaking in human language. God *knew* the conditions which prevailed in Sodom, and His eyes had witnessed its fearful sins, yet He is pleased to use terms here that are taken from our own vocabulary.

Again; in Gen. 22:12 we read, "And He (God) said, Lay not thine hand upon the lad, neither do thou anything unto him: for *now* I know that thou fearest God, seeing thou hast not withheld thy son, thine only son, from Me." Here again, God is speaking in the language of men, for *He* "knew" *before* He tested Abram exactly how the patriarch would act. So too the expression used *of God* so often in Jeremiah (7:13 etc.), of Him "rising up early", is manifestly an accommodation of terms.

Once more: in the parable of the vineyard Christ Himself represents its Owner as saying, "Then said the Lord of the vineyard, What shall I do? I will send My beloved Son: *it may be* they will reverence Him when they see Him" (Luke 20:13), and yet, it is certain that God knew perfectly well that the "husbandmen" of the vineyard—the Jews—would *not* "reverence His Son" but, instead, would "despise and reject" Him, as His own Word had declared!

In the same way we understand the words in Gen. 6:6— "It *repented* the Lord that He had made man on the earth" —as an accommodation of terms to human comprehension. This verse does not teach that God was confronted with an unforeseen contingency, and therefore *regretted* that He had made man, but it expresses the *abhorrence* of a holy God at the awful wickedness and corruption into which man had fallen. Should there be any doubt remaining in the minds of our readers as to the legitimacy and soundness of our interpretation, a direct appeal to Scripture should instantly and entirely remove it—"The Strength of Israel (a Divine title) will not lie nor repent: *for He is not a man, that He should repent*" (1 Sam. 15:29)! "Every good and perfect gift is from above, and cometh down from the Father of lights, *with Whom is no variableness, neither shadow of turning*" (Jas. 1:17)!

Careful attention to what we have said above will throw light on numerous other passages which, if we ignore their *figurative* character and fail to note that God *applies to Himself* human modes of expression, will be obscure and perplexing. Having commented at such length upon Gen. 6:6 there will be no need to give such a detailed exposition of other passages which belong to the same class, yet, for the benefit of those of our readers who may be anxious for us to examine several other scriptures, we turn to one or two more.

One scripture which we often find cited in order to overthrow the teaching advanced in this book is our Lord's lament over Jerusalem: "O Jerusalem, Jerusalem, thou that killest the prophets, and stonest them that are sent unto thee, *how often would I* have gathered thy children together, even as a hen gathereth her chickens under her wings, *and ye would not!*" (Matt. 23:37). The question is asked, Do not these words show that the Saviour *acknowledged the defeat* of His mission, that as a people the Jews resisted all His gracious overtures toward them? In replying to this question, it should first be pointed out that our Lord is here referring not so much to His *own* mission, as He is upbraiding the Jews for having *in all ages* rejected His grace—this is clear from His reference to the "prophets." The Old Testament bears full witness of how graciously and patiently Jehovah dealt with His people, and with what extreme obstinacy, from first to last, they refused to be "gathered" unto Him, and how in the end He (temporarily) abandoned them to follow their own devices, yet, as the same Scriptures declare, the counsel of God *was not frustrated* by their wickedness, for it had been foretold (and therefore, decreed) by Him—see, for example, 1 Kings 8:33.

Matthew 23:37 may well be compared with Isaiah 65:2 where the Lord says, "I have spread out My hands all the day unto a rebellious people, which walketh in a way that was not good, after their own thoughts." But, it may be asked, Did God seek to do that which was in opposition to His own eternal purpose? In words borrowed from Calvin we reply, "Though to our apprehension the will of God is manifold and various, yet He does not in Himself will things at variance with each other, but astonishes our faculties with His various and *'manifold'* wisdom, according to the expression of Paul, till we shall be enabled to understand that He mysteriously wills what now seems contrary to His will." As a further illustration of the same principle we would refer the reader to Isa. 5:1-4: "Now will I sing to my well Beloved a song of my Beloved touching His vineyard. My well Beloved hath a vineyard in a very fruitful hill: And He fenced it, and gethered out the stones thereof, and planted it with the choicest vine and built a tower in the midst of it, and also made a winepress therein: and *He looked that it should bring forth grapes,* and it brought forth wild grapes. And now, O inhabitants of Jerusalem, and men of Judah, judge, I pray you, betwixt Me and My vineyard. *What could have been done more* to My vineyard, that I have not done in it? wherefore, when I looked that it should bring forth grapes, brought it forth wild grapes?" Is it not plain from this language that God reckoned Himself to have done enough for Israel to warrant an expectation—speaking after the manner of men—of better returns? Yet, is it not equally evident when Jehovah says here "He looked that it should bring forth grapes" that He is accommodating Himself to a form of finite expression? And, so also when He says "What could have been done more to My vineyard, that I have not done in it?" we need to take note that in the previous enumeration of what He *had* done—the "fencing" etc.—He refers *only* to *external* privileges, means, and opportunities, which had been bestowed upon Israel, for, of course, He *could* even then have taken away from them their stony heart and given them a new heart, even a heart of flesh, as He will yet do, had He so pleased.

Perhaps we should link up with Christ's lament over Jerusalem in Matt. 23:37, His tears over the City, recorded in Luke 19:41: "He beheld the city, and wept over it." In the verses which immediately follow, we learn *what* it was that occasioned His tears: "Saying, If thou hadst known, even thou, at least in this thy day, the things which belong unto thy peace! but now they are hid from thine eyes. For the days shall come upon thee, that thine enemies shall cast a trench about thee, and compass thee round, and keep thee in on every side." It was the prospect of the fearful judgment which Christ knew was impending. But did those tears make manifest a disappointed God? Nay, verily. Instead, they displayed a perfect Man. The Man Christ Jesus was no emotionless stoic, but One "filled with compassion." Those tears expressed the sinless sympathies of His real and pure humanity. Had He *not* "wept", He had been less than human. Those "tears" were one of many proofs that "in *all* things it behoved Him to be made like unto His brethren" (Heb. 2:17).

In chapter one we have affirmed that God is sovereign in the exercise of His *love,* and in saying this we are fully aware that many will strongly resent the statement and that, furthermore, what we have now to say will probably meet with more criticism than anything else advanced in this book.

Nevertheless, we must be true to our convictions of what
we believe to be the teaching of Holy Scripture, and we can
only ask our readers to examine diligently in the light of
God's Word what we here submit to their attention.

One of the most popular beliefs of the day is that God
loves everybody, and the very fact that it is so *popular* with
all classes ought to be enough to arouse the suspicions of
those who are subject to the Word of Truth. God's Love toward *all* His creatures is the fundamental and favorite ten-
et of Universalists, Unitarians, Theosophists, Christian Sci-
entists, Spiritualists, Russellites, etc. No matter how a man
may live—in open defiance of Heaven, with no concern
whatever for his soul's eternal interests, still less for God's
glory, dying, perhaps with an oath on his lips,—notwithstanding, God loves him, we are told. So widely has this
dogma been proclaimed, and so *comforting* is it to the heart
which is at enmity with God, we have little hope of convinc-
ing many of their error. That God loves everybody, is, we
may say, quite a *modern* belief. The writings of the church-
fathers, the Reformers or the Puritans will (we believe)
be searched in vain for any such concept. Perhaps the late
D. L. Moody—captivated by Drummond's "The Greatest
Thing in the World"—did more than anyone else last century to popularize this concept.

It has been customary to say God loves the sinner, though
He hates his sin.* But that is a meaningless distinction.
What is there in a sinner but sin? Is it not true that his
"whole head is sick", and his *"whole* heart faint", and that
"from the sole of the foot even unto the head there is *no
soundness"* in him? (Isa. 1:5, 6). Is it true that God *loves*
the one who is *despising* and rejecting His blessed Son?
God is Light as well as Love, and therefore His love must be
a *holy* love. To tell the Christ-rejector that God loves him is
to cauterise his conscience, as well as to afford him a sense
of security in his sins. The fact is, that the love of God,
is a truth for the saints only, and to present it to the enemies
of God is to take the children's bread and cast it to the dogs.
With the exception of John 3:16, not once in the four Gos-

---

*Rom. 5:8 is addressed to *saints,* and the "we" are the same ones
as those spoken of in 8:29, 30.

pels do we read of the Lord Jesus—the perfect Teacher—
telling sinners that God loved them! In the book of Acts,
which records the evangelistic labors and messages of the
apostles, God's love is never referred to at all! But, when
we come to the Epistles, which are addressed to *the saints,*
we have a full presentation of this precious truth—God's
love *for His own.* Let us seek to *rightly* divide the Word
of God and then we shall not be found taking truths which
are addressed to believers and *mis*-applying them to unbelievers. That which sinners need to have brought before
them is, the ineffable holiness, the exacting righteousness,
the inflexible justice and the terrible wrath of God. Risk-
ing the danger of being mis-understood, let us say—and
we wish we could say it to every evangelist and preacher
in the country—there is far too much presenting of Christ
to sinners today (by those sound in the faith), and far too
little showing sinners their *need* of Christ, i.e., their absolutely ruined and lost condition, their imminent and awful
danger of suffering the wrath to come, the fearful guilt resting upon them in the sight of God—to present Christ to
those who have never been shown their *need* of Him, seems
to us to be guilty of casting pearls before swine.*

If it be true that God loves every member of the human
family then why did our Lord tell His disciples, "He that
hath My commandments, and keepeth them, he it is that
loveth Me: and he that loveth Me shall be loved of My Father. . . . . If a man love Me, he will keep My words:
and My Father will love him" (John 14:21, 23)? Why say
"he that loveth Me shall be loved of My Father" if the Father loves *everybody?* The same limitation is found in Prov.
8:17: "I love them that love Me." Again; we read, "Thou
hatest all *workers* of iniquity"—not merely the works of
iniquity. Here, then, is a flat repudiation of present teach-

---

*Concerning the rich young ruler of whom it is said Christ *"loved
him"* (Mark 10:21), we fully believe that he was one of God's elect,
and was "saved" sometime after his interview with our Lord. Should
it be said this is an arbitrary assumption and assertion which lacks
anything in the Gospel record to substantiate it, we reply, It is written, "Him that cometh to Me I will in no wise cast out," and this man
certainly *did* "come" to Him. Compare the case of Nicodemus. He,
too, came to Christ, yet there is nothing in John 3 which intimates he
was a saved man when the interview closed; nevertheless, we know
from his later life that *he* was not "cast out."

ing that, God hates sin but loves the sinner; Scripture says, "Thou *hatest* all *workers* of iniquity" (Ps. 5:5)! "God is *angry* with the wicked every day." "He that believeth not the Son shall not see life, but *the wrath of God*"—not *"shall* abide," but even now—"abideth on him" (Ps. 5:5; 7:11; John 3:36). Can God "love" the one on whom His "wrath" abides? Again; is it not evident that the words "The love of God *which is in Christ Jesus*" (Rom. 8:39) mark a limitation, both in the sphere and objects of His love? Again; is it not plain from the words "Jacob have I loved, *but Esau have I hated*" (Rom. 9:13) that God does *not* love everybody? Again; it is written, "For *whom* the Lord loveth He chasteneth, and scourgeth *every son* whom He receiveth" (Heb. 12:6). Does not this verse teach that God's love is *restricted* to the members of His own family? If He loves all men without exception, then the distinction and limitation here mentioned is quite meaningless. Finally, we would ask, Is it conceivable that God will love the damned in the Lake of Fire? Yet, if He loves them now He will do so then, seeing that His love knows no change—He is *"without variableness* or shadow of turning"!

Turning now to John 3:16, it should be evident from the passages just quoted, that this verse will not bear the construction usually put upon it. "God so loved *the world*". Many suppose that this means, The entire human race. But "the entire human race," includes all mankind from Adam till the close of the earth's history: it reaches backward as well as forward! Consider, then, the history of mankind *before* Christ was born. Unnumbered millions lived and died before the Saviour came to the earth, lived here "having no hope and without God in the world", and therefore passed out into an eternity of woe. If God "loved" *them,* where is the slightest proof thereof? Scripture declares, "Who (God) in times past (from the tower of Babel till after Pentecost) suffered *all* nations to walk in their own ways" (Acts 14:16). Scripture declares that, "And even as they did not like to retain God in their knowledge, *God gave them over* to a reprobate mind, to do those things which are not convenient" (Rom. 1:28). To Israel God said, "You *only* have I known of all the families of the earth" (Amos 3:2). In view of these plain passages, who will be so foolish as to insist that God in the past loved all mankind! The same applies with equal force to the future. Read through the book of Revelation, noting especially chapters 8 to 19, where we have described the judgments which will yet be poured out from heaven on this earth. Read of the fearful woes, the frightful plagues, the vials of God's wrath, which shall be emptied on the wicked. Finally, read the 20th chapter of the Revelation, the great white throne judgment, and see if you can discover there the slightest trace of *love*.

But the objector comes back to John 3:16 and says, "World *means world*". True, but we have shown that "the world" does not mean the whole human family. The fact is that "the world" is used in a *general* way. When the brethren of Christ said, "Shew Thyself to *the world*" (John 7: 4), did they mean "shew Thyself to *all mankind*"? When the Pharisees said, "Behold, *the world* is gone after Him" (John 12:19), did they mean that "*all the human family*" were flocking after Him? When the apostle wrote, "Your faith is spoken of throughout *the whole world*" (Rom. 1:8), did he mean that the faith of the saints at Rome was the subject of conversation by every man, woman, and child on the earth? When Rev. 13:3 informs us that "*all the world* wondered after the beast*", are we to understand that there will be no exceptions? What of the godly Jewish Remnant, who will be slain (Rev. 20:4) rather than submit? These, and other passages which might be quoted, show that the term "the world" often has a *relative* rather than an *absolute* force.

Now the first thing to note in connection with John 3:16 is that our Lord was there speaking to Nicodemus—a man who believed that God's mercies were *confined* to his own nation. Christ there announced that God's love in giving His Son had a larger object in view, that it flowed beyond the boundary of Palestine, reaching out to "regions beyond". In other words, this was Christ's announcement that God had a purpose of grace toward Gentiles as well as Jews. "God so loved the world", then, signifies, God's love is *international* in its scope. But does this mean that God loves every individual among the Gentiles? Not necessarily, for as we have seen, the term "world" is general rather than specific, relative rather than absolute. The term "world"

in itself is not conclusive.   To ascertain *who* are the objects
of God's love other passages where *His love* is mentioned
must be consulted.

In 2 Peter 2:5 we read of "the world of the *ungodly*".   If
then, there is a world of the *ungodly* there must also be a
world of the *godly*.   It is the latter who are in view in the
passages we shall now briefly consider.   "For the bread of
God is He which cometh down from heaven, and giveth
life unto *the world*" (John 6:33).   Now mark it well, Christ
did not say, "*offereth* life unto the world", but "giveth".
What is the difference between the two terms?   This: a
thing which is "offered" may be *refused,* but a thing "given",
necessarily implies its *acceptance.*   If it is not *accepted,* it
is *not* "given", it is simply proffered.   Here, then, is a scripture that positively states Christ giveth life (spiritual, eternal
life) "unto *the world.*"   Now He does not *give* eternal life
to the "world of the ungodly" for they will not have it, they
do not want it.   Hence, we are *obliged* to understand the
reference in John 6:33 as being to "the world of the godly",
i.e., God's own people.

One more: in 2 Cor. 5:19 we read, "To wit that God was
in Christ, reconciling *the world* unto Himself".   What is
meant by this is clearly defined in the words immediately
following, "not imputing *their* trespasses unto them".   Here
again, "the world" *cannot* mean "the world of the ungodly",
for *their* "trespasses" *are* "imputed" to them, as the judgment of the Great White Throne will yet show.   But 2 Cor.
5:19 plainly teaches there *is* a "world" which *are* "reconciled", reconciled unto God, because their trespasses are *not*
reckoned to their account, having been borne by their Substitute.   Who then are they?   Only one answer is fairly
possible—the world of God's people!

In like manner, the "world" in John 3:16 must, in the
final analysis, refer to the world of God's people. *Must*
we say, for there is no other alternative *solution.*   It cannot
mean the whole human race, for one half of the race was
already in hell when Christ came to earth.   It is unfair to
insist that it means every human being now living, for every
other passage in the New Testament where God's *love* is
mentioned *limits it to His own people*—search and see!
The objects of God's love in John 3:16 are precisely the

same as the objects of Christ's love in John 13:1: "Now before the Feast of the Passover, when Jesus knew that His time was come, that He should depart out of this world unto the Father, having *loved His own* which were in the world, He *loved them* unto the end". We may admit that our interpretation of John 3:16 is no novel one invented by us, but one almost uniformly given by the Reformers and Puritans, and many others since them.*

Coming now to chapter three—The Sovereignty of God in Salvation—innumerable are the questions which might be raised here. It is strange, yet it is true, that many who acknowledge the sovereign rule of God over material things, will cavil and quibble when we insist that God is also sovereign in the spiritual realm. But their quarrel is with God and not with us. We have given scripture in support of everything advanced in these pages, and if that will not satisfy our readers it is idle for us to seek to convince them. What we write now is designed for those who *do* bow to the authority of Holy Writ, and for their benefit we propose to examine several other scriptures which have purposely been held over for this chapter.

Perhaps the one passage which has presented the greatest difficulty to those who have seen that passage after passage in Holy Writ plainly teaches the election of a limited number unto salvation is 2 Peter 3:9: "not willing that *any* should perish, but that *all* should come to repentance".

The first thing to be said upon the above passage is that, like all other scripture, it must be understood and interpreted in the light of its context. What we have quoted in the preceding paragraph is only part of the verse, and the last part of it at that! Surely it must be allowed by all that the first half of the verse needs to be taken into consideration. In order to establish what these words are supposed by many to mean, viz., that the words "any" and "all" are to be received without any qualification, it *must* be shown that the *context* is referring to *the whole human race!* If this cannot be shown, if there is no *premise* to justify this, then the *conclusion* also must be unwarranted. Let us then ponder the first part of the verse.

*For a further discussion of John 3:16 see Appendix 3.

"The Lord is not slack concerning His promise". Note "promise" in the singular number, *not* "promises." *What* promise is in view? The promise of *salvation?* Where, in all Scripture, has God ever *promised* to save the whole human race!! Where indeed? No, the "promise" here referred to is *not* about *salvation*. What then is it? The context tells us.

"Knowing this, first, that there shall come in the last days scoffers, walking after their own lusts, and saying, Where is the promise of His coming?" (vv. 3, 4). The context then refers to God's promise *to send back His beloved Son*. But many long centuries have passed, and this promise has not yet been fulfilled. True, but long as the delay may seem to *us*, the interval is short in the reckoning of *God*. As the proof of this we are reminded, "But, beloved, be not ignorant of this one thing, that one day is with the Lord as a thousand years, and a thousand years as one day" (v. 8). In God's reckoning of time, less than two days have yet passed since He promised to send back Christ.

But more, the delay in the Father sending back His beloved Son is not only due to no "slackness" on His part, but it is also occasioned by His "longsuffering". His longsuffering to whom? The verse we are now considering tells us: "but is longsuffering *to usward*". And whom are the "usward"?—the human race, or God's own people? In the light of the context this is *not* an open question upon which each of us is free to form an opinion. The Holy Spirit has defined it. The opening verse of the chapter says, "This second Epistle, *beloved,* I now write unto you". And, again, the verse immediately preceding declares, "But, *beloved,* be not ignorant of this one thing etc.," (v. 8). The "usward" then are the "beloved" of God. They to whom this Epistle is addressed are "them that have *obtained* (not "exercised", but "obtained" as God's sovereign *gift*) like precious faith with us through the righteousness of God and our Saviour Jesus Christ" (2 Pet. 1:11). Therefore we say there is no room for a doubt, a quibble or an argument—the "usward" are the elect of God.

Let us now quote the verse as a whole: "The Lord is not slack concerning His promise, as some men count slackness; but is longsuffering to usward, not willing that any should

perish, but that all should come to repentance." Could anything be clearer? The "any" that God is not willing should
perish, are the "usward" to whom God is "longsuffering",
the "beloved" of the previous verses. 2 Peter 3:9 means,
then, that God will not send back His Son until "the fulness
of the Gentiles be come in" (Rom. 11:25). God will not
send back Christ till that "people" whom He is now "taking
out of the Gentiles" (Acts 15:14) are gathered in. God
will not send back His Son till the Body of Christ is complete, and that will not be till the ones whom He has elected
to be saved in this dispensation shall have been brought to
Him. Thank God for His "longsuffering to us-ward". Had
Christ come back twenty years ago the writer had been left
behind to perish in His sins. But that *could not* be, so God
graciously delayed the Second Coming. For the same reason
He is still delaying His Advent. His decreed purpose is that
all His elect will come to repentance, and repent they *shall.*
The present interval of grace will not end until the last of
the "other sheep" of John 10:16 are safely folded,—*then*
will Christ return.

In expounding *the sovereignty of God the Spirit in Salvation* we have shown that His power is *irresistible,* that, by
His gracious operations upon and within them, He "compels" God's elect to come to Christ. The sovereignty of the
Holy Spirit is set forth not only in John 3:8 where we are
told "The wind bloweth where it pleaseth . . . . . . so is every
one that is born of the Spirit," but is affirmed in other passages as well. In 1 Cor. 12:11 we read, "But all these worketh that one and the selfsame Spirit, dividing to every man
severally *as He will."* And again; we read in Acts 16:6, 7—
"Now when they had gone throughout Phrygia and the
region of Galatia, and were *forbidden of the Holy Spirit to
preach the Word in Asia.* After they were come to Mysia,
they assayed to go in to Bithynia: *but the Spirit suffered
them not."* Thus we see how the Holy Spirit interposed
His imperial will in opposition to the determination of the
apostles.

But, it is objected against the assertion that the will and
power of the Holy Spirit are *irresistible* that there are two
passages, one in the Old Testament and the other in the
New, which appear to militate against such a conclusion.

God said of old, "My Spirit shall not always *strive* with man" (Gen. 6:3), and to the Jews Stephen declared, "Ye stiffnecked and uncircumcised in heart and ears, ye do *always resist the Holy Spirit:* as your fathers did, so do ye. Which of the prophets have not your fathers persecuted?" (Acts 7:51, 52). If then the Jews "resisted" the Holy Spirit, how can we say His power is *irresistible?* The answer is found in Neh. 9:30—"Many years didst Thou forbear them, and testifiedst against them by Thy Spirit *in Thy Prophets:* yet would they not give ear." It was the *external* operations of the Spirit which Israel "resisted." It was the Spirit speaking by and through *the prophets* to which they "would not give ear." It was not anything which the Holy Spirit wrought *in them* that they "resisted," but the motives *presented to them* by the inspired messages of the prophets. Perhaps it will help the reader to catch our thought better if we compare Matt. 11:20-24—"Then began He to upbraid the cities wherein most of His *mighty works* were done, because they repented not. Woe unto thee Chorazin!" etc. Our Lord here pronounces woe upon these cities for their failure to repent *because of* the "mighty works" (miracles) which He had done in their sight, and *not* because of any *internal* operations of His grace! The same is true of Gen. 6:3. By comparing 1 Pet. 3:18-20 it will be seen that it was *by and through Noah* that God's Spirit "strove" with the antediluvians. The distinction noted above was ably summarized by Andrew Fuller (another writer long deceased from whom our moderns might learn much) thus: "There are *two kinds* of influences by which God works on the minds of men. First, That which is common, and which is effected by the ordinary use of motives presented to the mind for consideration; Secondly, That which is special and supernatural. The one contains nothing mysterious, anymore than the influence of our words and actions on each other; the other is such a mystery that we know nothing of it but by its effects—The former *ought* to be effectual; the latter *is* so." The work of the Holy Spirit *upon* or *towards* men is always "resisted," by them; His work *within* is always successful. What saith the scriptures? This: "He which hath begun a good work IN you, *will* finish it" (Phil. 1:6).

The next question to be considered is: *Why preach the Gospel to every creature?* If God the Father has predestined only a limited number to be saved, if God the Son died to effect the salvation of only those given to Him by the Father, and if God the Spirit is seeking to quicken none save God's elect, then what is the use of giving the Gospel to the world at large, and where is the propriety of telling sinners that *"Whosoever* believeth in Christ shall not perish but have everlasting life"?

First; it is of great importance that we should be clear upon the *nature* of the Gospel itself. The Gospel is God's good news concerning Christ and not concerning sinners,— "Paul a servant of Jesus Christ, called to be an apostle, separated unto the Gospel of God . . . . *concerning His Son,* Jesus Christ our Lord" (Rom. 1:1, 3). God would have proclaimed far and wide the amazing fact that His own blessed Son "became obedient unto death, even the death of the cross." A universal testimony must be borne to the matchless worth of the person and work of Christ. Note the word "witness" in Matt. 22:14. The Gospel is God's "witness" unto the perfections of His Son. Mark the words of the apostle: "For we are *unto God* a sweet savor of Christ, in them that are saved, *and* in them that *perish"* (2 Cor. 2:15)!

Concerning the character and contents of the Gospel the utmost confusion prevails today. The Gospel is not an "offer" to be bandied around by evangelistic peddlers. The Gospel is no mere *invitation,* but a *proclamation,* a proclamation concerning *Christ;* true, whether men believe it or no. No man is asked to believe that Christ died for him in particular. The Gospel, in brief, is this: Christ died for sinners, you are a sinner, believe in Christ, and you shall be saved. In the Gospel, God simply announces the terms upon which men may be saved (namely, repentance and faith) and, indiscriminately, all are commanded to fulfill them.

Second; repentance and remission of sins are to be preached in the name of the Lord Jesus "unto all the nations" (Luke 24:47), because God's elect are "scattered abroad" (John 11:52) *among* all nations, and it is by the preaching and hearing of the Gospel that they are called out of the world. The Gospel is the means which God uses in the saving of His own chosen ones. By nature God's elect are children of wrath "even as others"; they are lost sinners needing a Saviour, and apart from Christ there is no salvation for them. Hence, the Gospel must be believed by them *before* they can rejoice in the knowledge of sins forgiven. The Gospel is God's winnowing fan: it separates the chaff from the wheat, and gathers the latter into His garner.

Third; it is to be noted that God has other purposes in the preaching of the Gospel than the salvation of His own elect. The world exists for the elect's sake, yet others have the benefit of it. So the Word is preached for the elect's sake, yet others have the benefit of an external call. The sun shines, though blind men see it not. The rain falls upon rocky mountains and waste deserts, as well as on the fruitful valleys; so also, God suffers the Gospel to fall on the ears of the non-elect. The power of the Gospel is one of God's agencies for holding in check the wickedness of the world. Many who are never saved by it *are* reformed, their lusts are bridled, and they are restrained from becoming worse. Moreover, the preaching of the Gospel to the non-elect is made an admirable *test* of their characters. It exhibits the inveteracy of their sin: it demonstrates that their hearts *are* at enmity against God: it justifies the declaration of Christ that "men loved darkness rather than light, because their deeds were evil" (John 3:19).

Finally; it is sufficient for us to know that we are *bidden* to preach the Gospel to every creature. It is not for us to reason about the *consistency* between this and the fact that "few are chosen." It is for us to obey. It is a simple matter to ask questions relating to the ways of God which no finite mind can fully fathom. We, too, might turn and remind the objector that our Lord declared, "Verily I say unto you, All sins shall be forgiven unto the sons of men, and blasphemies wherewith soever they shall blaspheme. But he that shall blaspheme against the Holy Spirit *hath never forgiveness*" (Mark 3:28, 29), and there can be no doubt whatever but that certain of the Jews *were* guilty of this very sin (see Matt. 12:24 etc.), and hence their destruction was inevitable. Yet, notwithstanding, scarcely two months later, He commanded His disciples to preach the Gospel to *every* creature. When the objector can show us the con-

sistency of these two things—the fact that certain of the
Jews had committed the sin for which there is never forgiveness, and the fact that to *them* the Gospel was to be preached
—we will undertake to furnish a more satisfactory solution
than the one given above to the harmony between a *universal* proclamation of the Gospel and a *limitation* of its saving
power to those only that God has predestined to be conformed to the image of His Son.

Once more, we say, it is not for us to *reason about* the
Gospel; it is our business to *preach* it. When God ordered
Abraham to offer up his son as a burnt-offering, he might
have objected that this command was *inconsistent* with His
promise "In *Isaac* shall thy seed be called." But instead of
arguing he obeyed, and left God to harmonize His promise
and His precept. Jeremiah might have argued that God had
bade him do that which was altogether unreasonable when
He said, "Therefore thou shalt speak all these words unto
them; *but they will not hearken* to thee; thou shalt also call
unto them; *but they will not answer thee"* (Jer. 7:27), but
instead, the prophet obeyed. Ezekiel, too, might have com-
plained that the Lord was asking of him a hard thing when
He said, "Son of man, go, get thee unto the House of Israel,
and speak with My words unto them. For thou art not sent
to a people of a strange speech and of an hard language, but
to the House of Israel; Not to many people of a strange
speech and of a hard language, whose words thou cans't not
understand. Surely, had I sent thee to them, they would
have hearkened unto thee. *But the House of Israel will
not hearken unto thee;* for they will not hearken unto Me;
for all the House of Israel are impudent and hard hearted"
(Ezek. 3:4-7).

> "But, O my soul, if truth so bright
> Should dazzle and confound thy sight,
> Yet still His written Word obey,
> And wait the great decisive day."—Watts.

It has been well said, "The Gospel has lost none of its ancient power. It is, as much today as when it was first
preached, 'the power of God unto salvation'. It needs no
pity, no help, and no handmaid. It can overcome all ob-
stacles, and break down all barriers. No human device need
be tried to prepare the sinner to receive it, for if God has

sent it no power can hinder it; and if He has not sent it, no power can make it effectual." (Dr. Bullinger).

This chapter might be extended indefinitely, but it is already too long, so a word or two more must suffice. A number of other questions will be dealt with in the pages yet to follow, and those that we fail to touch upon the reader must take to the Lord Himself who has said, "If any of you lack wisdom, *let him ask of God,* that giveth to all liberally, and upbraideth not" (Jas. 1:5).

XII

THE VALUE OF THIS DOCTRINE

"All Scripture is given by inspiration of God,
And is profitable for doctrine,
For reproof, for correction, for instruction in righteousness:
That the man of God may be perfect,
Throughly furnished unto all good works" (2 Tim. 3:16, 17).

"ALL Scripture is given by inspiration of God, and *is profitable for doctrine,* for reproof, for correction, for instruction in righteousness: that the man of God may be perfect, throughly furnished unto all good works" (2 Tim. 3:16, 17). "Doctrine" means "teaching," and it is by doctrine or teaching that the great realities of God and of our relation to Him—of Christ, the Spirit, salvation, grace, glory, are made known to us. It is by doctrine (through the power of the Spirit) that believers are nourished and edified, and where doctrine is neglected, growth in grace and effective witnessing for Christ necessarily cease. How sad then that doctrine is now decried as "unpractical" when, in fact, doctrine is the very base of the practical life. There is an inseparable connection between belief and practice—"*As* he thinketh in his heart, *so* is he" (Pro. 23:7). The relation between Divine truth and Christian character is that of cause to effect—"And ye shall *know* the truth, *and* the truth shall make you free" (John 8:32)—free from ignorance, free from prejudice, free from error, free from the wiles of Satan, free from the power of evil; and if the truth is not "known" then such freedom will not be enjoyed. Observe the *order* of mention in the passage with which we have opened. All Scripture is profitable *first* for "doctrine"! The same order is observed throughout the Epistles, particularly in the great doctrinal treatises of the apostle Paul. Read the Epistle of "Romans" and it will be found that there is not a single admonition in the first five chapters. In the Epistle of "Ephesians" there are no exhortations till the fourth chapter is reached. The order is first doctrinal exposition and then admonition or exhortation for the regulation of the daily walk.

The substitution of so-called "practical" preaching for the doctrinal exposition which it has supplanted is the root cause of many of the evil maladies which now afflict the church of God. The reason why there is so little depth, so little intelligence, so little grasp of the fundamental verities of Christianity, is because so few believers have been established in the faith, through hearing expounded and through their own personal study of the doctrines of grace. While the soul is unestablished in the doctrine of the Divine Inspiration of the Scriptures—their full and verbal inspiration—there can be no firm foundation for faith to rest upon. While the soul is ignorant of the doctrine of Justification there can be no real and intelligent assurance of its acceptance in the Beloved. While the soul is un-acquainted with the teaching of the Word upon Sanctification it is open to receive all the crudities and errors of the Perfectionists or "Holiness" people. While the soul knows not what Scripture has to say upon the doctrine of the New Birth there can be no proper grasp of the two natures in the believer, and ignorance here inevitably results in loss of peace and joy. And so we might go on right through the list of Christian doctrine. It is *ignorance* of doctrine that has rendered the professing church helpless to cope with the rising tide of infidelity. It is *ignorance* of doctrine which is mainly responsible for thousands of professing Christians being captivated by the numerous false isms of the day. It is because the time has now arrived when the bulk of our churches *"will not endure* sound doctrine" (2 Tim. 4:3) that they so readily receive *false* doctrines. Of course it is true that doctrine, like anything else in Scripture, may be studied from a merely cold intellectual viewpoint, and *thus* approached, doctrinal teaching and doctrinal study will leave the *heart* untouched, and will naturally be "dry" and profitless. But, doctrine properly received, doctrine studied with an *exercised* heart, will ever lead into a deeper knowledge of God and of the unsearchable riches of Christ.

The doctrine of God's sovereignty then is no mere metaphysical dogma which is devoid of practical value, but is one that is calculated to produce a powerful effect upon Christian character and the daily walk. The doctrine of God's sovereignty lies at the foundation of Christian theology, and in importance is perhaps second only to the Divine Inspiration of the Scriptures. It is the centre of gravity in the system of Christian truth—the sun around which all the lesser orbs are grouped. It is the golden milestone to which every highway of knowledge leads and from which they all radiate. It is the cord upon which all other doctrines are strung like so many pearls, holding them in place and giving them unity. It is the plumbline by which every creed needs to be measured, the balance in which every human dogma must be weighed. It is designed as the sheet-anchor for our souls amid the storms of life. The doctrine of God's sovereignty is a Divine cordial to refresh our spirits. It is designed and adapted to mould the affections of the heart and to give a right direction to conduct. It produces gratitude in prosperity and patience in adversity. It affords comfort for the present and a sense of security respecting the unknown future. It is, and it does all, and much more than we have just said, because it ascribes to God—Father, Son, and Holy Spirit—the glory which is His due, and places the creature in his proper place before Him—in the dust.

We shall now consider the Value of the doctrine in detail.

1. IT DEEPENS OUR VENERATION OF THE DIVINE CHARACTER.

The doctrine of God's sovereignty as it is unfolded in the Scriptures affords an exalted view of the Divine perfections. It maintains *His creatorial rights*. It insists that "to us there is but one God, the Father, *of whom are all things,* and we in Him; and one Lord Jesus Christ, *by whom are all things,* and we by Him" (1 Cor. 8:6). It declares that His rights are those of the "potter" who forms and fashions the clay into vessels of whatever type and for whatever use He may please. Its testimony is, "Thou hast created all things, *and for Thy pleasure* they are and were created" (Rev. 4:11). It argues that none has any right to "reply" against God, and that the only becoming attitude for the creature to take is one of reverent submission before Him. Thus the apprehension of the absolute supremacy of God is of great practical importance, for unless we have a proper regard to His high sovereignty He will never be honored in our thoughts of Him, nor will He have His proper place in our hearts and lives.

It exhibits the *inscrutableness of His wisdom*. It shows that while God is immaculate in His *holiness,* He has permitted *evil* to enter His fair creation; that while He is the Possessor of *all power*, He has allowed the Devil to wage war *against Him* for six thousand years at least; that while He is the perfect embodiment of *love*, He spared not His own Son; that while He is the God of *all grace*, multitudes will be tormented for ever and ever in the Lake of Fire. High mysteries are these. Scripture does not deny them, but acknowledge their existence—"O the depth of the riches both of the wisdom and knowledge of God! how *unsearchable* are His judgments, and His ways *past finding out!*" (Rom. 11:33).

It makes known the *irreversibleness of His will*. "Known unto God are all His works from the beginning of the world" (Acts 15:18). From the beginning God purposed to glorify Himself "in the Church by Christ Jesus, throughout all ages, world without end" (Eph. 3:21). To this end, He created the world, and formed man. His all-wise plan was not defeated when man fell, for in the Lamb "slain from the foundation of the world" (Rev. 13:8) we behold the Fall anticipated. Nor will God's purpose be thwarted by the wickedness of men since the Fall, as is clear from the words of the Psalmist, *"Surely the wrath of man shall praise Thee: the remainder of wrath shalt Thou restrain"* (Ps. 76:10). Because God is the Almighty His will cannot be withstood. "His purposes originated in eternity, and are carried forward without change to eternity. They extend to all His works, and control all events. He 'worketh all things after the counsel of His own will.'" (Dr. Rice). Neither man nor devil can successfully resist Him, therefore is it written, "The Lord reigneth; *let the people tremble."* (Ps. 99:1).

It magnifies *His grace*. Grace is un-merited favor, and because grace is shown to the un-deserving and Hell-deserving, to those who have *no claim* upon God, therefore is grace *free* and can be manifested toward the chief of sinners. But because grace is exercised toward those who are *destitute* of worthiness or merit, grace is *sovereign;* that is to say, God bestows grace upon whom He pleases. Divine sovereignty has ordained that *some* shall be cast into the Lake of Fire to show that *all* deserved such a doom. But grace comes in like a drag-net and draws out from a lost humanity a people for God's name, to be throughout all eternity the monuments of His inscrutable favor. Sovereign grace reveals God breaking down the opposition of the human heart, subduing the enmity of the carnal mind, and bringing us to love Him because He first loved us.

2. IT IS THE SOLID FOUNDATION OF ALL TRUE RELIGION.

This naturally follows from what we have said above under the first head. If the doctrine of Divine sovereignty alone gives God His rightful place, then it is also true that it alone can supply a firm base for practical religion to build upon. There can be no progress in Divine things until there is the personal recognition that God is Supreme, that He is to be feared and revered, that He is to be owned and served *as Lord*. We read the Scriptures in vain unless we come to them earnestly desiring a better knowledge of God's will for us—any other motive is selfish and utterly inadequate and unworthy. Every prayer we send up to God is but carnal presumption unless it be offered "according to *His* will"—anything short of this is to ask 'amiss,' that we might consume upon our *own* lusts the thing requested. Every service we engage in is but a "dead work" unless it be done for the glory of God. Experimental religion consists mainly in the perception and performance of the Divine will—performance both active and passive. We are predestinated to be "conformed to the image of God's Son", whose meat it ever was to do the will of the One that sent Him, and the measure in which each saint is becoming "conformed" practically, in his daily life, is largely determined by his response to our Lord's word—"Take My yoke upon you, *and learn of Me;* for I am meek and lowly in heart."

3. IT REPUDIATES THE HERESY OF SALVATION BY WORKS.

"There is a way which seemeth right unto a man; but the end thereof are the ways of death" (Pro. 14:12). The way which *"seemeth right"* and which ends in *"death,"* death eternal, is salvation by human effort and merit. The belief in salvation by works is one that is common to human nature. It may not always assume the grosser form of Popish penances, or even of Protestant "repentance"—i.e., sorrowing for sin, which is never the meaning of repentance in Scripture—anything which gives man a place at all is but a vari-

ety of the same evil genus. To say, as alas! many preachers
are saying, God is willing to do His part if you will do yours,
is a wretched and excuseless *denial* of the Gospel of His
grace. To declare that God helps those who help themselves, is to *repudiate* one of the most precious truths taught
in the Bible, and in the Bible alone; namely, that God helps
those who are *unable* to help themselves, who have tried
again and again only to fail. To say that the sinner's salvation turns upon the action of his *own* will, is another
form of the God-dishonoring dogma of salvation by human
efforts. In the final analysis, any movement of the will is
a work: it is something *from me,* something which *I do.* But
the doctrine of God's sovereignty lays the axe at the root of
this evil tree by declaring, *"It is not of him that willeth, nor*
of him that runneth, but of God that sheweth mercy" (Rom.
9:16). Does some one say, Such a doctrine will drive sinners to *despair.* The reply is, Be it so; it is just such despair the writer longs to see prevail. It is not until the sinner
despairs of any help from himself, that he will ever fall
into the arms of sovereign mercy; but if once the Holy Spirit
convicts him that there is *no help* in himself, then he will
recognize that he is *lost,* and will cry, "God be merciful to
me a sinner," and *such* a cry will be heard. If the author
may be allowed to bear personal witness, he has found during the course of his ministry that, the sermons he has
preached on human depravity, the sinner's helplessness to do
anything himself, and the salvation of the soul turning upon
the sovereign mercy of God, have been those most owned
and blessed in the salvation of the lost. We repeat, then,
a sense of utter *helplessness* is the first prerequisite to any
sound conversion. There is no salvation for any soul until
it looks away from itself, looks to something, yea, to Someone, *outside* of itself.

4. IT IS DEEPLY HUMBLING TO THE CREATURE.

This doctrine of the absolute sovereignty of God is a great
battering-ram against human pride, and in this it is in sharp
contrast from "the doctrines of men." The spirit of our
age is essentially that of boasting and glorying in the flesh.
The achievements of man, his development and progress,
his greatness and self-sufficiency, are the shrine at which the

world worships today. But the truth of God's sovereignty, with all its corollaries, removes every ground for human boasting and instills the spirit of humility in its stead. It declares that salvation is of the Lord—of the Lord in its origination, in its operation, and in its consummation. It insists that the Lord has to apply as well as supply, that He has to complete as well as begin His saving work in our souls, that He has not only to reclaim but to maintain and sustain us to the end. It teaches that salvation is by grace through faith, and that *all* our works (before conversion), good as well as evil, count for nothing toward salvation. It tells us we are "born, not of the will of the flesh, nor of the will of man, but of God" (John 1:13). And all this is most humbling to the heart of man, who wants to contribute something to the price of his redemption and do that which will afford ground for boasting and self-satisfaction.

But if this doctrine humbles *us,* it results in praise to *God.* If, in the light of God's sovereignty, we have seen our own worthlessness and helplessness, we shall indeed cry with the Psalmist, *"All* my springs are *in Thee"* (Ps. 87:7). If by nature we were "children of wrath," and by practice rebels against the Divine government and justly exposed to the "curse" of the Law, and if God was under *no* obligation to rescue us from the fiery indignation and yet, notwithstanding, He delivered up His well-beloved Son for *us* all; then how such grace and love will melt our hearts, how the apprehension of it will cause us to say in adoring gratitude, *"Not unto us,* O Lord, not unto us, *but unto Thy name give glory,* for Thy mercy, and for Thy truth's sake" (Psa. 115:1)! How readily shall each of us acknowledge, *"By the grace of God* I am what I am"! With what wondering praise shall we exclaim—

> "Why was I *made* to hear His voice,
> And enter while there's room,
> When thousands make a wretched choice,
> And rather starve than come?
> 'Twas the same love that spread the feast,
> That sweetly *forced* us in;
> Else we had still refused to taste
> And perished in our sin."

5. It affords a sense of absolute security.

God is infinite in power, and therefore it is impossible

to withstand His will or resist the outworking of His decrees. Such a statement as that is well calculated to fill the sinner with alarm, but from the saint it evokes naught but praise. Let us add a word and see what a difference it makes:—*My* God is infinite in power! *then* "I will not fear what man can do unto me." My God is infinite in power, *then* "what time I am afraid I will trust in Him." My God is infinite in power, *then* "I will both lay me down in peace, and sleep: for Thou, Lord, *only* makest me dwell in safety" (Ps. 4:8). Right down the ages *this* has been the source of the saints' confidence. Was not this the assurance of Moses when, in his parting words to Israel, he said—"There is none like unto the God of Jeshurun (Israel), who rideth upon the heaven in Thy help, and in His excellency on the sky. The eternal God is thy refuge, *and underneath are the everlasting arms*" (Deut. 33:26, 27)? Was it not this sense of security that caused the Psalmist, moved by the Holy Spirit, to write—"He that dwelleth in the secret place of the Most High shall abide under the shadow of the Almighty. I will say of the Lord, *He is my refuge and my fortress: my God: in Him will I trust. Surely* He shall deliver thee from the snare of the fowler, and from the noisome pestilence. He shall cover thee with His feathers, and under His wings shalt thou trust: His truth shall be thy shield and buckler: *Thou shalt not be afraid* for the terror by night; nor for the arrow that flieth by day; Nor for the pestilence that walketh in darkness; nor for the destruction that wasteth at noonday. A thousand shall fall at thy side, and ten thousand at thy right hand, *but it shall not come nigh thee.* Because thou hast made the Lord, which is my refuge, even the Most High *thy Habitation;* There shall no evil befall thee (instead, all things will work together for *good),* neither shall any plague come nigh thy dwelling" (Psa. 91)?

> "Death and plagues around me fly,
> Till He bid, I cannot die;
> Not a single shaft can hit,
> Till the God of love sees fit."

O the preciousness of this truth! Here am I, a poor, helpless, senseless "sheep," yet am I *secure* in the hand of Christ. And *why* am I secure *there?* None can pluck me thence *because* the hand that holds me is that of the Son

of God, and all power in heaven and earth is *His!* Again;
I have no strength of my own: the world, the flesh, and the
Devil, are arrayed against me, so I commit myself into the
care and keeping of the Lord and say with the apostle, "I
know Whom I have believed, and am persuaded *that He is
able* to keep that which I have committed unto Him against
that day" (2 Tim. 1:12). And what is the ground of my
confidence? *How* do I *know* that He is able to keep that
which I have committed unto Him? I know it because God
is *almighty,* the King of kings and Lord of lords.

6. IT SUPPLIES COMFORT IN SORROW.

The doctrine of God's sovereignty is one that is full of
consolation and imparts great peace to the Christian. The
sovereignty of God is a foundation that nothing can shake
and is more firm than the heavens and earth. How blessed
to know there is no corner of the universe that is out of His
reach! as said the Psalmist, "Whither shall I go from Thy
Spirit? *or whither shall I flee from Thy presence?* If I
ascend up into heaven, *Thou art there:* if I make my bed in
hell, behold, *Thou art there.* If I take the wings of the
morning, and dwell in the uttermost parts of the sea; *even
there shall Thy hand lead me,* and Thy right hand shall hold
me. If I say surely the darkness shall cover me; *even the
night shall be light about me.* Yea, the darkness hideth not
from Thee: but the night shineth as the day: the darkness
and the light are both alike to Thee" (Ps. 139:7-12). How
blessed it is to know that God's strong hand is upon every
one and every thing! How blessed to know that not a spar-
row falleth to the ground without His notice! How blessed
to know that our very *afflictions* come not by chance, nor
from the Devil, but are ordained and ordered *by God:*—
"That no man should be moved by these afflictions: for
yourselves *know* that we are *appointed* thereunto" (1 Thess.
3:3)!

But our God is not only infinite in power, He is infinite
in wisdom and goodness too. And herein is the preciousness
of this truth. God wills only that which is good and His
will is irreversible and irresistible! God is too wise to err
and too loving to cause His child a needless tear. Therefore

if God be perfect wisdom and perfect goodness how blessed is the assurance that everything *is* in *His* hand, and moulded by His will according to His eternal purpose! *"Behold, He taketh away,* who can hinder Him? who will say unto Him what doest Thou?"* (Job 9:12). Yet, how comforting to learn that *it is* "He", and not the Devil, who "taketh away" our loved ones! Ah! what peace for our poor frail hearts to be told that the number of our days is with Him (Job 7:1; 14:5); that disease and death are His messengers, and always march under *His* orders; that it is the Lord who gives and the Lord who takes away!

7. It begets a spirit of sweet resignation.

To bow before the sovereign will of God is one of the great secrets of peace and happiness. There can be no real submission with contentment until we are broken in spirit, that is, until we are willing and *glad* for the Lord to have *His* way with us. Not that we are insisting upon a spirit of *fatalistic acquiescence;* far from it. The saints are exhorted to *"prove* what is that *good,* and *acceptable,* and *perfect will of God"* (Rom. 12:2).

We touched upon this subject of resignation to God's will in the chapter upon our Attitude towards God's Sovereignty, and there, in addition to the supreme Pattern, we cited the examples of Eli and Job: we would now supplement their cases with further examples. What a word is that in Lev. 10:3—"And Aaron held his peace." Look at the circumstances: "And Nadab and Abihu, the sons of Aaron, took either of them his censer, and put fire therein, and put incense thereon, and offered strange fire before the Lord, which He commanded them not. And there went out fire from the Lord, and devoured them, and they died before the Lord. . . . . *And Aaron held his peace."* Two of the high priests' sons were slain, slain by a visitation of *Divine judgment,* and they were probably *intoxicated* at the time; moreover, this trial came upon Aaron *suddenly,* without anything to *prepare* him for it; yet, he "held his peace." Precious exemplification of the power of God's all-sufficient grace!

Consider now an utterance which fell from the lips of David: "And the king said unto Zadok, Carry back the ark

of God into the city: if I shall find favor in the eyes of the
Lord, He will bring me again, and shew me both it, and
His habitation. But if He thus say, I have no delight in
thee; behold, here am I, *let Him do to me as seemeth good
unto Him"* (2 Sam. 15:25, 26). Here, too, the circumstances which confronted the speaker were exceedingly trying to the human heart. David was sore pressed with sorrow. His own son was driving him from the throne, and
seeking his very life. Whether he would ever see Jerusalem
and the Tabernacle again he knew not. But he was so
yielded up to God, he was so fully assured that *His* will was
best, that even though it meant the loss of the throne and
the loss of his life he was content for Him to have His way
—"let Him do to me as seemeth Him good."

There is no need to multiply examples, but a reflection
upon the last case will be in place. If amid the shadows of
the Old Testament dispensation, David was content for the
Lord to have *His* way, now that the *heart* of God has been
fully revealed at the Cross, how much more ought *we* to delight in the execution of His will! Surely we shall have no
hesitation in saying—

> "*Ill* that *He* blesses is *our good*,
> And *un*blest good is ill,
> And all is right that seems most wrong,
> If it be His sweet will."

8. IT EVOKES A SONG OF PRAISE.

It could not be otherwise. Why should I, who am by
nature no different from the careless and godless throngs
all around, have been chosen in Christ before the foundation
of the world and now blest with all spiritual blessings in the
heavenlies in Him! Why was I, that once was an alien and
a rebel, singled out for such wondrous favors! Ah, that is
something I cannot fathom. Such grace, such love, "passeth
knowledge." But if my mind is unable to discern a reason,
my heart can express its gratitude in praise and adoration.
But not only should I be grateful to God for His grace toward me in the past, His present dealings will fill me with
thanksgivings. What is the force of that word *"Rejoice in
the Lord alway"* (Phil. 4:4)? Mark it is not "Rejoice *in the
Saviour,"* but we are to "Rejoice in the Lord," *as* "Lord,"

as the *Master* of every circumstance. Need we remind the
reader that when the apostle penned these words he was himself a prisoner in the hands of the Roman government. A
long course of affliction and suffering lay behind him. Perils on land and perils on sea, hunger and thirst, scourging
and stoning, had all been experienced. He had been persecuted by those within the church as well as by those without:
the very ones who ought to have stood by him had forsaken
him. And still he writes, *"Rejoice in the Lord alway"*! What
was the secret of his peace and happiness? Ah! had not
this same apostle written, "And we know that all things
work together for good to them that love God, to them who
are the called according to His purpose" (Rom. 8:28). But
how did he, and how do we, "know," that *all* things work
together for *good?* The answer is, Because *all things* are under the control of and are being regulated by the Supreme
Sovereign, and because *He* has naught but thoughts of love
toward His own, then "all things" are so ordered by Him
that they are *made to minister to our ultimate good.* It is
for this cause we are to give "thanks *always* for *all things*
unto God and the Father in the name of our Lord Jesus
Christ" (Eph. 5:20). Yes, give thanks for "all things" for,
as it has been well said "Our disappointments are but *His*
appointments." To the one who delights in the sovereignty
of God the clouds not only have a 'silver lining' but they are
silvern all through, the darkness only serving to offset the
light—

> "Ye fearful saints fresh courage take
> The clouds ye so much dread,
> Are *big with mercy* and shall break
> In blessings o'er your head."

9. It guarantees the final triumph of good over evil.

Ever since the day that Cain slew Abel, the conflict on
earth between good and evil, has been a sore problem to the
saints. In every age the righteous have been hated and persecuted, whilst the unrighteous have appeared to defy God
with impugnity. The Lord's people, for the most part,
have been poor in this world's goods, whereas the wicked
in their temporal prosperity have flourished like the green
bay tree. As one looks around and beholds the oppression of
believers and the earthly success of unbelievers, and notes

how few are the former and how numerous the latter; as he sees the apparent defeat of the right, and the triumphing of might and the wrong; as he hears the roar of battle, the cries of the wounded, and the lamentations of the bereaved; as he discovers that almost everything down here is in confusion, chaos, and ruins, it seems as though Satan were getting the better of the conflict. But as one looks *above*, instead of around, there is plainly visible to the eye of faith a Throne, a Throne unaffected by the storms of earth, a Throne that is "set," stable and secure; and upon it is seated One whose name is the Almighty, and who "worketh all things after the counsel of His own will" (Eph. 1:11). This then is our confidence—*God is on the Throne.* The helm is in *His* hand, and being Almighty His purpose cannot fail, for "He is in one mind, and who can turn *Him?* and what His soul desireth, *even that He doeth*" (Job 23:13). Though God's governing hand is invisible to the eye of sense, it is real to faith, that faith which rests with sure confidence upon His Word, and therefore is assured *He cannot fail.* What follows below is from the pen of our brother Mr. Gaebelein.

"There can be no failure with God. 'God is not a man, that He should lie, neither the Son of man, that He should repent; hath He said and shall He not do it? or hath He spoken, and shall He not make it good?' (Num. 23:19). All will be accomplished. The promise made to His own beloved people to come for them and take them from hence to glory will not fail. He will surely come and gather them in His own presence. The solemn words spoken to the nations of the earth by the different prophets will also not fail. 'Come near, ye nations, to hear; and hearken ye people; let the earth hear, and all that is therein; the world, and all things that come forth of it. For the indignation of the Lord is upon all nations, and His fury upon all armies; He hath utterly destroyed them, He hath delivered them to the slaughter' (Is. 34:1, 2). Nor will that day fail in which 'the lofty looks of man shall be humbled and the haughtiness of men shall be bowed down and the Lord alone shall be exalted' (Is. 2:11). The day in which He is manifested, when His glory shall cover the heavens and His feet will stand again upon this earth, will surely come. His kingdom

will not fail, nor all the promised events connected with the
end of the age and the consummation.

"In these dark and trying times how well it is to remember that He is on the throne, the throne which cannot be
shaken, and that He will not fail in doing all He has spoken
and promised. 'Seek ye out of the book of the Lord and
read: Not one of these shall fail' (Isa. 34:16). In believing,
blessed anticipation, we can look on to the glory-time when
His Word and His Will is accomplished, when through the
coming of the Prince of Peace, righteousness and peace
comes at last. And while we wait for the supreme and
blessed moment when His promise to us is accomplished,
we trust Him, walking in His fellowship and daily find
afresh, that He does not fail to sustain and keep us in all
our ways."

10. IT PROVIDES A RESTING-PLACE FOR THE HEART.

Much that might have been said here has already been
anticipated under previous heads. The One seated upon
the Throne of Heaven, the One who is Governor over the
nations and who has ordained and now regulates all events,
is infinite not only in power but in wisdom and goodness as well. He who is Lord over all creation is the One
that was "manifest in the flesh" (1 Tim. 3:16). Ah! here
is a theme no human pen can do justice to. The glory of
God consists not merely in that He is Highest, but in that
being high He stooped in lowly love to bear the burden
of His own sinful creatures, for it is written *"God* was in
Christ, reconciling the world unto Himself" (2 Cor. 5:19).
The Church of *God* was purchased *"with His own Blood"*
(Acts 20:28). It is upon the gracious self-humiliation of
the King Himself that His kingdom is established. O
wondrous Cross! By it He who suffered upon it has become not the Lord of our destinies (He was that before),
but the Lord of our hearts. Therefore, it is not in abject
terror that we bow before the Supreme Sovereign, but in
adoring worship we cry, "Worthy is the Lamb that was
slain to receive power, and riches, and wisdom, and
strength, and honor, and glory, and blessing" (Rev. 5:12).
Here then is the refutation of the wicked charge that
this doctrine is a horrible calumny upon God and danger-

ous to expound to His people. Can a doctrine be "horrible" and "dangerous" that gives God His true place, that maintains His rights, that magnifies His grace, that ascribes *all* glory to Him and removes every ground of boasting from the creature? Can a doctrine be "horrible" and "dangerous" which affords the saints a sense of security in danger, that supplies them comfort in sorrow, that begets patience within them in adversity, that evokes from them praise at all times? Can a doctrine be "horrible" and "dangerous" which assures us of the certain triumph of good over evil, and which provides a sure resting-place for our hearts, and that place, the perfections of the Sovereign Himself? No; a thousand times, no. Instead of being "horrible and dangerous" *this* doctrine of the Sovereignty of God is glorious and edifying, and a due apprehension of it will but serve to make us exclaim with Moses, *"Who is like unto thee, O Lord, among the gods?* who is like Thee, glorious in holiness, fearful in praises, doing wonders?" (Ex. 15:11).

CONCLUSION

"Halleluia: for the Lord God omnipotent reigneth" (Rev. 19:6).

IN our Foreword to the second edition (pages 13, 14) we acknowledge the need for *preserving the balance* of Truth. Two things are beyond dispute: God is sovereign, man is responsible. In this book we have sought to expound the former; in our other works we have frequently pressed the latter. That there is real danger of over-emphasising the one and ignoring the other, we readily admit; yea, history furnishes numerous examples of cases of each. To emphasise the sovereignty of God, without also maintaining the accountability of the creature tends to fatalism; to be so concerned in maintaining the responsibility of man, as to lose sight of the sovereignty of God, is to exalt the creature and dishonor the Creator.

Almost all doctrinal error, is, really, Truth perverted, Truth wrongly divided, Truth *disproportionately* held and taught. The fairest face on earth, with the most comely features, would soon become ugly and unsightly, if one member continued growing while the others remained undeveloped. Beauty is, primarily, a matter of proportion. Thus it is with the Word of God: its beauty and blessedness are best perceived when its manifold wisdom is exhibited in its true proportions. Here is where so many have failed in the past. A single phase of God's Truth has so impressed this man or that, that he has concentrated his attention upon it, almost to the exclusion of everything else. Some portion of God's Word has been made a "pet doctrine", and often this has become the distinctive badge of some party. But it is the duty of each servant of God to "declare *all* the counsel of God" (Acts 20:27).

It is true that the degenerate days in which our lot is cast, when on every side man is exalted, and "superman" has become a common expression, there is real need for a *special* emphasis upon the glorious fact of God's supremacy. The more so where this is expressly denied. Yet even here much wisdom is required, lest our zeal should not be "according to knowledge." The words "meat in due season" should ever be before the servant of God. What is needed, primarily, by one congregation, may not be specifically needed by another. If called to labor where Arminian preachers have preceded, then the neglected truth of God's sovereignty should be expounded—though with caution and care, lest too much "strong meat" be given to "babes". The example of Christ in John 16:12, "I have yet many things to say unto you, but ye cannot bear them *now*", must be borne in mind. On the other hand, if I am called to take charge of a distinctly Calvinistic pulpit, then the truth of human responsibility (in its many aspects) may be profitably set forth. What the preacher needs to give-out is not what his people most *like* to hear, but what they most *need*, i.e. those aspects of truth they are least familiar with, or least exhibiting in their walk.

To carry into actual practice what we have inculcated above will, most probably, lay the preacher open to the charge of being a Turncoat. But what matters that if he has his Master's approval? He is not called upon to be "consistent" with himself, nor with any rules drawn up by man; his business is to be consistent with *Holy Writ*. And in Scripture each part or aspect of truth is balanced by another aspect of truth. There are two sides to everything, even to the character of God, for He is "light" (1 John 1:5) as well as "love" (1 John 4:8), and therefore are we called upon to "Behold, therefore the goodness *and* severity of God" (Rom. 11:22). To be all the time preaching on the one to the exclusion of the other, caricatures the Divine character.

When the Son of God became incarnate He came here in "the form of a *servant*" (Phil. 2:6); nevertheless, in the manger He was "Christ *the Lord*" (Luke 2:11)! All things are possible with God (Matt. 19:26), yet God "cannot lie" (Titus 1:2). Scripture says, "Bear ye one another's burdens (Gal. 6:2), yet the same chapter insists "every man shall bear his own burden" (Gal. 6:5). We are enjoined to take "no thought for the morrow" (Matt. 6:34), yet "if any provide not for his own, and specially for those of his own house, he hath denied the faith, and is worse than an infidel" (1 Tim. 5:8). No sheep of Christ's can perish (John 10:28, 29), yet the Christian is bidden to make his "calling and election *sure*" (2 Peter 1:10). And so we might go on multiplying illustrations. These things are not contradictions, but complementaries: the one "balances the other". Thus, the Scriptures set forth *both* the sovereignty of God and the responsibility of man. So too should every servant of God, and that, in their proper proportions.

But we return now to a few closing reflections upon our present theme. "And Jehoshaphat stood in the congregation of Judah and Jerusalem, in the house of the Lord, before the new court, And said, O Lord God of our fathers, art not Thou God in heaven? and rulest not Thou over all the kingdoms of the heathen? and in Thine hand is there not power and might, *so that none is able to withstand Thee?*" (2 Chron. 20:5,6). Yes, the Lord *is* God, ruling over all the kingdoms of men, ruling in supreme majesty and might. Yet in our day, a day of boasted enlightenment and progress, this is denied on every hand. A materialistic science and an atheistic philosophy have bowed God out of His own world, and everything is regulated, forsooth, by (impersonal) laws of nature. So in human affairs: at best God is a far-distant spectator, and a *helpless* one at that. God could not help the launching of the dreadful war, and though He longed to put a stop to it He was unable to do so—and this in the face of 1 Chron. 5:22; 2 Chron. 24:24! Having endowed man with "free agency" God is obliged to let man make his own choice and go his own way, and He cannot interfere with him, or otherwise his moral responsibility would be destroyed. Such are the popular beliefs of the day. One is not surprised to find these sentiments emanating from German neologians, but how sad that they should be taught in many of our Seminaries, echoed from many of our pulpits, and accepted by many of the rank and file of professing Christians.

One of the most flagrant sins of our age is that of irreverence—the failure to ascribe the glory which is due the august majesty of God. Men limit the power and activities of the Lord in their degrading concepts of His being and character. Originally, man was made in the image and likeness of God, but today we are asked to believe in a god made in the image and likeness of man. The Creator is reduced to the level of the creature: His omniscience is called into question, His omnipotency is no longer believed in, and

His absolute sovereignty is flatly denied. Men claim to be the architects of their own fortunes and the determiners of their own destiny. They know not that their lives are at the disposal of the Divine Despot. They know not they have no more power to thwart Hs secret decrees than a worm has to resist the tread of an elephant. They know not that "The Lord hath prepared His throne in the heavens; and His kingdom *ruleth over all"* (Psa. 103:19).

In the foregoing pages we have sought to repudiate such paganistic views as the above-mentioned, and have endeavored to show from Scripture that God *is* God, on the Throne, and that so far from the recent war being an evidence that the helm had slipped out of His hand, it was a sure proof that He still lives and reigns, and is now bringing to pass that which He had fore-determined and fore-announced (Matt. 24:6-8 etc.). That the carnal mind is enmity against God, that the un-regenerate man is a rebel against the Divine government, that the sinner has no concern for the glory of his Maker, and little or no respect for His revealed will, is freely granted. But, nevertheless, behind the scenes, God is ruling and over-ruling, fulfilling His eternal purpose, not only in spite of but, also by means of, those who are His enemies.

How earnestly are the claims of man contended for against the claims of God! Has not man power and knowledge, but what of it? Has God no will, or power, or knowledge? Suppose man's will conflicts with God's—then what? Turn to the Scripture of Truth for answer. Men had a will on the plains of Shinar and determined to build a tower whose top should reach unto heaven, but what came of *their* purpose? Pharaoh had a will when he hardened his heart and refused to allow Jehovah's people to go and worship Him in the wilderness, but what came of his rebellion? Balak had a will when he hired Balaam to come and curse the Hebrews, but of what avail was it? The Canaanites had a will when they determined to prevent Israel occupying the land of Canaan, but how far did they succeed? Saul had a will when he hurled his javelin at David, but it entered the wall instead! Jonah had a will when he refused to go and preach to the Ninevites, but what came of it? Nebuchadnezzar had a will when he thought to destroy the three Hebrew children, but God had a will too, and the fire did not harm them. Herod had a will when he sought to slay the Child Jesus, and had there been no living, reigning God, his evil desire would have been effected; but in daring to pit his puny will against the irresistible will of the Almighty, his efforts came to nought. Yes, my reader, and you, too, had a will when you formed your plans *without* first seeking counsel of the Lord, therefore did He *overturn* them! "There are many devices in a man's heart: *nevertheless* the counsel of the Lord, that shall stand" (Prov. 19:21).

What a demonstration of the irresistible sovereignty of God is furnished by that wonderful statement found in Rev. 17:17—"*For God hath put in their hearts to fulfill His will, and to agree, and give their kingdom unto the Beast, until the words of God shall be fulfilled.*" The fulfillment of any single prophecy is but the sovereignty of God in operation. It is the demonstration that what He has decreed He is able also to perform. It is proof that none can withstand the execution of His counsel or prevent the accomplishment of His pleasure. It is the evidence that God *inclines* men to fulfill that which He has ordained and perform that which He has fore-determined. If God were not absolute Sovereign, then Divine prophecy would be valueless, for in such case no guarantee would be left that what He had predicted *would* surely come to pass.

"*For God hath put in their hearts to fulfill His will and, to agree, and give their kingdom unto the Beast, until the words of God shall be fulfilled*" (Rev. 17:17). Even in that terrible time, when Satan has been cast down to the earth itself (Rev. 12:9), when the Antichrist is reigning in full power (Rev. 13), when the basest passions of men are let loose (Rev. 6:4), even then God is supreme above all, working "*through all*" (Eph. 4:6), controlling men's hearts and directing their counsels to the fulfilling of *His own* purpose. We cannot do better than quote here the excellent comments of our esteemed friend Mr. Walter Scott upon this verse — "God works unseen, but not the less truly, in all the political changes of the day. The astute statesman, the clever diplomatist, is simply an agent in the Lord's hands. He knows it not. Self-will and motives of policy may influ-

ence to action, but God is steadily working toward an end—
to exhibit the heavenly and earthly glories of His Son.
Thus, instead of kings and statesmen thwarting God's purpose, they unconsciously forward it. God is not indifferent,
but is behind the scenes of human action. The doings of
the future ten kings in relation to Babylon and the Beast—
the ecclesiastical and secular powers—are not only under
the direct control of God, but all is done in fulfillment of
His words."

Closely connected with Rev. 17:17 is that which is
brought before us in Micah 4:11, 12—"Now also many nations are gathered against thee, that say, Let her be defiled,
and let our eye look upon Zion. *But they know not the
thoughts of the Lord,* neither understand they His counsel:
for *He* shall gather them as the sheaves into the floor."
**Here is another instance which demonstrates God's absolute
control of the nations, of His power to fulfill His secret
counsel or decrees through and by them, and of His inclining
men to perform His pleasure though it be performed blindly
and unwittingly by them.**

Once more. What a word was that of the Lord Jesus
as He stood before Pilate! Who can depict the scene!
There was the Roman official, and there also was the Servant of Jehovah standing before him. Said Pilate, "Whence
art Thou?" And we read, "Jesus gave him no answer."
Then said Pilate unto Him, "Speakest Thou not unto *me?*
Knowest Thou not *that I have power* to crucify Thee, and
have power to release Thee?" (John 19:10). Ah! that is
what Pilate thought. That is what many another has
thought. He was merely voicing the common conviction
of the human heart—the heart which leaves *God* out of its
reckoning. But hear the Lord Jesus as He *corrects* Pilate,
and at the same time *repudiates* the proud boasting of men
in general—*"thou couldest have no power* against Me, *except it were given thee from above"* (John 19:11). How
sweeping is this assertion! Man—even though he be a
prominent official in the most influential empire of his day—
has *no power* except that which is given him from above,
no power, even, to do that which is evil, i.e., carry out *his
own* evil designs, unless God empowers him so that *His*

purpose may be forwarded. It was *God* who gave Pilate
the power to sentence to death His well-beloved Son! And
how this rebukes the sophistries and reasonings of men,
who argue that God does nothing more than *permit* evil!
Why, go right back to the very first words spoken by the
Lord God to man after the Fall, and hear Him saying, "*I
will put ENMITY* between thee and the woman, and between thy seed and her seed" (Gen. 3:15)! Bare permission of sin does not cover all the facts which are revealed
in Scripture touching this mystery. As Calvin succinctly
remarked, "But what reason shall we assign for His permit-
ting it *but because it is His will?*"

At the close of chapter eleven we promised to give attention to one or two other Difficulties which were not examined at that time. To them we now turn. If God has
not only pre-determined the salvation of His own, but has
also fore-ordained the good works which they are to walk
in (Eph. 2:10), then what incentive remains for us to strive
after practical godliness? If God has fixed the number of
those who are to be saved, and the others are vessels of
wrath fitted to destruction, then what encouragement have
we to preach the Gospel to the lost? Let us take up these
questions in the order of mention.

1 GOD'S SOVEREIGNTY AND THE BELIEVER'S GROWTH IN
GRACE.

If God has fore-ordained everything that comes to pass,
of what avail is it for *us* to "exercise" ourselves "unto godliness" (1 Tim. 4:7)? If God has before ordained the
good works in which we are to walk (Eph. 2:10), then why
should *we* be "careful to maintain good works" (Titus
3:8)? This only raises once more the problem of human
responsibility. Really, it should be enough for us to reply, God has *bidden* us do so. Nowhere does Scripture
inculcate or encourage a spirit of fatalistic indifference.
Contentment with our present attainments is expressly dis-
allowed. The word to every believer is, "*Press* toward the
mark for the prize of the high calling of God in Christ
Jesus" (Phil. 3:14). This was the apostle's aim, and it
should be ours. Instead of hindering the development of
Christian character, a proper apprehension and appreciation

of God's sovereignty will forward it. Just as the sinner's *despair* of any help from himself is the first prerequisite of a sound conversion, so the loss of all confidence in himself is the first essential in the believer's growth in grace; and just as the sinner despairing of help from himself will cast him into the arms of sovereign mercy, so the Christian, conscious of his own frailty, will turn unto the Lord for power. It is when we are weak, we are strong (2 Cor. 12: 10) : that is to say, there must be *consciousness* of our weakness before we shall turn to the Lord for help. While the Christian allows the thought that he is sufficient in himself, while he imagines that by mere force of will he shall resist temptation, while he has any confidence in the flesh then, like Peter who *boasted* that though all forsook the Lord yet should not he, so we shall certainly fail and fall. Apart from Christ we can do *nothing* (John 15:5). The promise of God is, "He giveth power to the faint; and *to them that have no might* (of their own) He increaseth strength" (Is. 40:29).

The question now before us is of great practical importance, and we are deeply anxious to express ourselves clearly and simply. The secret of development of Christian character is the realization of our own *powerlessness,* acknowledged powerlessness, and the consequent turning unto the Lord for help. The plain fact is that of ourselves we are utterly unable to practice a single precept or obey a single command that is set before us in the Scriptures. For example: "Love your enemies"—but of ourselves we cannot do this, or make ourselves do it. "In nothing be anxious"—but who can avoid and prevent anxiety when things go wrong? "Awake to righteousness and sin not"—but who can help sinning? These are merely examples selected at random from scores of others. Does then God *mock* us by bidding us do what He knows we are *unable* to do? The answer of Augustine to this question is the best we have met with—"God gives commands we cannot perform, that we may know *what* we ought to request from Him." A consciousness of our powerlessness should cast us upon Him who has all power. Here then is where a vision and view of God's sovereignty *helps,* for it reveals *His* sufficiency and shows us our *in*sufficiency.

2 GOD'S SOVEREIGNTY AND CHRISTIAN SERVICE.

If God has determined before the foundation of the world the precise number of those who shall be saved, then why should *we* concern ourselves about the eternal destiny of those with whom we come into contact? What place is left for *zeal* in Christian service? Will not the doctrine of God's sovereignty, and its corollary of predestination, *discourage* the Lord's servants from faithfulness in evangelism? No; instead of *dis*couraging His servants, a recognition of God's sovereignty is most *en*couraging to them. Here is one, for example, who is called upon to do the work of an evangelist, and he goes forth believing in the freedom of the will and in the sinner's own ability to come to Christ. He preaches the Gospel as faithfully and zealously as he knows how; but, he finds the vast majority of his hearers are utterly indifferent and have no heart at all for Christ. He discovers that men are, for the most part, thoroughly wrapt up in the things of the world, and that few have any concern about the world to come. He beseeches men to be reconciled to God, and pleads with them over their soul's salvation. But it is of no avail. He becomes thoroughly disheartened, and asks himself, What is the use of it all? Shall he quit, or had he better change his mission and message? If men will not respond to the Gospel, had he not better engage in that which is more popular and acceptable to the world? Why not occupy himself with humanitarian efforts, with social uplift work, with the purity campaign? Alas! that so many men who once preached the Gospel are now engaged in these activities instead.

What then is God's corrective for His discouraged servant? First, he needs to learn from Scripture that God is not now seeking to convert the world, but that in this Age He is "taking out of the Gentiles" a people for His name (Acts 15:14). What then is God's corrective for His discouraged servant? This—a proper apprehension of *God's* plan for this Dispensation. Again: what is God's remedy for dejection at apparent failure in our labors? This—the assurance that *God's* purpose *cannot* fail, that God's plans *cannot* miscarry, that God's will *must* be done. *Our* labors are not intended to bring about that which *God* has not decreed. Once more: what is God's word of cheer for the one who is thoroughly disheartened at the lack of response to his appeals and the absence of fruit for his labors? This— that *we* are not responsible for results: that is *God's* side, and *God's* business. Paul may "plant," and Apollos may "water," but it is *God* who "gave the increase" (1 Cor. 3:6). Our business is to obey Christ and preach the Gospel to every creature, to emphasise the "Whosoever believeth", and then to leave the sovereign operations of the Holy Spirit to apply the Word in quickening power to whom *He* wills, resting on the sure promise of Jehovah—"For as the rain cometh down, and the snow from heaven, and returneth not thither, but watereth the earth, and maketh it bring forth and bud, that it may give seed to the sower, and bread to the eater: So shall My Word be that goeth forth out of My mouth: *it shall not return unto Me void,* but it shall accomplish *that which I please* (it may not that which *we* please), and it shall prosper in the thing *whereto I sent it*" (Is. 55:10, 11). Was it not this assurance that sustained the beloved apostle when he declared "Therefore (see context) I endure all things *for the elect's sake*" (2 Tim. 2: 10)! Yea, is not this same lesson to be learned from the blessed example of the Lord Jesus! When we read that He said to the people, "Ye also have seen Me, *and believe not*", He fell back upon the sovereign pleasure of the One who sent Him, saying, *"All* that the Father giveth Me *shall* come to Me, and him that cometh to Me I will in no wise cast out" (John 6:36, 37). He knew that His labor would not be in vain. He knew God's Word would not return unto Him "void." He knew that "God's elect" *would* come to Him and believe on Him. And this same assurance fills the soul of every servant who intelligently rests upon the blessed truth of God's sovereignty.

Ah fellow-Christian-worker, God has not sent us forth to "draw a bow at a venture". The success of the ministry which He has committed into our hands is not left contingent on the fickleness of the wills in those to whom we preach. How gloriously encouraging, how soul-sustaining the assurance are those words of our Lord's, if we rest on them in simple faith: "And other sheep I have ("have" mark you, *not* "will have"; "have," because given to Him by the Father before the foundation of the world), which are not of this fold (i.e. the Jewish fold then existing) : them also I *must* bring, and they *shall* hear My voice" (John 10: 16). Not simply, "they *ought* to hear My voice," not simply "they *may* hear My voice", not "they will do so *if* they are willing." There is no "if", no "perhaps", no uncertainty about it. "They *shall* hear My voice" is His own positive, unqualified, absolute promise. Here then, is where *faith* is to rest! Continue your quest, dear friend, after the "other sheep" of Christ's. Be not discouraged because the "goats" heed not His voice as you preach the Gospel. Be faithful, be scriptural, be persevering, and Christ may use even you to be His mouthpiece in calling some of His lost sheep unto Himself. "Therefore, my beloved brethren, be ye stedfast, unmoveable, always abounding in the work of the Lord, forasmuch as ye *know* that your labor is *not in vain* in the Lord" (1 Cor. 15:58).

It now remains for us to offer a few closing reflections and our happy task is finished.

God's sovereign election of certain ones to salvation is a MERCIFUL provision. The sufficient answer to all the wicked accusations that the doctrine of Predestination is cruel, horrible, and unjust, is that, *unless* God had chosen certain ones to salvation, *none* would have been saved, for "there is none that seeketh after God" (Rom. 3:11). This is no mere inference of ours but the definite teaching of Holy Scripture. Attend closely to the words of the apostle in Romans 9, where this theme is fully discussed—"Though the number of the children of Israel be as the sand of the sea, *a remnant* shall be saved. . . . And as Isaiah said before, *Except* the Lord of hosts *had left us a seed,* we had been as Sodom, *and been made like unto Gomorrah*" (Rom. 9:27, 29). The teaching of this passage is unmistakable: but for Divine interference, Israel would have become as Sodom and Gomorrah. Had God left Israel alone, human depravity would have run its course to its own tragic end. But God left Israel a "remnant" or "seed." Of old the cities of the plain had been obliterated for their sin, and none was left to survive them; and so it would have been in Israel's case had not God "left" or spared a remnant. Thus it is with the human race: but for God's sovereign grace in sparing a remnant, *all* of Adam's descendants had perished in their sins. Therefore, we say that God's sovereign election of certain ones to salvation is a *merciful* provision. And, be it noted, in choosing the ones He did, God did no *injustice* to the others who were passed by, for *none* had any *right* to salvation. Salvation is by *grace,* and the *exercise* of grace is a matter of pure *sovereignty*—God might save all or none, many or few, one or ten thousand, just as He saw best. Should it be replied, But surely it were "best" to save *all.* The answer would be: *We* are not capable of judging. *We* might have thought it "best" never to have created Satan, never to have allowed sin to enter the world, or having entered, to have brought the conflict between good and evil to an end long before now. Ah! God's ways are not ours, and His ways are "past finding out."

God fore-ordains everything which comes to pass. His sovereign rule extends throughout the entire Universe and is over every creature. "For *of* Him, and *through* Him, and *to* Him, are *all things*" (Rom. 11:36). God initiates all things, regulates all things, and all things are working unto His eternal glory. "There is but one God, the Father, *of whom are all things,* and we in Him; and one Lord Jesus Christ, *by whom are all things,* and we by Him" (1 Cor. 8: 6). And again, "According to the purpose of Him who *worketh all things after the counsel of His own will*" (Eph. 1:11). Surely if anything could be ascribed to *chance* it is the *drawing of lots,* and yet the Word of God expressly declares, "The lot is cast into the lap; *but the whole disposing thereof is of the Lord*" (Pro. 16:33)!!

God's wisdom in the government of our world shall yet be completely vindicated before all created intelligences. God is no idle Spectator, looking on from a distant world at the happenings on our earth, but is Himself shaping everything to the ultimate promotion of His own glory. Even now He is working out His eternal purpose, not only in spite of human and Satanic opposition, but by means of them. How wicked and futile have been all efforts to resist His will shall one day be as fully evident as when of old He overthrew the rebellious Pharaoh and his hosts at the Red Sea.

It has been well said, "The end and object of all is the

glory of God. It is perfectly, divinely true, that 'God hath
ordained for His own glory whatsoever comes to pass.'
In order to guard this from all possibility of mistake, we
have only to remember who is this God, and what the glory
that He seeks. It is He who is the God and Father of our
Lord Jesus Christ,—of Him in whom divine love came seeking *not* her own, among us as 'One that serveth.' It is
He who, sufficient in Himself, can receive no real accession
of glory from His creatures, but from whom—'Love', as
He is 'Light,'—cometh down every good and every perfect
gift, in whom is no variableness nor shadow of turning.
Of His own alone can His creatures give to Him."

"The glory of such an one is found in the display of His
own goodness, righteousness, holiness, truth; in manifest-
ing Himself as in Christ He has manifested Himself and
will forever. The glory of this God is what of necessity
all things must serve—adversaries and evil as well as all
else. *He has ordained it;* His power will insure it; and
when all apparent clouds and obstructions are removed, then
shall He rest—'rest in His love' forever, although eternity
only will suffice for the apprehension of the revelation. *'God
shall be all in all'* (italics ours throughout this paragraph)
gives in six words the ineffable result" (F. W. Grant on
"Atonement").

That what we have written gives but an incomplete and
imperfect presentation of this most important subject we
must sorrowfully confess. Nevertheless, if it results in a
clearer apprehension of the majesty of God and His sovereign mercy we shall be amply repaid for our labors. If
the reader *has* received blessing from the perusal of these
pages, let him not fail to return thanks to the Giver of every
good and every perfect gift, ascribing *all* praise to His
inimitable and sovereign grace.

"The Lord, our God, is clothed with might,
The winds and waves obey His will;
He speaks, and in the shining height
The sun and rolling worlds stand still.
Rebel ye waves, and o'er the land
With threatening aspect foam and roar,
The Lord hath spoken His command
That breaks your rage upon the shore.
Ye winds of night, your force combine—
Without His holy high behest
You shall not in a mountain pine
Disturb the little swallow's nest.
His voice sublime is heard afar;
In distant peals it fades and dies;
He binds the cyclone to His car
And sweeps the howling murky skies.
Great God! how infinite art Thou,
What weak and worthless worms are we,
Let all the race of creatures bow
And seek salvation now from Thee.
Eternity, with all its years
Stands ever-present to Thy view,
To Thee there's nothing old appears

Great God! There can be nothing new.
Our lives through varied scenes are drawn,
And vexed with mean and trifling cares;
While Thine eternal thought moves on
Thy fixed and undisturbed affairs."

"Halleluia: for the Lord God omnipotent reigneth" (Rev. 19:6).

APPENDIX I

THE WILL OF GOD

IN treating of the Will of God some theologians have differentiated between His *decretive* will and His *permissive* will, insisting that there are certain things which God has positively fore-ordained, but other things which He merely suffers to exist or happen. But such a distinction is really no distinction at all, inasmuch as God only permits that which is according to His will. No such distinction would have been invented had these theologians discerned that God could have *decreed* the existence and activities of sin *without* Himself being the *Author* of sin. Personally, we much prefer to adopt the distinction made by the older Calvinists between God's secret and revealed will, or, to state it in another way, His disposing and His preceptive will.

God's revealed will is made known in His Word, but His secret will is His own hidden counsels. God's revealed will is the definer of our duty and the standard of our responsibility. The primary and basic reason why I should follow a certain course or do a certain thing is because it is *God's will* that I should, His will being clearly defined for me in His Word. That I should not follow a certain course, that I must refrain from doing certain things, is because they are *contrary* to God's revealed will. But suppose I *disobey* God's Word, then do I not *cross* His will? And if so, how can it still be true that God's will is *always* done and His counsel accomplished at all times? Such questions should make evident the necessity for the distinction here advocated. God's *revealed* will *is* frequently crost, but His *secret* will is *never* thwarted. That it is legitimate for us to make such a distinction concerning God's will is clear from Scripture. Take these two passages: "For this is the will of God, even your sanctification" (1 Thess. 4:3); "For who hath resisted His will?" (Rom. 9:19). Would any thoughtful reader declare that God's "will" has precisely the same meaning in both of these passages? We surely hope not. The first passage refers to God's revealed will, the latter to His secret will. The first passage concerns our duty, the latter declares that God's secret purpose is

243

immutable and must come to pass notwithstanding the creature's insubordination. God's revealed will is never done perfectly or fully by any of us, but His secret will never fails of accomplishment even in the minutest particular. His secret will mainly concerns *future* events; His revealed will, our *present* duty: the one has to do with His irresistible purpose, the other with His manifested pleasure: the one is wrought upon us and accomplished through us, the other is to be done by us.

The secret will of God is His eternal, unchanging purpose concerning all things which He hath made, to be brought about by certain means to their appointed ends: of this God expressly declares "My counsel shall stand, and I will do *all* My pleasure" (Isa. 46:10). This is the absolute, efficacious will of God, always effected, always fulfilled. The revealed will of God contains not His purpose and decree but our duty,—not what *He* will do according to His eternal counsel, but what *we* should do if we would please Him, and this is expressed in the precepts and promises of His Word. Whatever God has determined within Himself, whether to do Himself, or to do by others, or to suffer to be done, whilst it is in His own breast, and is not made known by any event in providence, or by precept, or by prophecy, is His secret will. Such are the deep things of God, the thoughts of His heart, the counsels of His mind, which are impenetrable to all creatures. But when these are made known they become His revealed will: such is almost the whole of the book of Revelation, wherein God has made known to us "things which must shortly come to pass" (Rev. 1:1—"must" because He has eternally purposed that they should).

It has been objected by Arminian theologians that the division of God's will into secret and revealed is untenable, because it makes God to have two different wills, the one opposed to the other. But this is a mistake, due to their failure to see that the secret and revealed will of God respect entirely different objects. If God should require and forbid the same thing, or if He should decree the same thing should and should not exist, then would His secret and revealed will be contradictory and purposeless. If those who object to the secret and revealed will of God being inconsistent would only make the same distinction in this case that they do in many other cases, the seeming inconsistency would at once disappear. How often do men draw a sharp distinction between what is desirable in *its own nature* and what is not desirable *all things considered.* For example, the fond parent does not desire *simply considered* to punish his offending child, but, *all things considered,* he knows it is his bounden duty, and so corrects his child. And though he tells his child he *does not desire* to punish him, but that he is satisfied it is for the best *all things considered* to do so, then an intelligent child would see no inconsistency in what his father says and does. Just so the All-wise Creator may consistently decree to bring to pass things which He hates, forbids and condemns. God chooses that some things shall exist which He thoroughly hates (in their intrinsic nature), and He also chooses that some things shall not yet exist which He perfectly loves (in their intrinsic nature). For example: He commanded that Pharaoh should let His people go, because that was right *in the nature of things,* yet, He had secretly declared that Pharaoh should *not* let His people go, not because it was right in Pharaoh to refuse, but because it was best *all things considered* that he *should not* let them go—i.e. best because it subserved God's larger purpose.

Again; God commands us to be perfectly holy in this life (Matt. 5:48), because this is right *in the nature of things,* but He has decreed that no man shall be perfectly holy in this life, because this is best *all things considered* that none shall be perfectly holy (experimentally) before they leave this world. Holiness is one thing, the taking place of holiness is another; so, sin is one thing, the taking place of sin is another. When God requires holiness His preceptive or revealed will respects the nature or moral excellence of holiness; but when He decrees that holiness shall not take place (fully and perfectly) His secret or decretive will respects only the event of it not taking place. So, again, when He forbids sin, His preceptive or revealed will respects only the nature or moral evil of sin; but when He decrees that sin *shall* take place, His secret will respects only its actual occurrence to serve His good purpose. Thus the secret and revealed will of God respect entirely different objects.

God's will of decree is not His will in the same sense as His will of command is. Therefore, there is no difficulty in supposing that one may be contrary to the other. His will, in both senses, is His inclination. Everything that concerns His revealed will is perfectly agreeable to His nature, as when He commands love, obedience, and service from His creatures. But that which concerns His secret will has in view His ultimate end, that to which all things are now working. Thus, He decreed the entrance of sin into His universe, though His own holy nature hates all sin with infinite abhorrence, yet, because it is one of the means by which His appointed end is to be reached He suffered it to enter. God's *revealed* will is the measure of our responsibility and the determiner of our duty. With God's secret will we have nothing to do: that is His concern. But, God knowing that we should fail to perfectly do His revealed will ordered His eternal counsels accordingly, and these eternal counsels, which make up His secret will, though unknown to us are, though unconsciously, fulfilled in and through us.

Whether the reader is prepared to accept the above distinction in the will of God or not he must acknowledge that the commands of Scripture declare God's revealed will, and he must also allow that sometimes God *wills not to hinder* a breach of those commands, because He *does not* as a fact so hinder it. God wills to permit sin as is evident, for He *does* permit it. Surely none will say that God Himself does what He does not *will* to do.

Finally, let it be said again that, my responsibility with regard to the will of God is measured by what He *has* made known in His Word. There I learn that it is my duty to *use* the means of His providing, and to humbly *pray* that He may be pleased to bless them to me. To refuse so to do on the ground that I am ignorant of what may or may not be His secret counsels concerning me, is not only absurd, but the height of presumption. We repeat: the secret will of God is none of our business; it is His *revealed* will which measures our accountability. That there is no conflict whatever between the secret and the revealed will of God is made clear from the fact that, the former is accomplished by my use of the means laid down in the latter.

THE CASE OF ADAM

IN our chapter on God's Sovereignty and Human Responsibility we dealt only with the responsibility of man considered as a fallen creature, and at the close of the discussion it was pointed out how that the measure and extent of our responsibility varies in different individuals, according to the advantages they have received and the privileges they have enjoyed, which is a truth clearly established by the declaration of the Saviour recorded in Luke 12:47, 48, "And that servant, which knew his lord's will, and prepared not himself, neither did according to his will, shall be beaten with many stripes. But he that knew not, and did not commit things worthy of stripes, shall be beaten with few stripes. For unto whomsoever much is given, of him shall be much required: and to whom men have committed much, of him they will ask the more".

Now, strictly speaking, there are only two men who have ever walked this earth which were endowed with full and unimpaired responsibility, and they were the first and last Adam's. The responsibility of each of the rational descendants of Adam, while real, and sufficient to establish them accountable to their Creator is, nevertheless, limited in degree, limited because impaired through the effects of the Fall.

Not only is the responsibility of each descendant of Adam *sufficient* to constitute him, *personally* an accountable creature (that is, as one so constituted that he *ought* to do right and *ought not* to do wrong), but originally every one of us was also endowed, *judicially,* with full and *unimpaired* responsibility, not in ourselves, but, *in Adam.* It should ever be borne in mind that not only was Adam the father of the human race *seminally,* but he was also the head of the race *legally.* When Adam was placed in Eden he stood there *as our representative,* so that what he did is reckoned to the account of each for whom he acted.

It is beside our present purpose to enter here into a lengthy discussion of the Federal Headship of Adam*,

*Though there is deep and widespread *need* for this, and we hope ere long to write upon this subject in another book.

suffice it now to refer the reader to Romans 5:12-19 where this truth is dealt with by the Holy Spirit. In the heart of this most important passage we are told that Adam was "*the figure* of Him that was to come" (v. 14), that is, of Christ. In *what* sense, then, was Adam "the figure" of Christ? The answer must be, In that he was a Federal Head; in that he acted on the behalf of a race of men; in that he was one who has legally, as well as vitally, affected all connected with him. It is for this reason that the Lord Jesus is in 1 Cor. 15:45 denominated "the last *Adam*", that is, the Head of the new creation, as the first Adam was the Head of the old creation.

In Adam, then, each of us stood. As the representative of the human race the first man acted. As then Adam was created with full and unimpaired responsibility, unimpaired because there was no evil nature within him; and as we were all "in Adam", it necessarily follows that all of us, *originally*, were also endowed with full and unimpaired responsibility. Therefore, in Eden, it was not merely the responsibility of Adam as a single person that was tested, but it was Human Responsibility, the Responsibility of the Race, as a whole and in part, which was on trial.

Webster defines responsibility first, as "liable to account"; second, as "able to discharge an obligation". Perhaps the meaning and scope of the term responsibility might be expressed and summed up in the one word *oughtness*. Godwards, responsibility respects that which is *due* the Creator from the creature, and which the creature is under moral obligations to render.

In the light of the above definition it is at once apparent that responsibility is something that must be *placed on trial*. And as a fact, this is, as we learn from the Inspired Record, exactly what transpired in Eden. Adam was placed on probation. His obligations to God were put to the test. His loyalty to the Creator was tried out. The test consisted of obedience to his Maker's command. Of a certain tree he was forbidden to eat.

But right here a very formidable difficulty confronts us. From *God's* standpoint the *result* of Adam's probation was not left in uncertainty. Before He formed him out of the dust of the ground and breathed into his nostrils the breath

of life, God knew exactly how the appointed test would
terminate. With this statement every Christian reader must
be in accord, for, to deny God's foreknowledge is to deny
His omniscience, and this is to repudiate one of the fundamental attributes of Deity. But we must go further: not
only had God a perfect foreknowledge of the outcome of
Adam's trial, not only did His omniscient eye see Adam
eating of the forbidden fruit, but He *decreed* beforehand
that he *should* do so. This is evident not only from the
general fact that *nothing happens* save that which the Creator and Governor of the universe has eternally purposed,
but also from the express declaration of Scripture that
Christ as a *Lamb* "verily was foreordained before the foundation of the world" (1 Peter 1:20). If, then, God had
foreordained before the foundation of the world that
Christ should, in due time, be offered as a Sacrifice for sin,
then it is unmistakably evident that God had also foreordained sin should enter the world, and if so, that Adam
should transgress and fall. In full harmony with this,
God Himself placed in Eden the tree of the knowledge of
good and evil, and also allowed the Serpent to enter and
deceive Eve.

Here then is the difficulty: If God has eternally decreed
that Adam *should* eat of the tree, how could he be held
responsible *not* to eat of it? Formidable as the problem
appears, nevertheless, it is capable of a solution, a solution,
moreover, which can be grasped even by the finite mind.
The solution is to be found in the distinction between God's
secret will and His revealed will. As stated in Appendix
I, human responsibility is measured by our knowledge of
God's *revealed* will; what God *has* told us, not what He has
not told us, is the definer of our duty. So it was with Adam.

That God had decreed sin should enter this world through
the disobedience of our first parents was a *secret* hid in His
own breast. Of this Adam knew nothing, and *that made all
the difference* so far as his responsibility was concerned.
Adam was quite unacquainted with the Creator's hidden
counsels. What concerned him was God's *revealed* will.
And that was plain! God had *forbidden* him to eat of the
tree, and that was enough. But God went further: He even
warned Adam of the dire consequences which would fol-

low should he disobey—death would be the penalty. Trans-
gression, then, on the part of Adam was entirely *excuse-less*. Created with no evil nature in him, with a will in perfect equipoise, placed in the fairest environment, given do-
minion over all the lower creation, allowed full liberty with
only a single restriction upon him, plainly warned of what
would follow an act of insubordination to God, there was
every possible inducement for Adam to preserve his inno-
cence; and, should he fail and fall, then by every principle of righteousness his blood must lie upon his own head,
and his guilt be imputed to all in whose behalf he acted.

Had God disclosed to Adam His purpose that sin would
enter this world, and that He had decreed Adam *should* eat
of the forbidden fruit, it is obvious that Adam could not
have been held responsible *for* the eating of it. But in that
God *withheld* the knowledge of His counsels from Adam,
his accountability *was not* interfered with.

Again; had God created Adam with a bias toward evil,
then human responsibility had been impaired and man's
probation merely one in name. But inasmuch as Adam
was included among that which God, at the end of the sixth
day, pronounced "Very good", and, inasmuch as man was
made "upright" (Ecc. 7:29), then every mouth must be
"stopped" and "the whole world" must acknowledge itself
"guilty before God" (Rom. 3:19).

Once more, it needs to be carefully borne in mind that
God did not decree that Adam should sin *and then inject into Adam an inclination to evil,* in order that His decree
might be carried out. No; "God cannot be tempted, neither
tempteth *He* any man" (Jas. 1:13). Instead, when the
Serpent came to tempt Eve, God caused her *to remember*
His command forbidding to eat of the tree of the knowledge of good and evil and of the penalty attached to disobedience! Thus, though God *had* decreed the Fall, in no
sense was He the *Author* of Adam's sin, and at no point
was Adam's responsibility impaired. Thus may we admire
and adore the *"manifold* wisdom of God", in devising a way
whereby His eternal decree should be accomplished, and
yet the responsibility of His creatures be preserved intact.

Perhaps a further word should be added concerning the
decretive will of God, particularly in its relation to evil.

First of all we take the high ground that, whatever things God does or permits, are right, just, and good, simply because *God* does or permits them. When Luther gave answer to the question, "Whence it was that Adam was permitted to fall, and corrupt his whole posterity; when God could have prevented him from falling, etc", he said, "God is a Being whose will acknowledges no cause: neither is it for us to prescribe rules to His sovereign pleasure, or call Him to account for what He does. He has neither superior nor equal; and His will is the rule of all things. He did not thus will such and such things because they were right, and He was bound to will them; but they are therefore equitable and right because He wills them. The will of man, indeed, may be influenced and moved; but God's will never can. To assert the contrary is to undeify Him" (De Servo, Arb. c/ 153).

To affirm that God decreed the entrance of sin into His universe, and that He foreordained all its fruits and activities, is to say that which, at first may shock the reader; but reflection should show that it is far more shocking to insist that sin has invaded His dominions *against* His will, and that its exercise is *outside* His jurisdiction: for in such a case where would be His omnipotency? No; to recognise that God has foreordained all the activities of evil, is to see that He is the *Governor* of sin: His will determines its exercise, His power regulates its bounds (Psa. 76:10). He is neither the Inspirer nor the Infuser of sin in any of His creatures, but He *is* its Master, by which we mean God's management of the wicked is so entire that, they can do nothing save that which His hand and counsel, from everlasting, determined should be done.

Though nothing contrary to holiness and righteousness can ever emanate from God, yet He has, for His own wise ends, ordained His creatures to fall into sin. Had sin never been permitted, how could the justice of God have been displayed in punishing it? How could the wisdom of God have been manifested in so wondrously over-ruling it? How could the grace of God have been exhibited in pardoning it? How could the power of God have been exercised in subduing it? A very solemn and striking proof of *Christ's* acknowledgment of God's decretal of sin is seen in His treatment of Judas. The Saviour knew full well that Judas would betray Him, yet we never read that He expostulated with him! Instead, He said to him, "That thou doest, *do* quickly" (John 13:27)! Yet, mark this was said *after* he had received the sop and Satan had taken possession of his heart. Judas was already prepared for and determined on his traiterous work, therefore did Christ permissively (bowing to His Father's ordination) bid him go forth to his awful work.

Thus, though God is *not* the Author of sin, and though sin is contrary to His holy *nature,* yet the existence and operations of it are not contrary to His *will,* but subservient to it. God never tempts man to sin, but He has, by His eternal counsels (which He is now executing), *determined its course.* Moreover, as we have shown in chapter 8, though God has decreed man's sins, yet is man responsible not to commit them, and blameable because he does. Strikingly were these two sides of this awful subject brought together by Christ in that statement of His: "Woe unto the world because of offences! for it *must needs be* that offences come (because God has foreordained them); *but woe to that man* by whom the offence cometh" (Matt. 18:7). So, too, though all which took place at Calvary was by the "determinate counsel and foreknowledge of God" (Acts 2:23), nevertheless, "wicked hands" crucified the Lord of glory, and, in consequence, His blood has righteously rested upon them and on their children. High mysteries are these, yet it is both our happy privilege and bounden duty to humbly receive whatsoever God has been pleased to reveal concerning them in His Word of Truth.

APPENDIX III

THE MEANING OF "KOSMOS" IN JOHN 3:16

IT may appear to some of our readers that the exposition we have given of John 3:16 in the chapter on
"Difficulties and Objections" is a forced and unnatural one,
inasmuch as our definition of the term "world" seems to
be out of harmony with the meaning and scope of this
word in other passages, where, to supply *the world of believers* (God's elect) as a definition of "world" would
make no sense. Many have said to us, "Surely, 'world'
means world, that is, you, me, and everybody." In reply
we would say: We know from experience how difficult it
is to set aside the "traditions of men" and come to a passage
which we have heard explained in a certain way scores of
times, and study it carefully for ourselves *without bias.*
Nevertheless, this is essential if we would learn the mind
of God.

Many people suppose they *already know* the simple meaning of John 3:16, and therefore they conclude that no diligent study is required of them to discover the precise teaching of *this* verse. Needless to say, such an attitude shuts
out any further light which they otherwise might obtain on
the passage. Yet, if anyone will take a Concordance and
read carefully the various passages in which the term
"world" (as a translation of "kosmos") occurs, he will
quickly perceive that to ascertain the precise meaning of the
word "world" in any given passage is not nearly so easy
as is popularly supposed. The word "kosmos," and its
English equivalent "world," is *not* used with a *uniform* significance in the New Testament. Very far from it. It is
used in quite a number of *different* ways. Below we will
refer to a few passages where this term occurs, suggesting
a tentative definition in each case:

1 "Kosmos" is used of the Universe as a whole: Acts 17:
24—
"God that made *the world* and all things therein, seeing
that He is Lord *of heaven and earth.*"
2 "Kosmos" is used of the earth: John 13:1; Eph. 1:4,
etc., etc.—
"When Jesus knew that His hour was come that He

253

should depart *out of this world* unto the Father, having loved His own which were *in the world* He loved them unto the end." "Depart out of this world" signifies, leave this earth.

"According as He hath chosen us in Him before *the foundation of the world.*" This expression signifies, before the earth was founded—compare Job 38:4 etc.

3 "Kosmos" is used of the world-system: John 12:31 etc.

"Now is *the judgment* of this *world:* now shall *the Prince of this world* be cast out"—compare Matt. 4:8 and 1 John 5:19, R. V.

4 "Kosmos" is used of the whole human race: Rom. 3:19, etc.—

"Now we know that what things soever the law saith, it saith to them who are under the law: that *every* mouth may be stopped, and *all the world* may become guilty before God."

5 "Kosmos" is used of humanity *minus believers:* John 15:18; Rom. 3:6—

"If *the world hate* you, ye know that it hated Me before it hated you." Believers do not "hate" Christ, so that "the world" here *must* signify the world of *un*-believers in contrast from believers who love Christ.

"God forbid: for then how shall God *judge the world.*" Here is another passage where "the world" *cannot* mean "you, me, and everybody," for *believers will not* be "judged" by God, see John 5:24. So that here, too, it must be the world of *un*-believers which is in view.

6 "Kosmos" is used of Gentiles in contrast from Jews: Rom. 11:12 etc.

"Now if the fall of them (Israel) be *the riches of the world,* and the diminishing of them (Israel) *the riches of the Gentiles;* how much more their (Israel's) fulness." Note how the first clause in italics is *defined* by the latter clause placed in italics. Here, again, "the world" *cannot* signify all humanity for it *excludes* Israel!

7 "Kosmos" is used of believers only: John 1:29; 3:16, 17; 6:33; 12:47; 1 Cor. 4:9; 2 Cor. 5:19. We leave our readers to turn to these passages, asking them to note, carefully, exactly *what is said and predicated of* "the world" in each place.

Thus it will be seen that "kosmos" has at least seven clearly defined *different meanings* in the New Testament. It may be asked, Has then God used a word thus to confuse and confound those who read the Scriptures? We answer, No! nor has He written His Word for *lazy* people who are too dilitary, or too busy with the things of this world, or, like Martha, so much occupied with "serving," they have no time and no heart to "search" and "study" Holy Writ! Should it be asked further, But how is a searcher of the Scriptures to know *which* of the above meanings the term "world" has in any given passage? The answer is: This may be ascertained by a careful study of the context, by diligently noting *what is predicated* of "the world" in each passage, and by prayerfully consulting other parallel passages to the one being studied.

The principal subject of John 3:16 is *Christ as the Gift of God.* The first clause tells us *what* moved God *to* "give" His only begotten Son, and that was His great "love;" the second clause informs us *for whom* God "gave" His Son, and that is for, "whosoever (or, better, 'every one') believeth;" while the last clause makes known *why* God "gave" His Son (His purpose), and that is, that everyone that believeth "should not perish but have everlasting life."

That "the world" in John 3:16 refers to *the world of believers* (God's elect), in contradistinction from *"the world of the ungodly"* (2 Pet. 2:5), is established, unequivocally established, by a comparison of the *other* passages which speak of God's *"love."* "God commendeth His love *toward US"*—the saints, Rom. 5:8. *"Whom* the Lord loveth He *chasteneth"*—every son, Heb. 12:6. "We love Him, because He first loved *US"*—believers, 1 John 4:19. The wicked God "pities" (see Matt. 18:33). Unto the unthankful and evil God is "kind" (see Luke 6:35). The vessels of wrath He endures "with much long-suffering" (see Rom. 9:22). But "His own" God *"loves"!!*

1 JOHN 2:2

THERE is one passage more than any other which is appealed to by those who believe in universal redemption, and which at first sight appears to teach that Christ died for the whole human race. We have therefore decided to give it a detailed examination and exposition.

"And He is the propitiation for our sins: and not for ours only, but also for the sins of the whole world" (1 John 2:2). This is the passage which, apparently, most favors the Arminian view of the Atonement, yet if it be considered attentively it will be seen that it does so *only* in appearance, and not in reality. Below we offer a number of conclusive proofs to show that this verse *does not* teach that Christ has propitiated God on behalf of all the sins of all men.

In the first place, the fact that this verse opens with "and" necessarily links it with what has gone before. We, therefore, give a literal word for word translation of 1 John 2:1 from Bagster's Interlinear: "Little children my, these things I write to you, that ye may not sin; and if any one should sin, a Paraclete we have with the Father, Jesus Christ (the) righteous". It will thus be seen that the apostle John is here writing *to* and *about* the *saints* of God. His immediate purpose was two-fold: first, to communicate a message that would keep God's children from sinning; second, to supply comfort and assurance to those who might sin, and, in consequence, be cast down and fearful that the issue would prove fatal. He, therefore, makes known to them the provision which God has made for just such an emergency. This we find at the end of v. 1 and throughout v. 2. The ground of comfort is twofold: let the downcast and repentant believer (1 John 1:9) be assured that, first, he has an "Advocate with the Father"; second, that this Advocate is "the propitiation for our sins". Now *believers only* may take comfort *from this,* for they alone have an "Advocate", for them alone is Christ the propitiation, as is proven by *linking* the Propitiation ("and") with "the Advocate"!

In the second place, if other pasages in the New Testament which speak of "propitiation," be compared with

1 John 2:2, it will be found that it is *strictly limited* in its scope. For example, in Rom. 3:25 we read that God set forth Christ "a propitiation *through faith* in His blood". If Christ is a propitiation "through faith", then He *is not* a "propitiation" to those who have no faith! Again, in Heb. 2:17 we read, "To make propitiation for the sins of *the people*" (Heb. 2:17, R. V.).

In the third place, *who* are meant when John says, "He is the propitiation for *our* sins"? We answer, *Jewish believers*. And a part of the proof on which we base this assertion we now submit to the careful attention of the reader.

In Gal. 2:9 we are told that *John*, together with James and Cephas, were apostles "unto the circumcision" (i.e. *Israel*). In keeping with this, the Epistle of James is addressed to "the twelve tribes, which are scattered abroad" (1:1). So, the first Epistle of Peter is addressed to "the elect who are sojourners of the Dispersion" (1 Pet. 1:1, R.V.). And John also is writing *to* saved Israelites, but *for* saved Jews *and* saved Gentiles.

Some of the evidences that John *is* writing *to* saved Jews are as follows. (a) In the opening verse he says of Christ, "Which *we* have seen with *our* eyes . . . . and *our* hands have handled". How impossible it would have been for the Apostle Paul to have commenced any of *his* epistles to *Gentile* saints with such language!

(b) "Brethren, I write no new commandment unto you, but an old commandment which *ye* had *from the beginning*" (1 John 2:7). The "beginning" here referred to is the beginning of the public manifestation of Christ—in proof compare 1:1; 2:13, etc. Now these believers the apostle tells us, *had* the "old commandment" *from the beginning*. This was true of *Jewish* believers, but it was not true of *Gentile* believers.

(c) "I write unto you, fathers, because *ye have known* Him from the beginning" (2:13). Here, again, it is evident that it is *Jewish* believers that are in view.

(d) "Little children, it is the last time: and as ye *have heard* that Antichrist shall come, even now are there many antichrists; whereby we know that it is the last time. *They* went out from *us,* but they were not of us" (2:18, 19).

These brethren to whom John wrote *had* "heard" from Christ Himself that Antichrist should come (see Matt. 24). The "many antichrists" whom John declares "went out *from us*" were all *Jews,* for during the first century none but a *Jew* posed as the Messiah. Therefore, when John says "He is the propitiation for *our* sins" he can only mean for the sins of *Jewish believers**.

In the fourth place, when John added, "And not for ours only, but also for *the whole world*", he signified that Christ was the propitiation for the sins of *Gentile* believers *too,* for, as previously shown, "the world" is a term *contrasted* from Israel. This interpretation is unequivocally established by a careful comparison of 1 John 2:2 with John 11:51, 52, which is a strictly parallel passage: "And this spake he not of himself: but being high priest that year, he prophesied that Jesus should die for that nation; And not for that nation only, but that also He should gather together in one the children of God that were scattered abroad". Here Caiaphas, under inspiration, made known *for whom* Jesus should "die". Notice now the correspondency of his prophecy with this declaration of John's:

"He is the propitiation for our (believing Israelites) sins".

"He prophesied that Jesus should die for that nation".

"And not for ours only".

"And not for that nation only".

"But also for the whole world"—

That is, Gentile believers scattered throughout the earth.

"He should gather together in one the children of God that were scattered abroad".

In the fifth place, the above interpretation is confirmed by the fact that no other is consistent or intelligible. If the "whole world" signifies the whole human race, then the first clause and the "also" in the second clause are abso-

---

*It is true that many things in John's Epistle apply equally to believing Jews *and* believing Gentiles. Christ is the Advocate of the one, as much as of the other. The same may be said of many things in the Epistle of James which is also a *catholic,* or *general* epistle, though expressly addressed to the twelve tribes scattered abroad.

lutely meaningless. If Christ is the propitiation for *every-body*, it would be idle tautology to say, first, "He is the pro-pitiation for *our* sins and *also* for everybody". There could be no "also" if He is the propitiation for the entire human family. Had the apostle meant to affirm that Christ *is* a universal propitiation he had omitted the first clause of v. 2, and simply said, "He is the propitiation for the sins of the whole world." Confirmatory of "not for ours (Jewish believers) only, but also for the whole world"—Gentile be-lievers, too; compare John 10:16; 17:20.

In the sixth place, our definition of "the whole world" is in perfect accord with other passages in the New Testament. For example: "Whereof ye heard before in the word of the truth of the Gospel; which is come unto you, as it is in *all the world*" (Col. 1:5, 6). Does "all the world" here mean, absolutely and unqualifiedly, all mankind? Had all the human family heard the Gospel? No; the apostle's obvious meaning is that, the Gospel, instead of being con-fined to the land of Judea, had gone abroad, without re-straint, *into Gentile lands*. So in Rom. 1:8: "First, I thank my God through Jesus Christ for you all, that your faith is spoken of throughout *the whole world*". The apostle is here referring to the faith of these Roman saints being spoken of in a way of *commendation*. But certainly all mankind did not so speak of their faith! It was the whole world *of believers* that he was referring to! In Rev. 12:9 we read of Satan "which deceiveth *the whole world*". But again this expression cannot be understood as a universal one, for Matt. 24:24 tells us that Satan does not and can-not "deceive" God's elect. Here it is "the whole world" *of unbelievers*.

In the seventh place, to insist that "the whole world" in I John 2:2 signifies the entire human race is to undermine the very foundations of our faith. If Christ is the propiti-ation for those that are lost equally as much as for those that are saved, then what assurance have we that believers too may not be lost? If Christ is the propitiation for those now in hell, what guarantee have I that I may not end in hell? The blood-shedding of the incarnate Son of God is the *only* thing which can keep any one out of hell, and *if* many for whom that precious blood made propitiation are

now in the awful place of the damned, then may not that
blood prove inefficacious for me! Away with such a God-
dishonoring thought.

However men may quibble and wrest the Scriptures, one
thing is certain: The Atonement is no failure. God will
not allow that precious and costly sacrifice to fail in accomplishing, completely, that which it was designed to effect. Not a drop of that holy blood was shed in vain. In the
last great Day there shall stand forth no disappointed and
defeated Saviour, but One who *"shall* see of the travail of
His soul and *be satisfied"* (Isa. 53:11). These are not our
words, but the infallible assertion of Him who declares,
"My counsel shall stand, and I will do *all* My pleasure"
(Isa. 64:10). Upon this impregnable rock we take our
stand. Let others rest on the sands of human speculation
and twentieth-century theorising if they wish. That is their
business. But to God they will yet have to render an account. For our part we had rather be railed at as a narrow-
minded, out-of-date, hyper-Calvinist, than be found repu-
diating God's truth by reducing the Divinely-efficacious
atonement to a mere fiction.

INDEX OF SCRIPTURE

INDEX OF AUTHORS